A History of the Mississippi Governor's Mansion

A History of the Mississippi Governor's Mansion

by
DAVID G. SANSING
and
CARROLL WALLER

UNIVERSITY PRESS OF MISSISSIPPI
JACKSON

Copyright © 1977 by the
University Press of Mississippi
Manufactured in the United States of America
Designed by Barney McKee

Print-on-Demand Edition

Library of Congress Cataloging in Publication Data

Sansing, David G.
  A history of the Mississippi Governor's mansion.

  Includes bibliographical references and index.
    1. Jackson, Miss. Governor's Mansion.
2. Mississippi—Governors. 3. Mississippi—
Politics and government. I. Waller, Carroll,
joint author. II. Title.
F349.J13S26   976.2'51   77-12243
ISBN: 978-1-60473-380-8

Contents

Preface vii
I A Suitable House for the Governor 3
II Republican Simplicity in Grand Style 17
III The Years of Crisis 31
IV These are Wartimes 46
V A Fence Around the Mansion . . . A Wall Around Mississippi 57
VI Of Monuments and Men 72
VII The Mansion and the Myth 91
VIII A House of Glass 108
IX All the Changing Life of Mississippi 130
X And the Walls Came Tumbling Down 153
XI Home of Our Heritage 177
Notes 195
Index 213

Preface

WHEN I BEGAN collecting information to aid in the restoration of the Mississippi governor's mansion, I was surprised to learn that a full-length history of our antebellum mansion had never been written. As a native Mississippian with an interest in the state's past as well as its future, my personal thoughts turned toward some means of preserving and publishing the history of this building which has been used as the official residence of Mississippi governors since 1842.

Over the next two years, I was so preoccupied with the restoration of the mansion that I was not able to give the history much thought. But my interest in the project was revived in the fall of 1974 when Judge James P. Coleman, a former governor and resident of the mansion, wrote a letter to a Jackson paper in which he sketched its long and interesting past and suggested that it was an appropriate time for someone to write a history of the Mississippi executive mansion. I clipped the article and read it to Governor Waller as we were flying to the Gulf Coast for a "Move the Capital" day. Over the next few weeks we discussed the matter several times and became convinced that a book on the mansion was a project we would like to and felt should be undertaken. In January, 1975, we contacted Dr. David Sansing, a professor of history at the University of Mississippi, and asked him if he would undertake the project with me. He agreed to do so and we went to work immediately.

Over the next several months, while he researched the public records and documents, I interviewed former governors, first ladies, and the families and descendents of first families. I also talked with secretaries, hostesses, aides, inmates who had worked at the mansion, security of-

Preface

ficers, craftsmen, architects, interior designers, and many others who had some special knowledge about the mansion. In addition to being interesting and sometimes entertaining, these interviews were useful in the restoration of the mansion and were especially helpful in supporting our application to the U. S. Park Service requesting that the mansion be designated a National Landmark.

In order to acquire additional information about William Nichols, the mansion's architect, I visited Tuscaloosa, Alabama, to photograph the Gorgas home and the president's home on the campus of the University of Alabama, both of which were designed by Nichols. Additionally, I corresponded with archivists in several states where Nichols had been active in public architecture.

Throughout the three-year-long project of restoring the mansion to the period of its construction, compiling the material for both a pictorial history of the mansion and this full-length study, and trying to achieve the mansion's designation as a National Historic Landmark, there were many people who gave generously and graciously of their time and talents. Without them it could not have been done.

Dr. Sansing and I would especially like to thank the late Dr. R. A. McLemore, Director of the Department of Archives and History, his successor, Elbert Hilliard, Miss Charlotte Capers, Carl Ray (formerly State Archivist), Caroline Allen Killens, Michelle Hudson, Jean McDonald, and other staff members of the Department of Archives and History; the members of the Mississippi Executive Mansion Commission, Dr. R. A. McLemore, Chairman, Sherwood Wise, Elbert Hilliard, Arthur DeRosier, Robert B. McGehee, and Governor Bill Waller; James Chastain, Judy Shute, and the late Dewitt Hamilton of the State Building Commission; Charles Peterson, restoration consultant; Edwin Lewis, project architect; Terrell Wise, general contractor; Edward Jones, restoration consultant; Berl Smith, interior designer; and Bill Garbo, landscape architect; Frank Singleton, Sara Littlepage, Joe McReynolds, Alice McCardle, Shirley Walker, Charles McKellar, Anita Goodwin, H. L. Hill, Jr., Donald Garrett, Jack Giddens, Jimmy Williams, Hubert Worley, Mrs. Chester Mixon, Mrs. John E. Aldridge, Jimmy Wooldridge, Mrs. W. A. Miller, Jr., C. Doyle Hawkins, Gene Threadgill, Max Ewing, Judge John Holcomb, Jimmy Marquis, Charles C. McGonagill, and

Preface

Charles Henry. Special thanks are also due to Professor William K. Scarborough, University of Mississippi and Professor H. Dale Abadie, Associate Dean of the Graduate School, University of Mississippi.

Former first families, their descendents and former staff members, provided a great deal of information about the mansion which would not have been available anywhere else. For their assistance we would like to thank Judge and Mrs. James P. Coleman, Governor and Mrs. Paul B. Johnson, Jr., Mrs. Patricia Johnson Boykin, and Paul B. Johnson, III; Governor John Bell Williams and Mrs. Betty Wells Williams; Governor and Mrs. Ross Barnett and Ross Barnett, Jr.; Mrs. Charles Clark; Mrs. William T. Ratcliff; Mrs. Samuel Strite; Mrs. Gertrude Butler; Mrs. Theodore G. Bilbo and Colonel Theodore G. Bilbo, Jr.; Mrs. W. W. Ford; Mrs. Martin S. Conner and Mrs. Robert Biggs; Mrs. Robert Rushling; Mr. Sam Wilhite; Mrs. D. C. Lee; Mr. Harold Bailey and Mrs. Hunter Webb; Reverend Otis Goodwin; Mrs. Nan Wright King and Mrs. Charles Hunt; Mrs. Eula Poole; and Mrs. Gladys Seely.

And finally, Dr. Sansing and I would like to thank our families whose patience and understanding were sometimes tested during the restoration of the mansion and the production of this history. Especially to Governor Bill Waller, whose encouragement and assistance made it all possible, we acknowledge our debt; and to Bill Jr., Joy, Bob, Eddie, Don, and to Elizabeth, David Jr., Beth and Perry, we express our gratitude.

Carroll Waller
David Sansing
Jackson, Mississippi
August, 1977

A History of the
Mississippi Governor's Mansion

CHAPTER I

A Suitable House for the Governor

IT WAS THE first week of January, excitement was running high in the little capital city in the Mississippi wilderness. Newsmen from every part of the state had traveled muddy roads and ferried several rivers to get to the place, formerly known as Le Fleur's Bluff but more recently as Jackson, to cover the inauguration of Tilghman M. Tucker, scheduled for January 10. A reporter for the *Natchez Free Trader*, John F. H. Claiborne, described the scene: "I love the excitement that pervades everything around me—the life, the enthusiasm, the strife of rival interest." Inaugurals were always gay and festive affairs, but this one seemed even more so and attracted large crowds. Claiborne noted, "Artists, modistes, milliners, attitudinizers, Adonis, dancing masters, sky scrapers, fiddlers, fancy pieces, *maitres de ceremonie* and professors of etiquette are daily arriving, and I never turn a corner without having to apologize for coming too suddenly in contact with some professor of the fine arts, in pants or petticoats. . . . The theatre last night was a perfect jam."[1]

In anticipation of the inaugural crowd, local merchants had ordered extra stock, and some had even painted their storefronts. Saloons were doing a booming business, especially the one connected to the back door of the Mississippi House of Representatives by a plank walk three or four feet wide. The legislature was in session. Activity in the 300 block of Capitol Street was feverish. Builders, plasterers, and painters were keeping a rapid pace. A haggard William Nichols, the state architect, would be seen coming and going, early and late and in between.[2]

The unusual excitement attending Tucker's inauguration was occasioned by the grand opening of the Mississippi governor's mansion.

A History of the Mississippi Governor's Mansion

Almost ten years in the planning stage and three in construction, the "suitable house for the Governor" was at last ready for occupancy. Claiborne captures the mood and spirit of that occasion:

> Much is anticipated by the *elite* here from His Excellency, Governor Tucker's, taste and hospitality, when the Executive Mansion shall be ready for his reception. Levees, re-unions, routs, *conversationes, dejeuners* and *soirees*, will be the order of the day, and our political metropolis will become more gay, fashionable and attractive. . . . After this a new era will commence, and nothing is to be tolerated but the waltz, polanaise and gallopade. . . . I have serious ideas of removing hither.[3]

Since its admission to the Union in 1817, Mississippi's chief magistrates had been responsible for providing their own residence while conducting affairs of state at the capital. Because their duties and responsibilities were rather limited, the governors rarely maintained a residence at Jackson (which had been temporarily designated the capital in 1822) except when the legislature was in session. At other times they remained at their domicile residence and came to Jackson only when necessary to conduct official business. However, in 1832 the new state constitution greatly expanded the duties of the office and required the governor to maintain his official residence in the capital during his tenure in office. That same constitution also established Jackson as the seat of government until 1850, at which time the location of the capital could be reconsidered. If significant demographic changes warranted such action, the capital could then be moved to a site nearer the center of population.[4]

The 1832 constitution, considered by a contemporary historian as the freest in the world at that time, embraced the full range of Jacksonian reforms that characterized the "rise of the common man." The constitution was also adopted just as Mississippi was entering upon the most spectacular land boom in the history of the lower Mississippi valley. Contemporary chronicles described the early 1830s as an era of "Flush Times" when prosperity covered the land "with a golden canopy." During these years over 7.5 million acres of public land were sold and the state's population soared from 136,621 to 375,651. The effect was electrifying. At a banquet in Natchez celebrating the acquisition of vast Indian lands in north Mississippi, Robert J. Walker proclaimed, "Already the feet of thousands press upon the borders of this purchase . . . to pitch their tents

A Suitable House for the Governor

in the wilderness . . . Kentucky's coming, Tennessee's coming, Alabama's coming, and they're coming to join the joyous crowds of Mississippians."[5]

Anticipating the heavy demands that a burgeoning population and geographic expansion would place upon state government, the framers of Mississippi's new constitution multiplied the service agencies and redesigned the structural organization of state government. And to preclude a continuing controversy over the location of the state capital, the lawmakers established Jackson as the seat of government until 1850. However, the impending establishment of several new counties in north Mississippi and the imminent shift in legislative control from southern to northern representatives predisposed the location of the capital to legislative maneuvering. In 1852, by the narrow margin of only thirteen votes, Jackson retained its tenuous title as the capital city.[6]

Jackson was only a small hamlet consisting of about a dozen families in 1832. Since it was the capital by statutory rather than constitutional provision and thus subject to change by a simple majority in the legislature, the city had experienced only minimal growth as few merchants and manufacturers were willing to gamble on its remaining the permanent capital. Furthermore, Mississippi's government under the 1817 constitution was so simple and streamlined that all public offices had been housed in a two-story, wood-framed state house, the lone public building standing in Jackson when the legislature convened in 1833.[7]

It soon became obvious that such a structure could not accommodate all the departments and agencies established by the new constitution. Consequently, the first legislature to meet following its adoption provided for the "erection of a state capitol and other public buildings in the town of Jackson." The constitutional provision requiring the governor to maintain an official residence in Jackson added an interestin dimension to the state's initial building program.

On January 17, 1833, a bill was introduced to appropriate $95,000 for the construction of a capitol. The measure also included an allocation of $10,000 to build "a suitable house for the Governor." In assuming the responsibility of providing an official executive residence, the legislature considered several factors. The governor was elected for a two-year term but was constitutionally restricted to only four years in office during any six-year period. Since rental property in Jackson was virtually nonexis-

A History of the Mississippi Governor's Mansion

tent, a governor would find it necessary to buy a residence if the state did not provide one. Such a purchase might well consume a year's salary thus making the office unattractive to the "common man," a prospect inconsistent with the principles of Jacksonian Democracy then prevailing in the public mind. State pride was also a factor in the legislature's decision; several other southern states had already provided mansions for their chief executives.[8]

All other considerations aside, however, the fundamental motivation to provide an official executive residence was rooted in that strong sense of hospitality that is characteristic of the people of Mississippi. Three days before the expiration of his term, Governor Alexander G. McNutt reported to the legislature on the progress of the mansion's construction. McNutt reminded the lawmakers that the mansion was not being built for the "benefit of the Chief Magistrate alone, but to enable him to receive his fellow citizens on suitable occasions."[9]

Although construction of both the capitol and the mansion was to be financed by the sale of public lots in Jackson and not from general revenue sources, the bill evoked some opposition. Delegates from northern counties realized that the expenditure of $105,000 on public buildings in Jackson would be used in later years as an argument against moving the capitol to a more northern location. In an effort to prevent its passage, Tilghman M. Tucker, then a representative from Lowndes County, challenged the ruling of the Speaker of the House who had taken a voice vote on the measure. Tucker objected that appropriation bills required a two-thirds majority and that the voice vote had not indicated such a majority. The House sustained the chair's ruling and the bill was then sent to the Senate which concurred on February 26, 1833. Several days later Governor Abram Scott signed the bill into law. Ironically, Tucker, who attempted to defeat the bill authorizing its construction, would become the first governor to live in the executive mansion.[10]

Under the terms of the law, the governor was authorized to appoint a state architect of his own choosing to design and supervise the construction of public buildings in Jackson. What should have been a simple appointment became a complicated process, extending over the terms of three different governors and causing a delay of two years.

On May 20, 1833, after considering several applications, Governor

A Suitable House for the Governor

Scott offered the position of state architect to David Morrison of Nashville, Tennessee, who was widely known for his renovation of Jackson's Hermitage. Morrison accepted the post on the condition that his appointment be delayed until he could complete the work in which he was then engaged. During the negotiations, however, Governor Scott died.[11] Scott's successor, Charles Lynch, wrote Morrison on June 22, 1833, asking for a more definite commitment. After the letter went unanswered for several weeks, Lynch sent an agent to Nashville to confer personally with Morrison. The architect said that he was ill and asked for further delays. Dissatisfied with Morrison's response, Lynch withdrew the appointment and offered the commission to John Lawrence, also of Nashville, on October 9, 1833. Lawrence immediately accepted the appointment.[12]

Lynch's timing was unfortunate. Only a few days after his appointment of Lawrence, Lynch received a letter from the architect who would eventually design both the capitol and the governor's mansion. Sometime earlier Lynch had written to Governor John Gayle of Alabama, asking him to recommend someone experienced in public architecture. Gayle forwarded the letter to William Nichols with a suggestion that he get in touch with Lynch. On October 12, 1833, Nichols wrote to Lynch, rather immodestly claiming to have more experience in designing state capitols than any other architect in the country. Two years later, after a costly and frustrating series of delays, Governor Hiram G. Runnels dismissed John Lawrence and appointed William Nichols.[13]

Soon after his appointment, John Lawrence arrived in Jackson and established a private practice, in addition to his duties as state architect. The advertisement for his private business appeared in the Jackson *Mississippian* in December, 1833, even before he published the specifications for the state house, and ran for a year after his dismissal. Lawrence's dual practice prompted a great deal of criticism. Construction of the capitol had been given priority over the mansion, and the legislature, after almost a year's delay, was anxious to see the work on the state house begin. Through the spring and summer bids were let, and construction began in the early fall of 1834.[14]

The cornerstone of the capitol was laid in a Masonic ceremony on November 21, 1834. Construction had barely begun, however, before it was suspended, as the anticipated revenue from the sale of public lots had not materialized. The Planters Bank would not discount the promissory notes which the state had accepted as payment for the public lots. Bank officials informed Governor Runnels that those notes which were to be redeemed in three annual installments were not negotiable in the money market and could not be rediscounted by the bank. As a temporary solution, Governor Runnels signed a personal note offering state securities as collateral and obtained a short-term loan enabling the architect to proceed with the contracts then in progress, though work beyond that point was halted.[15]

To deal with this and other problems, Governor Runnels called a special session of the legislature for January, 1835. But the session was aborted when the Senate refused to seat the delegates from the recently organized northern counties and adjourned in protest of the action by the House of Representatives which seated the delegates. The controversy involved the eligibility of the new members to sit in the special session. The Senate held that the recently elected members were not eligible until the regular session scheduled for the fall. The House thought otherwise. The legislature's inaction was disappointing to the Speaker of the House, who adjourned his branch of the lawmaking body by saying, "I had hoped to have been able to congratulate you on . . . the . . . fiscal aid which we were expected to give to the erection of the State Capitol. . . . These sanguine anticipations have, however, for the present been blasted [by] an unhappy collision of opinion."[16]

As the construction made available by Runnels' personal loan proceeded, still another and more pressing problem arose. During the spring of 1835 the design of the state house came under heavy criticism in the press. The *Mississippian* offered the opinion that the design required major "revisal and alterations." For several months the advisability of altering the present plans or starting over was bandied about in the press and discussed among those public officials who would occupy the building. Finally, Governor Runnels became convinced that Lawrence possessed neither the architectural skill nor the administrative ability to complete the capitol within a reasonable time and in a manner satisfactory to the legislature. On October 9, 1835, Runnels dismissed Lawrence

A Suitable House for the Governor

and offered the appointment to William Nichols, who accepted and was commissioned on November 11.[17]

The legislature, again meeting by special call of the governor, approved Lawrence's dismissal and confirmed Nichols' appointment in January, 1836. The *Mississippian*, after congratulating both Runnels and the legislature for their decisive action, conceded that Lawrence was honest but surmised that "nature never intended him an 'architeck.'" That quip, presumably, was a reference to Lawrence's misspelling of the word architect on his application to Governor Scott in 1833. The special committee which approved Nichols' appointment urged the legislature to make an additional appropriation for the state house and also, for the first time since 1833, mentioned the executive mansion. The reference was to the "government house" and merely reaffirmed the legislature's support for its construction.[18]

When William Nichols assumed the office of state architect, he was instructed by the legislature to prepare a new set of plans for a capitol. He was also assigned the additional responsibility of designing and constructing a state penitentiary. These two structures, both given priority over the mansion, were under construction when the economic disruption caused by the Panic of 1837 bankrupted the state and again necessitated the suspension of all public works.[19]

As the strictures of financial exigencies waned, Nichols resumed construction on both buildings during the summer of 1838. The capitol was completed, or at least to the point that the legislature could occupy the assembly chambers, during the session which convened in January, 1839. By December, 1840, the penitentiary was also far enough along to accommodate about thirty inmates. As these buildings were nearing completion, Nichols directed his efforts toward the executive mansion.[20]

In 1838 the legislature approved the architect's design for the mansion, and construction began in September, 1839. Unfortunately, Nichols' original drawings and sketches of the mansion have not been found. If they still exist, their location would constitute an important discovery in American architectural history. In a special report to the legislature while seeking a supplemental appropriation in 1840, Nichols described the mansion:

A History of the Mississippi Governor's Mansion

The mansion house for the residence of the Governor is now being built agreeably with the plan approved last Legislature. The building will be 72 by 53 feet. The ground or basement story is eight feet high and is divided into servant's rooms, store room and cellar.

On the principal floor the main entrance is from a portico 28 by 12 feet into an octagon vestibule, which communicates with a drawing room 50 by 24 feet, with a dining room, which by means of folding doors, may be made of the same size, and with the great stair-case leading to the upper floor; in rear of these will be a suite of comfortable family rooms; the upper floor will contain four spacious chambers, a wardrobe and a private stair-case, communicating with the basement story.

The portico on the principal front, will be supported by columns of the Corinthian order. In finishing the building, it is intended to avoid a profusion of ornament, and to adhere to a plain republican simplicity, as best comporting with the dignity of the State.[21]

While adhering to republican simplicity, Nichols designed the mansion in that period's most popular architectural style—Greek Revival. This style is typical of many antebellum southern mansions but had its greatest triumphs in public architecture. Talbot Hamlin, an architectural historian, has asserted that Greek Revival architecture was a revival only in the sense that "its decorative vocabulary was based upon classic Greek detail." Greek Revival, especially in the South, was more derivative than imitative and reflected a "frank acceptance of climates and ways of life" in an "attempt to create a new and American architecture." In light of this analysis of southern architecture, Nichols occupies a position of prominence in American architectural history for which he has not yet been recognized. Only recently has he attracted the attention of architectural historians, but there are several studies on Nichols now in progress. Perhaps these studies will document his achievements and enhance his reputation among the nation's early architects.[22]

William Nichols was born in Bath, England, in 1776. He first surfaces in the records of architectural history in the Commonwealth of North Carolina, where he also served as state architect (a position he held in at least three states). Employed to remodel the North Carolina capitol in 1821, Nichols added stucco and a dome to what originally was a plain brick building. He next appears in Alabama, again as state architect. In the late 1820s and early 1830s, Nichols designed the second Alabama state house and is also credited with the original buildings on the campus of the

A Suitable House for the Governor

University of Alabama, including the president's mansion. Following his work in Alabama, he received the appointment as state architect in Mississippi.

When his term as Mississippi's state architect expired in 1842, Nichols probably continued a private practice in and around Jackson. However, there is no evidence available, for the time being at least, to document his private practice. He resurfaces in the records of public architecture in January, 1845, when he was appointed by the Board of Trustees of the State University to design the original buildings for the University of Mississippi at Oxford. He designed the Lyceum and several other structures on the Oxford campus, including dormitories, faculty houses, and lecture halls. These buildings were completed by 1848 when the University held its first session.

Following his work with the state university, Nichols was retained by officials in Yazoo County to design a courthouse which was later described by the *Yazoo Democrat* as "an edifice . . . of unsurpassed beauty and convenience." He next emerges in Lexington, Holmes County, Mississippi. The Holmes County courthouse was completed in 1853. It was at Lexington, the county seat, that William Nichols died on December 12, 1853, and it is in the Lexington cemetery that he is buried. The only evidence available that Nichols was the architect of the courthouse derives from oral tradition among the county's oldest citizens, but the probability that he designed the structure is very great. If this was the case, it is only a matter of time before documentary evidence is discovered.

There is also no evidence presently available to document the Philadelphia phase of Nichols' career, yet there are spicy references here and there to "Captain Nichols of Philadelphia." During the late eighteenth and early nineteenth centuries, many fortune-seeking Pennsylvanians were lured into the Old Southwest. Such a rapidly developing area would seem especially enticing to an architect. However, such sketchy references can only suggest the possibility that Nichols may have moved down the "Great Philadelphia Wagon Road" to North Carolina, thence to Alabama, and finally to Mississippi. Perhaps at one time there was a trail of buildings marking his progress westward, though it is unlikely that very many of those structures have survived. One of them, however, has proven to be a building of remarkable endurance. Designed at the zenith

A History of the Mississippi Governor's Mansion

of his career, the Mississippi governor's mansion may be Nichols' greatest achievement.[23]

Although he considered the mansion as a single structure, Nichols' original design actually included two buildings connected by a veranda. The front or principal structure—with a basement, main floor, and second story—was designed primarily for state functions and visiting dignitaries. The extension on the north side—a basement and a suite of four family rooms—was to be used for the personal accommodation of the first family. This extension, or north wing, was replaced in 1908 by a two-story annex which was in turn replaced by a townhouse addition in 1975.

To "avoid a profusion of ornament," Nichols employed the Greek Revival style with restraint and taste. The mansion's front portico is supported by four fluted Corinthian columns with delicately carved capitals. Its semicircular design lends a graceful touch to the mansion's square, massive form. The mansion's interior was adorned by hand-crafted cornices, lintels, and friezes. A pleasure garden of roses and honeysuckle, a stable, chicken house, cook house, and other outbuildings were planned for the east lawn but were not constructed until several years later. The grounds were enclosed by a wooden fence until 1855, at which time a brick-based, wrought iron enclosure was added.[24]

It is difficult to determine the progress of construction through the often confusing records. The journal of expenditures kept by the Commissioners of Public Buildings indicates that Howell and Graves began excavation of the mansion square in September and completed their work in October, 1839. The brick and stone work was then contracted to S. D. Howell and Walker and McLacklan. Apparently, the foundation and exterior frame were completed by the fall of 1840. The commissioners authorized payments of $7,604.84 to S. D. Howell from December 4, 1839, to February 7, 1841, and of $2,000 to Walker and McLacklan from April 6, 1840, to June 10, 1840. Walker and McLacklan had another claim of $4,325 which had not been paid as of February 12, 1842. It seems certain, however, that this compensation was for carved freestone work which had been completed much earlier. Interior woodwork was done by Reuben Clark at a cost of approximately $6,500, which he received from October 21, 1840, to May 12, 1841. In addition to these earlier payments,

A Suitable House for the Governor

Clark claimed that the state still owed him $15,653 in February, 1842. Carpentry work accounted for one of the largest outlays in the construction of the mansion; material alone cost $6,265.[25]

The mansion's ornamental carving and plaster work, which have received high praise from architectural historians, were done by William Gibbon and Ezra Williams. As best determined from the records, Gibbon did most of the plastering and Williams carved the capitals for the four columns supporting the front portico, the ornamental door frames, some of the modillions, cornices, trusses, and the one hundred banisters for the grand staircase. However, Williams' payment of only $1,155 could not account for all of the mansion's interior ornamentation. Reuben Clark, who did most of the carpentry and joiners work, should also be credited with some of the craftsmanship which has distinguished the mansion's interior.[26]

Records kept by the commissioners of public buildings indicate only a minimal use of slave labor in building the governor's mansion. There are only two entries in the journal of expenditures that reflect the use of slaves. A Jackson woman was authorized two payments totaling $222.66 for the service of a young Negro man. It is possible, of course, that various contractors may have made use of slave craftsmen but there is no documentary evidence for such a practice.[27]

In accordance with the provisions of the 1833 law, which stipulated that the mansion must be covered with a fireproof material, Nichols ordered large quantities of zinc which he used to cover the exterior walls and the roof. Unfortunately, zinc was later found to be an inappropriate roofing material in the humid southern climate. Until a new slate roof was added in 1854, the first families experienced continued inconvenience during the spring and fall rains when heavy leakage caused damage to interior walls and furnishings.[28]

However, the use of zinc was not the only factor contributing to the problem of leakage. After the $20,000 supplemental appropriation of 1840 was exhausted, the financial condition of the state precluded any additional allocation for the mansion. Consequently, during the fall of 1840 construction was temporarily suspended and the building hastily covered to prevent damage from winter rains. But the roofing was not carefully installed and the attic gallery was so hurriedly enclosed and improperly

A History of the Mississippi Governor's Mansion

joined to the roof that streams of water leaked through three stories, permanently damaging interior walls.[29]

As the state's economic prospects brightened in the spring of 1841, construction was resumed although no additional appropriations had been made. Both Governor McNutt and William Nichols assured various contractors that once the mansion was completed the legislature would honor its contracts. Nichols worked feverishly throughout the fall of 1841 to have the mansion ready for Governor Tucker's inauguration on January 10, 1842. He motivated contractors by the rather obvious implication that to have the building ready for Tucker would be a "means of interesting the new governor in endeavoring to get all claims discharged at the commencement of the Legislature." Although the mansion was not finished by Tucker's inauguration, Nichols was able to prepare six rooms for occupancy and the first family moved into the mansion sometime in February, 1842.[30]

The final cost of the mansion is practically impossible to determine. Nichols and the state treasurer engaged in a heated exchange of letters during the 1842 legislative session concerning the final or projected cost. In his annual report of January 27, 1842, Richard Graves, state treasurer and ex-officio commissioner of public buildings, presented a cost analysis that alarmed the legislature. Admitting that the figures represented only the best estimate he could derive from the confusing and conflicting figures in the commissioner's office, he advised the lawmakers that the mansion would, when all bills were paid, cost the state $85,156.21. The figures contained in Graves' report reflected the following schedule of payments:

Expended in 1839	$ 3,339.82
Expended in 1840	27,312.55
Expended in 1841	9,259.42
Total expended in 1839–1841	$39,911.79
Outstanding claims against the state in 1842	$42,244.42
Estimate necessary to landscape grounds	3,000.00
TOTAL PROJECTED COST	$85,156.21[31]

Graves conceded that his figures might include some duplication of payments which could reduce the final cost by about $5,000. If that were the case, the cost would then be only about $80,000. This report brought a blistering reply from William Nichols on February 12, 1842.[32]

In his rejoinder, Nichols charged that Graves' report was "calculated to mislead the public mind and place the subject in the worst possible light." Nichols advised the legislature that $11,000 of the claims Graves listed as outstanding had already been paid. An additional $11,000 had been cancelled by an agreement between the state and various individuals who provided material or labor on the mansion in lieu of cash payments for town lots during the hard times that followed the Panic of 1837. Nichols further accused Graves of overestimating by $1,500 the amount necessary to landscape the grounds. His adjusted figure, including the legitimate claims still outstanding, showed the approximate cost to be only $61,556 rather than $80,000.[33]

In response to Nichols' charge that his estimate was inaccurate by design, Graves sent another report to the legislature on February 26, 1842. The language of his second report indicated that a personal conflict between himself and Nichols, and not a cost analysis of the mansion, was the real point of issue. Graves referred to Nichols as "His Highness, the ex-State Architect." The conflict may have resulted from the fact that Graves had earlier recommended that the office of state architect be abolished because it was a useless and wasteful expense to the state. As a final retort, Graves recommended a legislative investigation of his charges. The treasurer pledged, in the meantime, to "faithfully discharge the duties of his office."[34]

In light of subsequent events it is remarkable that Graves would have been so brazen. For the legislature did conduct an investigation. But rather than finding Nichols negligent and malfeasant, they discovered a shortage in the state treasury. Graves was dismissed, arrested, and placed under guard in Jackson. In one of the most unspectacular episodes in the annals of great escapes, Graves soon regained his freedom. While under guard, the ex-treasurer was allowed a brief visit with his wife behind closed doors. A few moments later, dressed in his wife's clothing, Graves walked calmly past the guards, out of the building, and then fled the state to avoid prosecution.[35]

Even though the investigation which led to Graves' dismissal may have exonerated Nichols, it did not disentangle the confusion over the actual

A History of the Mississippi Governor's Mansion

cost of the mansion. To the original 1833 appropriation of $10,000 a supplemental appropriation of $20,000 was made in 1840. But two other special appropriations in 1842 and 1844, paying various claims against the state, undoubtedly ran the cost well above $50,000. Since several other claims paid during the next three legislative sessions appear to have been payment of mansion contracts, though not identified as such, the effort to arrive at a specific figure seems an exercise in futility.

The cost of the mansion, however, did not seem to be a major concern to most contemporary Mississippians. Only the Whig press, always critical of the Democratic party's extravagance, had harsh words for the completed project. The Whigs referred to the executive residence as a "palace" built for "Alexander The Great McNutt, Commander-in-Chief of the Army and Navy of Mississippi." Most contemporaries, however, local residents in particular, were very proud of the governor's mansion.[36]

After its completion, the Mississippi mansion became one of Jackson's two most notable landmarks, the other being the capitol located just three blocks up Capitol Street. The mansion's architectural grace and beauty received the accolades of both local citizens and visitors to the otherwise unimposing capital city. A correspondent of *De Bow's Review*, a monthly magazine published in New Orleans, considered the Mississippi governor's mansion the "handsomest abode to be seen in the Southern Country" and others compared it favorably with the White House.[37]

CHAPTER II

Republican Simplicity in Grand Style

THE GOLDEN CANOPY that covered the land in the early 1830s gave way to dark clouds and ill winds by the end of that decade. A reckless misuse of credit during the Flush Times generated an inflationary spiral that swept the economically naïve frontier farmers into a vortex of speculation. When the Panic of 1837 brought economic chaos to the state, thousands of Mississippians marching in double quick-step to the rhythmic sounds of the seller's hammer moved to Texas.[1]

During the height of the boom period, the state had issued several million dollars in bonds which were later invested in banks and railroad companies. When these corporations failed during the panic, the Democratic governor, Alexander G. McNutt, announced that the state would not honor the bonds. His action precipitated a bitter factional struggle which transcended party lines and threatened to "carry down the Democratic party."[2]

Divided and on the brink of dissolution, the Democratic party was held together by William Gwin, who persuaded a reluctant Tilghman Tucker to head the party's ticket in the election of 1841. Tucker's nomination was not a grass roots movement, nor even a compromise within the party; it was a last resort, as few prominent Democrats were willing to bear the party's standard and the onus of repudiation. In contrast, a unified Whig party was augmented by dissident Democrats. This coalition conducted a scathing campaign against Tucker, who not only favored repudiation of the bonds but had publicly accused his predecessor of being in league with speculators and in violation of the state constitution by allowing the issuance of the bonds in the first place.[3]

17

A History of the Mississippi Governor's Mansion

Recrimination and personal animosity characterized the campaign. The editor of the *Vicksburg Sentinel* was killed in an altercation prompted by an editorial. Not infrequently did the clash of issues degenerate to arbitrament by force and violence, so intense and heated was the electioneering. When the smoke cleared, Tucker had defeated his Whig opponent, David Shattuck, by 19,059 votes to 16,773; but the ill will engendered during the campaign lingered through Tucker's two years in office.[4]

Tilghman Tucker was born in North Carolina on February 2, 1802. Like thousands of his contemporaries, Tucker migrated through Alabama into Mississippi during his early youth. He took up the trade of a blacksmith, but forsook this to study law. He then entered politics, representing Lowndes County in the state legislature from 1830–41. In an age of great debaters and stump speakers, Tucker was distinguished for his lack of rhetorical skills and was often ridiculed for his "slow and prosy" speeches, though admired by others for his "fund of smutty anecdote."[5]

When Tucker was inaugurated as governor of Mississippi on January 10, 1842, a cold, rainy, winter day, the *Canton Creole* noted that "in an age of superstition, the physical gloom which enshrouded all nature" would have been interpreted "as ominous signs of an unhappy administration." Dismissing such forebodings as the legacy of an unlettered age, the *Creole*'s editor then proceeded, by implication at least, to betray his own suspicion that Tucker's administration would indeed be an unhappy one. The Whig editor ridiculed Tucker's inaugural address and accused him of "malice aforethought" since the speech had been written out beforehand and read to the legislature. It was humiliating to proud Mississippians, said the editor, to witness the governor "openly claim the infamous doctrine of repudiation."[6]

For over a month after his inauguration, Governor Tucker and his family boarded at the home of Mrs. David Dickson while the finishing touches were being applied to the six rooms in the mansion which Nichols had readied for their occupancy. As the carpets and drapes were being installed, Governor McNutt sent a special message to the legislature seeking an immediate appropriation of $6,000 based on Nichols' estimate of the amount necessary to furnish the mansion. Several legislators objected to such a large appropriation on the grounds that the governor's

Republican Simplicity in Grand Style

family had remained in Columbus and did not intend to live in the mansion. Supporters of the bill, however, assured their colleagues that Tucker's family was in Jackson and would occupy the mansion if adequately furnished. "Half-a-dozen members," according to the *Natchez Free Trader*, "spoke at full length on this subject, all of whom objected to wasting time."[7]

After the confusion over the first family's intention to occupy the executive mansion was settled, the legislature authorized an expenditure of $4,000 for the purchase of furniture. Despite the authorization, Governor Tucker refused to spend the money, arguing that the purchase of furniture for the mansion was an unnecessary and unjustified expense which the state could ill afford. Praising the governor for denying himself "the gratification of putting his house in splendid costume," the *Free Trader* reported that Tucker "contents himself with the simplest furniture, purchased at his own expense."[8]

If Nichols designed the mansion in "republican simplicity," Governor Tucker and the first lady, the former Sarah F. McBee, occupied it in similar fashion. Tucker was disinclined toward what one editor described as "those superfluous ceremonies so often attempted and so often burlesqued." In America, he added, anything beyond the "simplicity of our plain, republican institutions is ridiculous." Additionally, the lingering effects of Tucker's earlier bout with typhoid fever and a recurring illness which incapacitated the first lady disposed the Tuckers to a quiet and simple lifestyle. They spent much of their first year in office at their home in Columbus. Consequently, entertainment at the mansion was held to a minimum, a fact which seemed to disappoint local residents.[9]

A Jackson editor, vocalizing that disappointment, commended the "good people of Mississippi [who] at a very great expense, have erected in this city a most beautiful Mansion for the Executive of the State," and asserted that "the doors of the Governor's house [should] be thrown open occasionally." He also protested the governor's continued absence, beseeching "Come home, Governor Tucker, your friends want to see you. We are tired of traveling cabinets and migratory Governors."[10]

Although not to his personal liking, there were times when Governor Tucker could not avoid the ceremonial responsibilities attached to his office and, consequently, the use of the mansion. Among these occasions were the visits of prominent national figures to Jackson. On a return trip to Kentucky after a visit in New Orleans in February of 1843, Henry Clay passed through Natchez and Jackson. Although an inopportune time for the Whig leader to visit Jackson (the state convention of the Democratic party then being in progress), Clay was nevertheless accorded the honor of a public reception at the mansion "where he received the visits of hundred of his fellow citizens."[11]

Only two months later another popular national figure, Richard M. Johnson, former vice-president of the United States and reputed slayer of the Shawnee chief Tecumseh, was similarly entertained at the mansion. Johnson was greeted at the depot by a large delegation which escorted him first to the capitol, where he delighted his audience with a thirty-minute speech, and then to the mansion which "was thrown open for the accommodation of those who desired to exchange salutations with the Old Hero." As on the occasion of Clay's visit, a public ball was given in Johnson's honor in the evening. But in both cases, the evening events were held at a Jackson hotel and not at the mansion.[12]

Governor Tucker, a member of the local temperance society and a plain, unsophisticated man, was never comfortable at formal, public ceremonies. He was much more at ease swapping stories with his old personal and political friends who frequently called upon him at the mansion. And he usually insisted that they extend their visit as long as possible, as the pleasure derived from those occasions did not require receiving lines or depend upon fancy furnishings.[13]

Somewhat to the surprise of Tucker, the fancy furniture which he had earlier refused to buy began appearing at the mansion. Although the circumstances surrounding the purchase of furnishings during the fall of 1842 are obscure, Tucker surmised a relationship between their arrival at the mansion and his suspicion that something was amiss in the state treasurer's office. On January 8, 1843, Tucker wrote Senator Robert J. Walker in Washington:

> I have, myself, for somedays past been inclined to fear that all was not as it should be, on account of the fact, of some furniture having reached the Executive Mansion. This furniture has been purchased (as I suppose) by the Treasurer of this State. At all events the furniture has reached the Executive Mansion, without any knowledge or direction of the Governor, as to its pur-

Republican Simplicity in Grand Style

chase, or of the means with which it was purchased, though the law (Acts of 1842 page 139, Sec. 2) provides that the sum of four thousand dollars, shall be expended by the Commissioner of Public Buildings (who is the State Treasurer) under the direction of the Governor, in the purchase of furniture for the Executive Mansion. Though I have fears, yet I hope that nothing is wrong.[14]

Within a month after this letter was written a legislative investigation uncovered evidence that Richard Graves had diverted or otherwise misused approximately $44,000 of state funds. Although he removed Graves from office and ordered his arrest, Tucker was severely criticized for not acting sooner as speculation concerning Graves' malfeasance in office mounted through the month of January. Some of the criticism included thinly veiled accusations that Tucker was also implicated.[15]

It is difficult to ascertain just how much of the $4,000 was actually spent on furniture for the mansion. Records in the auditor's office show that three purchases were made on November 18, November 22, and December 29, 1842. Among the items listed on the invoices were a piano, a carriage, and several crates of furniture. The purchases were arranged through J. C. Buckles, a commissioner and forwarding merchant in Louisville, Kentucky; but these did not consume the entire appropriation. Whether Graves misappropriated any of the remaining funds or diverted any of the purchases to his personal use is not known.[16]

While incarcerated, Graves was in the custody of the Capitol Guards, a local militia unit. After the ex-treasurer's escape, Tucker not only publicly chastised the Capitol Guards but refused to authorize any compensation for their services. In what must have been the first demonstration at the mansion, an unidentified group paid an unscheduled call upon the governor. Under the caption WRONG, the Jackson *Southron*, a Whig paper, reported the visit:

> We have been informed that some individuals last night visited the Governor's Mansion, with tin pans, kettles and other musical instruments of a similar kind, to the great annoyance of the Governor's family and the citizens of the neighborhood. We do not know the individuals who constituted the serenading band, but it was a shameful proceeding, and it was condemned by almost every citizen in town.[17]

The *Southron* assured its readers that the Capitol Guards had not participated in the affair, although the editor did take the opportunity to express his support of the guards in their controversy with Tucker over their right to be paid for guarding Graves.

This incident and the way it was reported seem typical of Tucker's uneasy residence in the mansion and his relationship with the press, which was generally unfavorable and often abusive. During the Democratic state convention of 1843, the *Vicksburg Sentinel* published a mock version of a conversation in the mansion between the governor and the attorney general, John D. Freeman:

> Tucker: Don't you think, Freeman, that the d----d convention has refused to nominate me for Governor.
> Freeman: I wish the convention was at the devil. They refused to nominate me for Congress.
> Tucker: What do they say against me?
> Freeman: Why, that which they seem to harp on most, is that you are dull and stupid. Great many say that you have not sense enough for a good justice of the peace.
> Tucker: Come now, Freeman, help me out of this scrape. You know you have lived in the Executive Mansion, just as though it belonged to you.
> Freeman: Well now, Governor, you know it is the people's house; and what is more, I have furnished my share of the eatables; and as you belong to the temperance society, when there was any treating to do, I treated.
> Tucker: Oh, it has been sort of joint stock: what the whigs call an anti-bond mess, for they have talked about it in the papers, and accused me of keeping a boarding house. Speaking of newspapers, I think they ought to be put down. Sometimes I think that the art of printing should never have been invented.[18]

The Tucker portrayed in this mock conversation was not unlike the real Tucker, stammering in speech and halting in leadership. Finding himself presiding over a divided party, Tucker proved himself unable to reunite the rival factions. Still more significantly, Tucker's failure to provide effective leadership left a vacuum and prompted the development of a small clique whose influence within the party was so greatly expanded over the next few years that this group came to rule the party rather than lead it. To avert just such a development, Thomas Williams wrote to Tucker urging him to seek renomination. Williams argued that only Tucker's renomination could defeat that "corrupt clique . . . [who seek] to rule the democratic party with a rod of iron, and to *rule out* all who will not give in to their unholy design."[19] But the Democratic convention did

Republican Simplicity in Grand Style

not renominate Tucker, passing over him in favor of Albert Gallatin Brown, then serving in the United States Congress and probably the most popular Democrat in the state.

Tucker's unhappy term came to an end in January, 1844. On the eve of his departure from office, the first family held a farewell levee at the mansion. More in keeping with what the Jackson elite had anticipated from the residents of the beautiful mansion, the gala affair was described as the "largest and most brilliant assembly that ever graced the Executive Mansion since the late Governor's election."[20] A more detailed account appeared in the *Mississippian*:

> Every room was crowded, and the scene was one of rare animation, fashion and beauty. The number present was computed at some five or six hundred—with but little less than a hundred ladies—some as beautiful as beings of aerial mould and not of earth. Every one seemed full of enjoyment—no counterfeit smiles lighted the blooming cheeks—no regret mingled in the festivity.
>
> The dancing was carried on with much grace and spirit, and a little past midnight the thronged assemblage repaired up stairs to a dining hall, where plenty, taste and good feeling presided at the bounteous feast.[21]

Following this glowing description the editor asked, "If the sunset of official power throws off at its going down, such gorgeous and entrancing brightness, what . . . will be the splendor that shall attend the rising of another sun?"[22] Beneath this florid style is an intriguing insight into the nature of politics. In any political system, royal or popular, routine social currents are just as tricky and often more treacherous than an occasional political storm. How often an innocent social slight has ignited a bitter political struggle is not known, but it is evident that the ship of state must weather the social currents as well as the political storms.

Governor Tucker did not understand this, or the relationship between parties at the mansion and politics in the capitol, or the subtle impact of ladies on the passage of important legislation. He did not perceive the interaction between social cliques and political factions nor did he exploit the mansion's potential in dealing with either. His successor did, however, and accrued both political advantage and personal popularity as a natural result.[23]

Albert Gallatin Brown and his charming wife served a socio-political apprenticeship in the whirling world of Washington where they learned to correlate the seating arrangement at a dinner party to the seniority system in Congress. Although the stakes might not be as high at the state level, the same forces were at work. A perceptive Jackson editor wrote: "Should Mrs. Governor Brown find in our intellectual and accomplished female society the same love and deference which surrounded her when she moved a bright and graceful and particular star in the brilliant circles of the city of Washington, she will . . . wield power over society here more potent than the constitution and the laws allow to her honored husband."[24]

Roberta Young of Alexandria, Virginia, had married Albert Gallatin Brown while he was serving in the United States Congress. As the wife of a young and promising congressman and a member of one of Virginia's aristocratic families, Mrs. Brown moved in the best circles in Washington and Virginia society. Cognizant of her power over public affairs as first lady of Mississippi, she exercised that power skillfully, not at the capitol, but at the mansion. She exploited the social potential of an invitation requesting "the pleasure of your company at the Governor's Mansion," and afforded rival political factions many opportunities to socialize and thus minimize their personal animosity. Reuben Davis, whose presence enlivened many of those occasions, described the effects of Mrs. Brown's hospitality: "Those rejoicings were like a truce between two armies, during which the soldiers on each side laid down their arms and mingled freely in feast and dance."[25]

Although it is impossible to gauge the role that the mansion's hospitality may have played in reestablishing Democratic party unity, there is no question that such unity was in fact restored. The *Mississippian* noted on June 18, 1847, that the Democratic state convention "closed with great harmony" and that "many grave personal difficulties which had been festering for years were healed."[26] A corresponding reaction to the reestablishment of party unity was the rise in Brown's popularity during his first administration, a marvel in Mississippi politics by any measure.

By the time of Brown's second inauguration in January, 1846, the first family's reputation for hospitality was well known throughout the state. From the remote "province" of Panola County a correspondent came to Jackson to cover the second inauguration and filed the following report:

Republican Simplicity in Grand Style

The Governor gave a grand levee on Saturday night, which was attended by an immense number of ladys [sic] and gentlemen, and was emphatically a complete jam. There was a fine band of music in attendance for the benefit of those who wished to shake the fantastic toe, and the number was not small, as there were seldom less than forty on the floor at one time. Supper was announced at 10 o'clock, and from the rush that was made for the supper table, and the avidity with which the dishes were seized and devoured, I should suppose that many of the crowd had abstained from dinner, for the purpose of whetting their appetite for the feast. Mrs. Brown was entitled to high commendation for the display of taste in the preparation and management of the supper.[27]

A Jackson paper described the event in similar fashion but added that the mansion was filled with those who came to honor "the Chief Magistrate, whose administration for a single term had disarmed opposition to him, and who had now been installed for a second term."[28]

As popular as the Browns were for their gracious entertaining, they were equally appreciated, especially by Jacksonians, for their efforts to beautify the mansion grounds. During Tucker's administration virtually no landscaping had been done to the mansion square, which according to one account more closely resembled a "cow pasture full of ugly weeds" than the cultured lawn "which should grace such a majestic structure." Mrs. Brown planted several rose bushes and honeysuckle throughout the grounds and lined the walk from Capitol Street to the front portico with an avenue of cedars. The first lady's efforts were applauded by the *Mississippian* which observed the fruits of her labors in a May issue, noting "the tasteful and preserving appearance of the grounds" about the mansion. "No longer is the eye disgusted by the many noxious weeds which formerly cumbered the spot." In appreciation of her interest in beautification, a committee of local citizens presented a flower vase to the first lady at a public ball given in honor of Governor and Mrs. Brown just before the expiration of his second term.[29]

During the Browns' four-year residency, the mansion was sparsely furnished and included only the barest necessities. Many years later, during the heated controversy over Republican expenditures during Reconstruction, Brown (then retired from public life) recalled his first night in the mansion:

A History of the Mississippi Governor's Mansion

> I shall never forget my first night in that house. My wife slept on a shuck mattress, without sheets, and rested her head on a carpet sack. It was a bitter cold night in January, and she used woolen garments as a substitute for blankets. I remained in the Mansion four years and in all that time there was never appropriated one dollar to furnish it. I did not ask it, and would never have allowed it if it had been offered until the State was out of debt.[30]

Brown might also have added that the mansion had not been provided an outdoor privy prior to his occupancy in 1844, nor had the stables, carriage house, and fencing been completed. The only outbuilding which had been erected before he moved into the mansion was the kitchen located on the east lawn. The only expenditure during Brown's first two years was for the installation of a lightning rod at a cost of about $70.00. During his second term an appropriation of $2,240 was made available to complete the appurtenances as originally designed by Nichols, who was again employed by the state to supervise their construction.[31]

During Brown's last year in office, the location of the mansion became the focus of an interesting controversy. When the Democratic party nominated Brown for his old congressional seat in the Fourth District, the opposition asserted that Brown was not eligible to run for that particular seat. Because Brown's term of office would not expire until after the election for Congress, and since his official residence at the time of the election would be the Mississippi executive mansion in Jackson which was not located within the Fourth District, the Whigs argued that Brown could not maintain an official residence outside the district and be eligible to run in that district. On the other hand, they maintained that if Brown were actually a resident of Copiah County as he claimed, he was then in violation of the state constitutional provision requiring the governor to maintain his official residence at the capital city. The Whigs were content, however, to merely raise the issue. They took no judicial action to prevent Brown's candidacy and the governor easily won the election.[32]

The Democratic state convention, meeting in Jackson on June 7, 1847, faced a rather difficult decision in the choice of a successor to Albert Gallatin Brown, who had provided both the party and the state with four years of constructive leadership. The fact that the Mexican War was then in progress further complicated the situation, as most of the state's prominent Democrats were serving in the United States Army. The party finally

Republican Simplicity in Grand Style

settled on Joseph W. Matthews of Marshall County. A native of Alabama, Matthews had been employed by the federal government to survey the public domain in north Mississippi when the Chickasaw Cession opened millions of acres to white settlement. After establishing residence at Old Salem, in Marshall County, Matthews served two terms in the legislature before his gubernatorial nomination.[33]

The election of 1847 was relatively calm by Mississippi standards. Matthews and the Democratic party, unified and stronger than ever, easily carried the state. Matthews' Whig opponent, Major A. B. Bradford, also of Marshall County, had achieved a less than illustrious record in the Mexican War. A contemporary account of his exploits in that engagement affords an insight into the political importance antebellum Mississippians attached to military achievements. Reuben Davis, in his remarkably candid *Recollections of Mississippi and Mississippians*, wrote:

> Colonel [Jefferson] Davis had already received a wound at Buena Vista; and Bradford, although charging and encouraging his men all along the line with the most reckless bravery, was unwounded. It is the only case I ever heard of where a man was absolutely heart-broken because a bullet failed to hit him. Eye-witnesses reported that he actually charged up and down the line, waving his arms in the air, and exclaiming, 'My God, can't one bullet hit me?' In all this he was perfectly honest, and it is an actual fact that for the rest of his life his spirit was wounded because his body was whole. He always confessed that he never recovered from the disappointment of that day.[34]

The records do not reveal how much disappointment may have been added by Bradford's defeat at the hands of Joseph Matthews by a margin of two to one.

Throughout the campaign Matthews, like Tucker, came across as a rather plain and rugged frontiersman. Lacking the flair for oratory which Mississippians had come to expect from their statesmen, Matthews was derisively referred to as "Jo Salem," "Jo the well digger," and "Old Copperas Breeches." News accounts of Matthews' inaugural reception hinted that some apprehension had existed concerning the style of hospitality which the governor and the first lady would maintain at the mansion during their residency.[35]

But fears were assuaged during the first open house held by Matthews at the mansion. The local paper reported:

A History of the Mississippi Governor's Mansion

On Thursday last, the Executive Mansion was thrown open for the receipt of visitors, and on no occasion of the kind have we ever witnessed a more magnificent display. The crowd was too great. It seemed that the whole people had gathered to witness the "performances." Those who came through *curiosity*, rather than to do honor to the chief magistrate, went away "with their fingers in their mouths." "Old Copperas Breeches" was as much at home in the parlor as he ever was on the stump and his amiable lady pleasantly greeted all who were presented to her.[36]

The article continued with an analysis of the ideological origins of hospitality and unconsciously expressed the difficulty Mississippi's first family would have in measuring up to an unspoken but understood quality and style of hospitality. The writer admitted, "We do not favor grand display on the part of public officers. They look to us like apeing the magnificence of royalty; but we must confess we were highly gratified on this occasion. The Governor is a plain planter, and the invidious and curious were eager for scandal; they were disappointed."[37]

Loosely translated, that statement meant that Mississippi's first family must be able to entertain lavishly and in grand style, but in a manner that appeared consistent with "republican simplicity." In the vernacular of rural Mississippi, they must not "put on the dog." However, it does seem likely that if, in failing to achieve such a delicate balance, the first family tilted toward the grand rather than the simple style, the people in their munificence would forgive them. From all accounts Governor and Mrs. Matthews, the former Martha Ann Jones of Richmond, Virginia, and their two young daughters, Sallie and Elizabeth, achieved that balance.[38]

An earlier Mississippi historian evaluated Matthews' administration as "uneventful and covered the years from 1848–1850."[39] Although Matthews may be Mississippi's Millard Fillmore, several significant developments occurred during his tenure in office—the adoption of a new legal code for the state, the construction of the State Institute for the Blind, and the opening of the University of Mississippi. In addition, Jackson gained important links to the outside world. The construction of the Jackson–Brandon railroad made the capital much more accessible than it had been before and the installation of telegraph lines brought the city within minutes of the major news centers and important developments in the nation. By far, however, the most significant development during

Republican Simplicity in Grand Style

Matthews' administration was the culmination of the power elite within the Democratic party, which through Mississippi's stormy political history has been called at various times the "Jackson clique," the "capital crowd," and the "Capitol Street gang." Evidence of its impending culmination is derived from an unlikely source.

In early December, 1848, only eleven months into Matthews' two-year term and seven months before the next Democratic state convention was scheduled to meet, a traveling correspondent for the New York magazine, *Literary American*, filed the following report from Jackson: "This beautiful building on our right is the Capitol of the State, . . . As we stand at the main entrance of the capitol, casting our eyes forward, they rest upon the beautiful Mansion of the Governor. His Excellency, Joseph W. Matthews of Marshall County, now fills the Executive chair. . . . Governor Matthews, it is understood, will retire at the end of his present term, and give place to the heroic Quitman."[40] It bears repeating that this article was filed seven months prior to the nominating convention, which was held at Jackson on June 18, 1849.

One of the contributing factors to the success of the "Jackson clique" was the Democratic press. With one voice Democratic editors urged party members to concede all "points of difference" in the interest of party solidarity. The Marshall County *Jacksonian* asked those Democrats "with whom we differ on two or three points, if it is right and proper that this difference should prevent" the achievement of the party's " 'common object'—to keep the whigs from getting control of the state?" After urging all party members to work for harmony the paper concluded, unabashedly, "We also hope that they will aid us in extending the circulation of the *Jacksonian*." The most influential Democratic paper in the state, the Jackson *Mississippian*, expressed a similar position: "We have FIRST OF ALL, determined to save the state from Whig domination, and to postpone till a more suitable period, all questions among ourselves." The *Yazoo Democrat* was even more emphatic. That paper declared, "We will ask no other questions than is he a Democrat? is he honest? is he capable?"[41] In that order, it might be noted.

If compromise or concession was the price of victory, some element within the party must determine who would concede and on what points. Arbitrary power, which is not the same as the power to arbitrate, was assumed by the Jackson clique. Democratic papers condoned and few rank and file members either questioned or challenged their leadership. The action of the Democratic state convention in 1849 was stamped APPROVED and bore the great seal of the Jackson clique. After a spokesman for Matthews advised the convention that the governor did not desire a second term, John Anthony Quitman was nominated by acclamation. Forthwith, the convention nominated the secretary of state, state treasurer, auditor of public accounts, and attorney general, all by acclamation.[42] With that degree of party unity and the "Hero of Mexico" heading the ticket, the Democrats swept the state in the election of 1849.

CHAPTER III

The Years of Crisis

THROUGHOUT THE CAMPAIGN of 1849 the Democratic press publicized the military phase of Quitman's career almost to the exclusion of his public service, which at various times had included positions in the legislative, judicial, and executive branches of state government. In a manner that would excite the admiration of modern ad men, the party's papers based their appeal on the timeless tradition of rewarding military heroes with the laurels of public office.

Perhaps in few societies was this tradition more advanced than in the antebellum South. Mississippians were enthralled by the splendor and display associated with militarism. When local militia units were assembled for muster day, large crowds from miles around the field of review gathered to watch the close order drills. It was an important social event that brought a measure of excitement to the drudgery of their rural isolation. In his reminiscences of life in antebellum Mississippi, Reuben Davis recalled a typical muster day:

> Some time before, I had been elected brigadier of militia, and Major-General [A. B.] Bradford now sent me an order to call out for review the militia in the six counties which composed my brigade. . . . General Bradford had provided himself with a uniform so gorgeous as to smite the eyes of all beholders. His glittering chapeau was crowned with long white plumes, and the gilt scabbard of his sword was girt about him with a magnificent yellow sash. He was a tall and handsome man, and in his dazzling array looked, and felt, every inch a hero. . . . Although we travelled in the plain garb of peaceful citizens, I promise you we were not unprovided with the paraphernalia of magnificent regimentals. . . . We soon discovered that the people were disgusted by our appearance in citizen's clothes, and considered themselves defrauded of part of

A History of the Mississippi Governor's Mansion

the show. We hastened to repair this injustice, and soon appeared disguised in splendors that might have startled a Comanche Indian. This appeased the multitude, and we were greeted with thunders of applause.[1]

Although this intriguing account begs a more extended comment, it may be sufficient to say that it was at this "multitude" that Quitman's campaign was directed. Shortly before the November election, a quarter-page advertisement in a Jackson paper regaled the military exploits of that "brave and chivalrous soldier GENERAL JOHN ANTHONY QUITMAN." Aware of the process of transference long before pyschologists confirmed it, the paper then asked the Mississippi electorate, "Shall we not tell our sister states, by our vote for him in November, that we are a chivalrous people, and that we love and cherish our warriors with lively gratitude?" By a majority of 10,000 votes the people proclaimed their chivalry and expressed a gratitude lively enough even for the ambitious Quitman.[2]

When the governor-general was inaugurated on January 10, 1850, he wore the deep blue, full military dress of a major general. Sword at his side, girt about by a yellow sash, and mounted upon a dazzling white charger, Quitman led the inaugural parade to the riotous cheers of the largest inaugural crowd in the state's history.[3]

The following day Quitman wrote his wife who had remained with five of their children at their plantation in Adams County:

> All desire to see you and our family and it is very important you should be here as early as possible—I am sorry to say the Executive Mansion is not in as good order or furnished as I expected—I will however have the cottage part *clean* & fitted up for you by the time you arrive—You would be of greatest assistance to me here. I beg you therefore to come up immediately.[4]

Eliza Turner Quitman, born into a prominent Woodville family and accustomed to the affluence of a wealthy planter, had not anticipated leaving Monmouth, their 1,500-acre plantation with its 300 slaves. But a few days before the inauguration, Quitman's nineteen-year-old son had written his mother of the rumors that the general's lady refused to leave the cultured, sophisticated Natchez society to live among the "Rosin Heels in these partes." The loyal son consoled his mother, however, by assuring her that the complaints about her absence from the governor's mansion in Jackson were "got up no doubt to make political capital for the

The Years of Crisis

opposing party."[5] Both of these letters indicate the continuing political importance attached to social life at the mansion. Not even the governor-general was exempt; in fact more was expected from him in the way of grand hospitality.

Quitman's plea prevailed and the first lady with her five other children soon joined him at the mansion. Quitman's promise to have the building cleaned and repaired was an assurance often repeated by other governors over the years. The mansion seems never to have been ready for the first family at the time of their occupancy. Quitman's letter is also something of an index to the mansion's furnishings. He instructed the first lady to bring "your bed linen, towels & napkins [and] our china set." But he promised her a better set "when we leave here." "The state," he said, "will probably purchase it." Quitman presumed that the state would purchase their old china, which he would leave in the mansion; he would then use the money paid by the state to buy his wife a new set. The governor added, "If you doubt anything bring it along we will want it all," assuring his wife that the legislature would be "liberal to us" but "a little time is necessary."[6]

As it turned out, very little time was necessary. On January 21, 1850, the legislature authorized the expenditure of $3,500 to be used by the governor in repairing and furnishing the mansion. The law authorized the governor to sell the old and damaged furniture and transfer the proceeds from that sale to the state treasury. The law also specified that the appropriation be expended for such articles as cooking utensils, carpets, curtains, tables, chairs, bedsteads, and bureaus.[7] The first family's residency in the mansion had begun under promising circumtances.

With the exception of George Poindexter, probably no other Mississippian had a more varied background or held public office longer than John Quitman. Born in New York on September 1, 1798, Quitman came to Mississippi by way of Ohio and settled at Natchez in 1821. After marrying into a prominent Woodville family, he engaged in planting and was for a short time president of the railroad company that built the line from Natchez to Jackson. At the age of twenty-nine, he was elected to the state legislature and then served a short term as chancellor in the southern district. During the nullification controversy of 1832–33, Quitman supported Calhoun in his conflict with President Andrew Jackson; he was one of the few Mississippians whose career survived an anti-Jackson background. By virtue of his office as president of the Senate, Quitman also served as acting governor for a thirty-three-day interim when the inaugural date was changed from November to January in 1836.[8]

Quitman's success in public office, as outstanding as it was, stimulated rather than satisfied his inordinate ambition. John F. H. Claiborne, Mississippi's premier nineteenth-century historian and Quitman's biographer, wrote that "a more ambitious man never lived" than Quitman who "was greedy for military fame."[9] In a chauvinistic society military achievement was the measure of greatness. Quitman accepted this standard early in his life and sought its reward. At the age of twenty-six, only three years after coming to Natchez, he organized a local militia unit, the Natchez Fencibles, and then worked his way up to major general in the Mississippi militia. But despite his exploits in the Texas Revolution and the Mexican War, where he served with distinction, Quitman did not achieve military fame. Although his active military career ended when his application for appointment as a brigadier general in the regular army was declined shortly after the Mexican War, fate would again dangle an enticing offer before him—though again just beyond his grasp.

Quitman was in office only three months when emissaries representing the Cuban insurgency visited the mansion and offered him the military command of the Cuban revolutionary army. In March, 1850, Narciso Lopez and José Ambrosio Gonzales spent several days with Quitman trying to convince the governor-general of the great fame that would accrue to his already illustrious military career if he were to lead the Cubans in a war for independence against their Spanish oppressors. Their offer, later expanded to include compensation of one million dollars for his services, was appealing to Quitman. Although he declined to accept the military command, his interest in and support for Cuban independence continued and would eventually cause his arrest by federal authorities.[10]

As valuable as his services may have been to the Cubans, Quitman envisioned an even more important conflict that would afford still greater opportunity. He was convinced, as early as 1850, that secession or civil war—or maybe both—were imminent. After the enactment of the Compromise of 1850, which many southerners considered a northern victory

The Years of Crisis

with alarming ramifications, Quitman was even more certain that secession was the only alternative to war.[11]

While the debate over Mississippi's response to the compromise was raging, and possible alternatives were being considered, Quitman held a "magnificent levee" at the mansion. That occasion again underscored the importance of the social amenities in shaping public policy. The *Mississippian* noted that "A splendid entertainment was given at his Excellency's Mansion. . . . Quite a crowd of ladies were present, and their fair and beautiful forms well served to remind our gallant sons of the inestimable treasure at stake in this crisis of Northern invasion. The merry dance was kept up until a late hour, and was only interrupted by a magnificent supper . . . displaying the luxuries of our Southern soil, and sparkling with the wines of France. We were pleased to see the good feeling which abounded on the occasion." Hinting that weightier matters were also discussed during the course of the evening, the journal expressed its hope that amiability would "continue to characterize our social intercourse, notwithstanding all our conflicts of political views, which however serious, must proceed alone from patriotic hearts and minds."[12] There is no doubt that, while sipping the wines of France, small groups of men who would shape the state's destiny clustered in the hallways or in the corners of the mansion's spacious parlors where the inclination of national allegiance and the urgency of sectional interest were weighed, one against the other. Perhaps while the ladies and the connoisseurs in more polite conversation weighed the whites against the reds.

On the basis of the legislature's action taken shortly after this levee it can be assumed that the urgency of sectional interest was found weightier than national allegiance, at least among those groups dominated by Quitman's overbearing presence. The governor convened a special session of the legislature in December, 1850, and urged the lawmakers to call a constitutional convention for the purpose of seceding from the Union. The legislature acted favorably upon Quitman's suggestion, and an election for delegates was set for September, 1851.[13]

In February, 1851, however, Quitman was arrested for violating American neutrality in Cuba. The situation provided an opportunity to test state sovereignty against the power of the federal government to arrest a state's chief executive. However, Quitman did not contest his arrest. He resigned on February 3 and voluntarily surrendered to federal authorities who arraigned him in New Orleans. His family moved out of the mansion and returned to their home at Monmouth.[14]

In March, after all charges were dropped for lack of evidence necessary for indictment, Quitman returned in triumph to Jackson where a mass public meeting was held in his honor. The "great Quitman rally," as reported in the Democratic press, drew a crowd estimated at 3,000. The Whig paper, however, reported that there were only between 190 and 202 people at the rally. Since the evidence necessary to reconcile the discrepancies in these figures is not available, it can only be said with any degree of certainty that the great Quitman rally attracted a crowd numbering something between 190 and 3,000 people.[15]

Since 1851 was a general election year, there were to be two elections in the fall. First, there would be the September election for delegates to the convention and then the general election in November. Although the party leadership was less than unanimous in the choice of Quitman as the party's candidate for governor, they acceded to his nomination, which had strong support in a Democratic press generally favorable to secession. Almost immediately, traditional party lines were blurred by the overriding consideration of secession versus Union. A combination of Whigs and Union Democrats nominated Henry Stuart Foote, one of Mississippi's two senators and the only member of the state's congressional delegation who supported and voted for the Compromise of 1850.[16]

The election of delegates to the convention proved a resounding victory for the Union ticket. This defeat of the secession delegates so surprised and disgusted Quitman that he withdrew his candidacy for the governorship. The Democratic party then prevailed upon a reluctant and ill Jefferson Davis to replace Quitman. The still popular Davis was only barely defeated by Foote in the general election, losing by less than 1,000 votes. The first crisis of secession passed, and Mississippi voted to remain in the Union a little while longer.[17]

The first secession crisis was recalled years later by Quitman's daughter, Rosalie Quitman Duncan, who was only ten years old during her father's term of office. Although as a child she heard her father talk about civil war and remembered the "disquieted and anxious feeling" associated with those discussions, she could not understand why "he should feel as he did when all things seemed so calm, so serenely at peace in our lives" at the mansion. "But, alas!" she admitted, "he knew better than I. A few years later and the same home was taken as headquarters by our dire enemies, and a rough soldiery telling us we had 'bad names' took whatsoever they wanted."[18]

During the interim, between Quitman's resignation of February 3, 1851, and Foote's inauguration on January 10, 1852, the office of governor was held initially by John I. Guion, president of the Senate. However, when Guion's term in the Senate expired on November 4, a vacancy again occurred in the governorship. During Guion's term as acting governor, he may have occupied the executive mansion though it is doubtful. For one thing, he was a resident of Jackson and it seems unlikely that he would have moved into the mansion for such a short period of time. Moreover, during much of that time he was campaigning for a judgeship embracing several counties in central Mississippi. The only reference to the executive residence in Guion's correspondence occurs in a letter from the state auditor informing the acting governor that from the January, 1850, appropriation of $3,500 for furnishing and repairing the mansion a balance of $400 remained and was at the disposal of the governor.[19]

When Guion's term in the Senate expired on November 4, 1851, a crisis of sorts existed in the state. There was no chief executive and no president of the Senate, who by constitutional provision would be automatically elevated to the post upon a vacancy. For a period of twenty days the office was vacant. The state seemed not to have suffered unduly. Nevertheless, on November 24 a special session of the Senate convened in Jackson for the sole purpose of electing a president who would then exercise the duties of the chief executive. On the twenty-first ballot, James Whitfield of Columbus was elected. Whitfield continued as acting governor until January 10, 1852, but there is no indication that he and his family lived in the mansion during that time.[20] For almost a year following Quitman's resignation, the mansion had not been occupied, and there had been some damage and loss of furnishings resulting either from leakage, theft, or vandalism. It had also become customary for the outgoing first family to vacate the mansion before the expiration of their term to allow the incoming first family to situate themselves prior to the inaugural ceremonies. Thus there usually was a short period of time, varying from a few days to several weeks, when the mansion was subject to abuse through vandalism or theft.

In an attempt to eliminate the loss of state property and other damages to the mansion while the residence was unoccupied, John J. Pettus, a senator from Kemper County, introduced a resolution requiring the governor prior to his vacating the executive mansion "to employ some suitable person to take charge of and safe keep the same."[21] Strangely, this resolution did not pass. The only possible explanation is that such a requirement was an insinuation, however indirect, that the first family might be implicated in the loss of furnishings which at various times had been removed from the mansion.

When Governor Foote, First Lady Rachel Smiley of Nashville, Tennessee, and their young daughter occupied the mansion in January, 1852, the executive residence was ten years old. During that decade approximately $23,000 had been appropriated to finish, furnish, and repair the building, but still several problems remained.

When the legislature convened in January, 1852, a select committee was appointed to examine the executive mansion, determine its overall condition, and ascertain the repairs necessary to prevent any further deterioration. The committee found the wooden enclosures in a state of almost total disrepair; there were wide gaps where sections had been removed by pedestrians or riders taking a short cut across the mansion square. Rather than advocating repair of the existing wooden structure, the committee recommended the construction of a wrought iron, brick-based enclosure at an estimated cost of $3,000. The committee also recommended the purchase of "articles of fixed and heavy furniture." The legislation that was later enacted specified that $1,800 be appropriated for "tables, chairs, bedsteads, and bureaus" in addition to carpets, curtains, kitchenware, and cooking utensils. This law also provided for the repair of the existing fences rather than for their replacement as the committee had recommended.[22]

In addition to appropriating specific sums for these purchases and repairs, the legislature of 1852 also authorized the use of the Executive Contingency Fund for minor day-to-day repairs at the mansion. This system proved so effective in correcting minor problems before they

The Years of Crisis

became major ones that a subsequent legislature established a separate Executive Mansion Contingency Fund.[23]

The election of 1851, like that of 1841, was a bitter factional struggle that transcended party lines and left scars which took years to heal. The single issue was Union or secession. Foote's election was more than a personal triumph; it revealed that a majority of Mississippians were unwilling to sever their ties with the Union. Shortly after her family moved into the Mississippi executive mansion, Mrs. Foote planted a line of oaks on the four sides of the mansion square. It is not known if the first lady intended the oaks to symbolize the permanence of the Union, but the temptation to so speculate is irresistible. Although the Union victory was not permanent, the first lady's oaks survived long after the crisis of secession and war had passed. Ultimately, they were a casualty of progress. When the city of Jackson widened the streets in the downtown business district in 1902, the oaks were removed.[24]

The highlight of Foote's residence in the mansion was the visit of the Hungarian patriot Louis Kossuth. While a United States senator, Foote was instrumental in securing Kossuth's release from a Turkish prison. During his subsequent tour of the United States, Kossuth expressed a particular desire to visit his benefactor in Mississippi. After he made a speech in Washington defending states' rights, which was widely quoted in the Mississippi press, Kossuth was extended a special invitation to address a joint session of the Mississippi legislature. Upon his arrival in Jackson, Kossuth addressed a large crowd which had assembled to welcome the rebel in exile. During his three days in Jackson, March 24–26, 1852, Kossuth and his wife with a small entourage were the guests of the governor and first lady at the mansion.[25] A round of speeches and receptions crowded his brief visit. Like that of his predecessor, Foote's administration had opened on a note of optimism. Unfortunately, however, it would end—also like that of Foote's predecessor—with the governor's resignation.

A native Virginian, Foote had practiced law in Richmond prior to coming to Mississippi by way of Alabama. Settling in Vicksburg, where he practiced law and edited a newspaper, Foote soon became an outstanding criminal lawyer and one of the state's best stump orators. He frequently baited his opponents with biting sarcasm, a tactic which "resulted in four formal duels and other less formal encounters." After serving in the legislature, he was elected to the United States Senate in 1847. During the debate over the Compromise of 1850, Foote played a key role in enlisting southern support for the measure, and it was that handful of southern votes which provided the margin of victory. In view of Foote's strong stand against secession throughout the 1850s, it may seem strange that he would later serve in the Confederate Congress; yet many southern Unionists, when faced with the *fait accompli* of secession, chose to remain loyal to their native section. In addition to his active political career, Foote was also an author of several books including his sagacious memoirs, *A Casket of Reminiscences*.[26]

The Mississippi phase of Foote's public career ended by his own choice. John J. McRae's defeat of Francis M. Rogers in the election of 1853 was a repudiation of the policies Foote had counseled during his term in office. In disgust he resigned five days before his term expired and left the state, thus ending a long and stormy career in Mississippi politics.[27]

The election of 1853 which so disgusted Foote was quite delightful to many other Mississippians who saw perhaps their first folk hero elevated to the exhalted status of chief magistrate. A former riverboat pilot who sailed his steamer *Triumph* up and down the Chickasawhay River "as if he were on the Mississippi itself," John J. McRae was one of antebellum Mississippi's most popular governors. Known to his friends as "Johnny McRae of Chickasawhay," he was an engaging conversationalist and capable orator whose varied background included a short stint in journalism. Though he is sometimes incorrectly credited with founding the *Eastern Clarion*, which later became the Jackson *Clarion-Ledger*, he was one of its earliest owners. As the journal's second publisher he owned the paper less than a year before selling it in 1839.[28] In addition to his four-year term as governor, McRae also served in both houses of the state legislature, in the United States Senate and House of Representatives, and in the Confederate Congress.

During McRae's residency in the mansion, three problems of long standing were corrected. For several years first families had been inconvenienced during the rainy season, and previous governors had been known to command that infamous brigade of buckets on cold and wintry days. On March 1, 1854, the legislature authorized the removal of the original roof from the mansion and the replacement of the zinc-coated covering with a "substantial slate roof." The appropriation of $8,500 also included the removal of all wooden enclosures then on the mansion grounds and the construction of an iron-railing fence built on a wall of brick capped with stone. The fence, constructed by James T. Hull, was located inside the line of oaks planted by Mrs. Foote. Two carriage entrances (on West and on Congress streets), a pedestrian gate on Amite, and a more formal, elaborate entrance fronting Capitol Street provided access to the mansion grounds. All four gates were topped by eagles with outspread wings.[29]

Finally, to remedy the problems caused by the settling or shifting of the mansion's foundation, the legislature authorized funds to pave an area ten or fifteen feet around the mansion, thus halting the erosion, and to install iron braces and anchors to support the building. An additional $2,000 was also appropriated for the purchase of new furnishings and household utensils to be secured at the discretion of the governor.[30]

From the levee on the night of his first inauguration to the end of his four-year tenure, McRae maintained a virtual open house at the mansion. During political campaigns, the mansion was utilized to its fullest advantage, politically as well as socially. On one occasion the local Democratic paper announced that the "ladies of Jackson and vicinity . . . are requested to meet at the Executive Mansion" to design a banner to be presented to the county with the largest attendance at the great Democratic mass meeting which was soon to be held at Jackson.[31]

When the results of the 1855 gubernatorial election were announced, a large group of McRae supporters spontaneously called upon him at the mansion to congratulate him on his reelection. He met them at the steps of the front portico and made a rousing speech, thanking them for their continued support. On concluding he shouted, "Fellow citizens, I have returned to the capital of the state with the plume of victory in my hat. . . . Walk in, gentlemen, and partake of the hospitalities of the Mansion."[32]

McRae's victory in 1855 was especially pleasing to his supporters because the Know-Nothing party had posed a significant challenge to the continued control of the state by the Democratic party. His success prompted several other spontaneous visits to the mansion. One evening in particular, in contrast to the band that had visited Tucker several years earlier, a large procession of the "unterrified Democracy" led by a brass band marched to the mansion and insisted that the governor show himself to the admiring throng. For one of three reasons—either the crowd was too great, Mrs. McRae would not permit it, or the mood of the marchers dictated a continuation of the parade—McRae did not invite the multitude into the mansion. It was probably the latter, because the parade continued to wind through the streets of Jackson. After pausing before the office of the *Mississippian*, which was given a rousing three cheers, the crowd revelled in equally rousing oratory provided at the slightest prompting. Finally, "at a late hour, the meeting dispersed in the highest spirits."[33]

Other first families may have entertained with more flair than the McRaes, but none more freely. A friend and neighbor described McRae as "generous and hospitable to a fault," and ventured to guess that "when he retired from the Executive Mansion he may have been a wiser man, but he was certainly a poorer man."[34] However, McRae must have been consoled, if not compensated, for his generosity by the display of affection at a public ball given in honor of the first family just after they left the mansion. From their constituents the first lady received a silver service and the governor received a gift which all politicians interpret as the highest award the people can give—reelection to office, in this case to the U.S. Congress.[35]

Democratic party unity, weakened during the crisis years of Quitman and Foote, was largely restored during the two terms of John J. McRae. But another and potentially more serious obstacle to solidarity resurfaced during McRae's administration. Sectional rivalry between north and south Mississippi intensified as north Mississippi Democrats contemplated the fact that four of the previous six and three of the last four governors had all been from the southern part of the state. This long-standing rivalry complicated the party's state convention in 1857 and threatened the "Jackson clique's" continued control over party nominations. Northern delegates demanded that the gubernatorial nomination in 1857 be given to north Mississippi. However, since William McWillie, of Madison County, had been passed over in favor of John J. McRae in 1853 the party's leadership was committed to him. Yet his nomination

The Years of Crisis

might jeopardize the reappointment of Albert Gallatin Brown to the United States Senate.[36]

A native South Carolinian, William McWillie moved to Mississippi in 1845 and almost immediately became involved in the inner circles of Mississippi's Democratic party, which elected him to the United States Congress in 1849. From Kirkwood, his Madison County plantation, McWillie commanded a social and economic status which qualified him for a place among the leaders of his party. A contemporary, Joel M. Acker of Aberdeen, recognized in McWillie the same characteristics which typified many other Mississippi politicians during the years immediately preceding the Civil War. McWillie was "personally honest and upright," according to Acker, "but like most political partisans . . . somewhat warped by the intrigues incident to long political life."[37] McWillie's nomination in 1857 resulted from the very sort of intrigue to which Acker referred.

As a good party man, Governor McRae invited the Democratic leadership to a conference at the mansion on June 22, 1857 during the state convention in Jackson. Dominated by the "Three Great Democratic Lights of Mississippi," Jefferson Davis, Albert Gallatin Brown, and John Anthony Quitman, the meeting lasted most of the night and "many drowsy physiognomies were seen around town and at the convention" the next morning. Since minutes of such meetings are rarely recorded, the action of the convention is the only index as to what transpired in the smoke-filled parlors of the mansion where the destinies of several men, and perhaps even the destiny of Mississippi, may have been shaped during that long night.[38]

The next day the convention nominated McWillie and endorsed the renomination of Albert G. Brown, who would join Jefferson Davis in the United States Senate. All three were from south Mississippi. The power elite's control over the party was complete and the rank and file members concurred in its action.

The Whig party, dissipated during its sojourn in the secrecy of Know-Nothingism, was destroyed in the fall elections when the Democratic party, "like a fire in the woods," swept the state and consumed its opposition by a margin of two to one. Following the election of 1857, Mississippi's political leadership consisted of McWillie as governor, Davis and

A History of the Mississippi Governor's Mansion

Brown in the Senate, and McRae, Quitman, L. Q. C. Lamar, Otho Singleton, Reuben Davis, and William Barksdale in the Congress. All were ardent secessionists.

But life in the Mississippi executive mansion during the McWillie residency gave no indication of the impending crisis. The first lady, Catherine Anderson McWillie of South Carolina, was the mansion's most elegant hostess since Mrs. Brown. Moreover, as McWillie was a wealthy planter, the first family's lifestyle in the mansion was not regulated by the rather meager income attached to the office of governor. The governor's family included several young and beautiful daughters who entertained lavishly and made the mansion the social center of the state during McWillie's two years in office. Based on documents preserved in the auditor's records, McWillie's inaugural reception and dinner must rank as one of the grand affairs for which the mansion was by then well known and its reputation well deserved. Included on the menu were three gallons of rum, fifteen gallons of brandy, two gallons of champagne, twenty pounds of cheese, thirty-three pounds of mutton, twenty-eight pounds of beef, ten dozen oysters, ten large cakes, and an unspecified quantity of small cakes, candy, bread, crackers, etc.[39]

Other records also reveal the legislature's concern that the McWillies not be forced to compromise their standard of living. An appropriation of $2,000 was made available to the first family for the purchase of additional furnishings for the mansion. The acquisitions, secured through such New Orleans import merchants as J. D. Dameron, D. H. Holmes, and C. Boye, were primarily heavy furniture, though some drapery material was also purchased. As usual, the expenditures exceeded the appropriation and McWillie asked his successor, John J. Pettus, to reimburse him from the mansion contingency fund for the amount spent in excess of the appropriation. McWillie explained to Pettus that he needed the money to pay his taxes.[40]

During the McWillie residency, the mansion's social notoriety extended beyond that of any of his predecessors and lingered long after his administration. The impressive list of distinguished visitors to the mansion included Seargent S. Prentiss, Jefferson Davis, J. L. Alcorn, Bishop Otey of Tennessee, Bishop William Mercer Green, the first Episcopal bishop of Mississippi, Col. Alexander McClung, and many others. In the

The Years of Crisis

1930s, when a Jackson social club presented a pageant recalling the history of the capital city, life in the executive mansion was represented by a scene portraying a gala ball during the McWillie residency. While the Browns extended the mansion's hospitality for more pragmatic purposes, the McWillies seemed to entertain for purely social reasons.[41]

While the McWillie family occupied the executive residence, two important first events occurred. The marriage of Annie McWillie to Dr. Thomas J. Mitchell was the first wedding ceremony held in the mansion. And the Mitchells' first child became the first baby born in the executive residence.[42]

During the McWillie administration, the governor's mansion was a place of laughter and gaiety. However, before it would again be the scene of such happy times, the mansion would house the councils of war and shelter the wounded.

CHAPTER IV

These Are Wartimes

ON JULY 4, 1859, the Mississippi Democratic party convened in Jackson to nominate its candidate for governor and other state officers. Amid great excitement and enthusiasm the party nominated John J. Pettus of Kemper County. Four years later a London *Times* correspondent interviewed the governor at his office in the capitol. The correspondent described Pettus as a man who often missed the spittoon but did so with the style and flair of "a man who wished to show that he could have hit the center if he liked."[1] To many antebellum Mississippians style was often as important as accuracy and flair always an essential for leadership.

By 1859, for all practical purposes, opposition to secession was relegated to a voice in the wilderness, faintly prophesying of doom and destruction. But Mississippi's leadership, employing all the style and flair it could muster and charmed by its own rhetoric, did not hear that voice. Elected by a three-to-one margin over only token opposition gotten up at the last minute, Pettus led Mississippians confidently and defiantly toward war, defeat, and disillusionment. "England is no doubt a great country," Pettus conceded to the *Times* correspondent, "but the sovereign state of Mississippi could do a great deal better without England than England could do without her."[2] What makes this statement so remarkable is that a month before it was made Pettus had been driven from his capital city by an invading army and a month after it was made he would again be driven from the very office in which the conversation was taking place.

Pettus was a natural development of the social and political institutions in antebellum Mississippi. Like the great majority of his fellow citizens, he was essentially a frontiersman with characteristic rugged individuality

These Are Wartimes

and an exaggerated sense of honor. Before Pettus was inaugurated, the legislature inquired if he and his family intended to occupy the executive mansion. The inquiry was no doubt prompted by his Natty Bumppo-Davy Crockett lifestyle which had attracted so much comment during the campaign. It seemed somehow incongruous that a tobacco-chewing, rough-hewn outdoorsman would find the stately mansion to his convenience or that he would mimic the affluent and sophisticated Governor McWillie whose family had made the mansion the center of Mississippi's elite society. Nevertheless, Pettus advised the legislature that he, his wife, and their two daughters would occupy the governor's mansion. The first family moved into the executive residence just before Pettus' inauguration on November 21, 1859, little more than a month after John Brown's abortive raid at Harpers Ferry. Like their father, Sucky and Willie loved the outdoors and kept horses at the mansion for their afternoon riding pleasure.[3]

In his inaugural message Pettus addressed himself to the impending crisis and counseled resistance to what he considered a federal usurpation of states' rights. In his rhetoric, the first ten amendments to the Constitution were as equally inviolate as the Ten Commandments and the state faced only two alternatives—submission or secession. Throughout 1860, Governor Pettus and Mississippi's Democratic leadership carefully nurtured the supposition that the "peculiar institution" would be unsafe in a federal Union governed by a black Republican president. All the forces that mold public sentiment were marshalled in the effort to impose the logic of secession upon the Mississippi electorate—on the editorial pages, from the pulpit, in the classrooms, in the legislative chambers, and from the governor's mansion. There were other alternatives as well as other issues, but southern pride, under the taunts of fanatical abolitionists, was at stake and required satisfaction. In his classic study *Mississippi: The Storm Center of Secession*, Percy L. Rainwater wrote that southerners, "like a parcel of schoolboys," determined to make the "puritanical snobs" feel "Southern steele and smell Southern powder."[4]

After Abraham Lincoln's election in November, 1860, Governor Pettus called the Mississippi legislature into special session. Meeting in December, the legislature authorized the election of delegates to a state constitutional convention to be assembled in January, 1861, for the purpose of seceding from the federal Union. When the Ordinance of Secession drafted by L. Q. C. Lamar was approved by a vote of 84 to 15, the packed galleries burst into wild cheers and applause. A bonnie blue flag already prepared in anticipation of the vote was unfurled, and later that evening a torchlight parade with bands and singing wound through the streets of Jackson. The celebration was more becoming the end of a war than the beginning of one.[5]

Yet, remarkably, few men among Mississippi's leadership believed that secession would lead to war, especially John J. Pettus. About the time Mississippi seceded, H. S. Fulkerson began corresponding with a small arms manufacturer in Brussels, Belgium. With samples of the guns offered for sale by the Brussels firm, Fulkerson called upon Pettus and urged him to purchase a large supply before the Union blockaded southern ports. After shooting away "much ammunition trying to hit an imaginary Yankee at long range," Pettus told Fulkerson that the guns were not necessary as there would be no war. The two men then retired to the governor's office where Pettus entertained Fulkerson "with one of his best bear stories."[6]

The few Mississippians who did anticipate war were cautioned against stating such views. Shortly after the secession convention had adjourned, a Mississippi congressman made a speech at Brandon during which he advised his audience of the possibility of a prolonged and devastating war. When he concluded, a friend approached him and counseled, "I believe your opinions are correct, but do you not doubt the propriety of saying these things in public? Would it not be wiser to preserve a discreet silence until everything is ready?" The congressman responded that the state's leadership must give their citizens fair warning. "Otherwise," he said, "they might justly utter the reproach that they had been led blindfolded to the very brink of a precipice." For a moment the man looked at the congressman "as if in doubt, and then said, 'Well, that's honest, anyway.'"[7]

After the war did come, the people were led to believe that one Rebel could whip ten Yankees. Thus did Mississippians greet the war with such wild enthusiasm that the number of volunteers exceeded the state's logistical capacity and financial ability to bring them under arms. During the first flush of enthusiasm, local commanders wrote Pettus demanding

These Are Wartimes

that their units be enrolled and assigned to combat areas. Through the four years of war, approximately 78,000 Mississippians were inducted into the Confederate military forces. Almost half of them did not return.[8]

As the Union strategy to capture the lower Mississippi valley developed, Jackson became an important military and commercial center, and the atmosphere at the governor's mansion assumed a unique character. The horses kept on the mansion grounds for the pleasure of Sucky and Willie Pettus had already been ridden into battle by young cavalrymen. Within the same period of time, military conferences crowded the mansion's calendar and invitations to the executive residence read "the urgency of your presence" rather than "the pleasure of your company."

In October, 1862, General John C. Pemberton was placed in command of the Department of Mississippi and East Louisiana with headquarters in Jackson. His orders were to protect the rail system supplying Vicksburg and to defend the port city at all costs. Simultaneously, General U. S. Grant embarked upon his assault of Vicksburg. By May, 1863, federal movements against Vicksburg and the lines supplying the city brought the war in its full fury to Jackson and its environs.[9]

Military planning and other wartime emergencies absorbed Governor Pettus and other state officials. The governor's mansion soon became the focal point of strategy sessions. General Pemberton, and later Joseph E. Johnston, and their staff officers met frequently with Governor Pettus for nighttime conferences at the mansion during the months preceding Jackson's first occupation on May 14, 1863. Records in the auditor's office reflect the increasing level of that activity. In payment for fuel consumed at the mansion the state auditor issued warrants to the Jackson Gas Light Company as follows: January, $8.60; February, $8.79; March, $8.98; April, $9.18; and May, $9.38.[10] Pettus was literally burning the midnight oil.

With Jackson in danger of attack, Governor Pettus prepared for various contingencies. On May 5, 1863, he advised state officials to be ready to evacuate the city on thirty minutes' notice. On the same day he ordered penitentiary officials to transfer the most dangerous prisoners to Alabama and release all the others.[11] Naturally, such orders spawned rumors of the impending fall of Vicksburg. However, the Jackson *Mississippian* advised its readers that, although things looked bad, the situation was not hopeless and assured local citizens that the Confederate army was invincible, that Vicksburg was impregnable, and that reinforcements were on the way.[12] But within a week the capital was in chaos as the anticipated reinforcements were too few and came too late to save Jackson from federal attack.

When General Joseph E. Johnston arrived at Jackson on May 13, he found an almost deserted city. Dr. D. W. Yandell, a surgeon on the Confederate general's staff, described the situation: "We . . . reached Jackson on May 13 . . . and met the Governor of the State fleeing from his capital. . . . We found the Governor's family gone, his Mansion deserted . . . the militia was nowhere to be found. . . . Terror reigned supreme."[13] Many of Jackson's 3,191 residents had also fled when Pettus ordered state officials to evacuate the capital.[14]

After assessing the situation, General Johnston concluded that Jackson could not be defended and during the night of the thirteenth he withdrew from the city. Before he left, Johnston burned the depot and several other buildings containing military supplies. During his retreat he also burned several bridges across the Pearl River. The following day federal troops marched unhindered into Jackson. On the afternoon of May 14, General Grant summoned his staff officers to a meeting at the Bowman House, a Jackson hotel. After discussing the importance of Jackson as a supply route to Vicksburg, which was their primary objective, Generals Grant and Sherman walked through the city and together they decided what should be burned.[15] Grant described one rather remarkable stop on that stroll through Jackson:

> Sherman and I went together into a manufactory which had not ceased work on account of the battle. . . . Our presence did not seem to attract the attention of either the manager or the operatives, most of whom were girls. We looked on for a while to see the tent cloth which they were making roll out of the looms, with "C.S.A." woven in each bolt. There was an immense amount of cotton, in bales, stacked outside. Finally, I told Sherman they had done work enough. The operatives were told they could leave and take with them what cloth they could carry. In a few minutes cotton and factory were in a blaze.[16]

Although General Grant remained in Jackson only one night, and incidentally stayed at the Bowman House in the same room occupied the previous night by General Johnston, he ordered Sherman to remain until he had destroyed "that place as a railroad center, and manufacturing city of military supplies." During the city's first occupation, six manufacturing plants and several buildings containing military stores were burned on Sherman's orders. Additionally, railroad bridges and track for ten miles around Jackson were also destroyed. Some private residences, the Catholic church, and the Confederate House were also burned.[17] Although few specific details concerning the destruction of private property are available, Sherman himself explained the circumstances under which the Confederate House was burned:

> Just as I was leaving Jackson (May 16), a very fat man came to see me, to inquire if his hotel . . . were doomed to be burned. I told him we had no intention to burn it, or any other house, except the machine-shops, and such buildings as could easily be converted to hostile uses. He professed to be a law-abiding Union man, and I remember to have said that this fact was manifest from the sign of his hotel, which was the "Confederate House;" I remembered that hotel, as it was the supper-station for the New Orleans trains when I used to travel the road before the war. I had not the least purpose, however, of burning it, but just as we were leaving town, it burst into flames and was burned to the ground. I never found out exactly who set it on fire, but was told that in one of our batteries were some officers and men who had been made prisoners at Shiloh, . . . and had been carried past Jackson in a railroad-train; they had been permitted by the guard to go to this very hotel for supper, and had nothing to pay but greenbacks, which were refused, with insult, by this same law-abiding landlord. These men, it was said, had quietly and stealthily applied the fire underneath the hotel just as we were leaving the town.[18]

There is also an intriguing but elliptical reference in the *Natchez Daily Courier* to the burning of the Catholic church. The report states only that as a Union officer was applying the torch to the church an Irish officer "crossed swords" with him. The same article indicated that the Baptist printing press had been saved from destruction by a federal soldier stationed outside the press's office. The Jackson *Mississippian*, however, was not so fortunate. Federal soldiers broke into the paper's office and, after destroying the press, scattered the type in the streets.[19] This action could have been the work of some loyal Illinois soldiers who resented the paper's reference to President Lincoln as a "gorilla."

There is no question that Jackson suffered heavy damage during the May occupation, but there is some doubt that the extent of destruction

A History of the Mississippi Governor's Mansion

was as great as rumor had it. On May 21, 1863, the editor of the *Natchez Daily Courier* reported that "notwithstanding the thousand rumors afloat in relation to the city of Jackson," his best intelligence was that "a small portion only of Jackson appears to have been burnt." He then cautioned his readers to "candidly sift" all rumors "before giving them circulation."

Although the records are not quite clear, Pettus must have returned to Jackson on or just before May 29. When he did return he found the city damaged but not destroyed. It is also unclear if and when he reoccupied the governor's mansion. Dr. R. N. Anderson wrote Pettus on May 29 informing the governor that his mansion had been turned into a hospital during his absence from the capital. The physician, on behalf of the women of Jackson who were attending the wounded Confederate soldiers, requested the continued use of the mansion for ten or twelve more days. By that time the more seriously wounded could be transferred elsewhere. A note of urgency was sounded by Anderson, who asked for an immediate answer because he had been advised that the "wagons will be here at 7 in the morning."[20] Pettus' reply, if one was sent, did not survive the war.

If Pettus did reoccupy the executive mansion, he did so only briefly, as the uneasy peace at Jackson following the withdrawal of Union forces was short-lived. The fall of Vicksburg on July 4, 1863, again placed the capital in jeopardy. Several days after the surrender of General Pemberton at Vicksburg, Pettus again moved the capital to Meridian, temporarily, and then to Macon on August 11.[21] The second occupation of Jackson was more difficult for the Union forces and more costly to the city from the standpoint of destruction of property. Jackson was much more strongly defended in July than it had been in May. Consequently, Sherman shelled the city for several hours, eventually driving General Johnston from Jackson a second time.[22]

Governor Pettus and most of the town's population evacuated the city during the early stages of the bombardment. Since he did not intend to return to the capital city, Governor Pettus removed most of the mansion's interior furnishings, which eventually found their way to Macon.[23]

During the second occupation, which lasted just a few days, General Sherman and his staff officers set up a command post in the governor's mansion and federal troops bivouacked on the mansion grounds. From

These Are Wartimes

the mansion on July 19, Sherman wrote Admiral David Porter commending him for his naval support in the capture of Vicksburg. The letter also included a resumé of the assault of Jackson. "The enemy," wrote Sherman, "burned nearly all the handsome dwellings round about the town because they gave us shelter or to light up the ground to prevent night attacks. He [General Johnston] also set fire to a chief block of stores in which were commissary supplies, and our men, in spite of guards, have widened the circle of fire, so that Jackson, once the pride and boast of Mississippi, is now a ruined town." But, Sherman continued, "State house, Governor's Mansion, and some fine dwellings, well within the lines of intrenchment, remain untouched."[24]

After complaining of the severe heat and stifling dust, Sherman concluded, "Last night, at the Governor's Mansion, in Jackson, we had a beautiful supper and union of the generals of the army, and I assure you the 'Army and Navy forever' was sung with a full and hearty chorus."[25]

Although Jackson suffered heavy damage during its first two occupations by federal troops, the extent of that destruction was greatly exaggerated by contemporaries and has usually been uncritically accepted by historians. Understandably, Jackson residents accused Sherman of rapacious plundering and pillaging during a reign of terror. There is documentary evidence, however, that Sherman posted guards at public buildings and ordered his subordinates to prevent the plundering of private homes. Before leaving Jackson, Sherman provided Mayor C. H. Manship with 200 barrels of flour and 100 barrels of pork to be distributed among the citizens. He did the same for other nearby towns.

Military considerations, not hatred for the South, promoted his orders to burn buildings and destroy contraband goods. Sherman had passed through Jackson several times before the war. The city was the supper station for the Jackson and Great Northern Railroad, and Sherman often dined there when traveling from his home in Ohio to the Louisiana Academy at Baton Rouge where he was president before the war.[26] It was also there, on the outskirts of Jackson, that Sherman may have made his cryptic comment on war. While waiting for his troops to cross a makeshift bridge across the Pearl River, Sherman observed their labored march from his mount at the water's edge. Trying to bolster his troops, he shouted, "War is hell, boys."[27]

A History of the Mississippi Governor's Mansion

Shortly after Sherman evacuated Jackson on July 19, 1863, a modicum of order was reestablished by city authorities. The presence of federal troops in Vicksburg, however, prevented Pettus' return to the capital. For the remainder of the war, Mississippi's peripatetic capital was located at various times in Meridian, Macon, and Columbus. During those two years the mansion remained officially vacant and empty of furnishings. Undoubtedly, it provided shelter for Jacksonians left homeless in the wake of war's destruction.

Mayor Manship wrote Governor Pettus at Columbus asking permission to use his office in the capitol because the city hall was in use as a hospital. The mayor assured the governor that he was looking after the public buildings in Jackson and briefly described the condition of the capitol. He did not, however, mention the executive residence.[28]

Through the late summer of 1863, Jackson residents expected the legislature to convene at the capital city for its fall session. Mayor Manship had indicated that the state house had not been severely damaged by the siege of July. The Jackson *Mississippian* also assured its readers over the state that the capital city could accommodate the session scheduled for October, 1863. The paper reported that there were enough hotel rooms and private homes to board the two hundred visitors expected to attend the session. After warning the legislators that they might experience some inconvenience, the editor remarked, "These are wartimes, and even the members of the legislature should not shrink from hardships."[29]

War or no war, politics must go on, and as early as April 14, 1863, the *Mississippian* began asking "who will be our next governor?" Several names were being mentioned throughout the state. Among them were Reuben Davis, A. M. West, Jacob Thompson, T. J. Wharton, and Charles Clark. Realizing that the constitutional process must be honored as nearly as possible, Pettus ordered on June 27, while still at Jackson, an election for the first Monday of October.[30] The election of state officers occurred as scheduled but reflected the growing disenchantment with the war among Mississippi's citizenry.

Although elections did not take place in several counties, Charles Clark, a former Whig and anti-secessionist, was declared the winner and

One of the earliest photographs of the original Mansion and family cottage.

Early Mansion scene showing the wrought-iron enclosure added in 1855 and removed in 1908.

The Mansion as it appeared just before or during the 1908 renovation.

A southeast view of the Mansion showing the porte-cochere added in 1908.

The Mansion circa 1930.

A southeast view of the Mansion after the porte-cochere had been screened in.

Mrs. Earl Brewer

Mrs. Theodore G. Bilbo

Mrs. Benjamin H. Humphreys

Mrs. Adelbert Ames

Mrs. James L. Alcorn

Mrs. Henry Whitfield

Mrs. Anselm J. McLaurin

Mrs. Dennis Murphree

Mrs. P. Coleman

Mrs. P. B. Johnson

Mrs. Thomas L. Bailey

Mrs. Waller entertains former first ladies (left to right) Mrs. Waller, Mrs. Conner, Mrs. Barnett, Mrs. Johnson.

Former first ladies honored at a tea at the Mansion in April, 1948, left to right—Mrs. Earl Brewer, Mrs. Theodore G. Bilbo, Mrs. Lee Russell, Mrs. Dennis Murphree, Mrs. Hugh L. White, Mrs. Paul B. Johnson, Sr., Mrs. Thomas L. Bailey, Mrs. Fielding L. Wright.

Two of the Waller boys, Don and Eddie, add their names to the attic's "honor roll."

Ben and George Yarborough, Jr. enjoy a ten-day stay in the Mansion when their father served as acting governor in 1961.

Daisy McLaurin Stevens, who was married in the Mansion, with her daughter Daisy, who was born in the Mansion.

These Are Wartimes

was inaugurated at Columbus on November 16, 1863. Only a month later, as federal troops converged on Columbus, Governor Clark again moved the capital back to Macon where it remained until May, 1865. During the intervening two years, popular support for the war diminished as Confederate defeats mounted. On May 6, 1865, two days after General Richard Taylor surrendered Confederate troops in Alabama, Mississippi, and Louisiana to General Edward Canby at Citronelle, Alabama, Governor Clark ordered all state officials to return to Jackson with the state archives in their possession.[31]

Clark's proclamation also called a special session of the legislature for May 18. But by the time the lawmakers finally assembled on May 20, Jackson was again occupied by federal troops. Nevertheless, the federal commander, General E. D. Osband, allowed the legislature to convene briefly and permitted Governor Clark to occupy the mansion for several days. After the Union general sent word that he was under orders to arrest the legislators, the lawmakers hastily adjourned after meeting for little more than an hour on the morning of May 20. General Osband also sent word to Governor Clark that all state property and archives, including the executive mansion, must be surrendered. Consequently, at 9:00 A.M. on May 22, Governor Clark "delivered all public property [to General Osband] under protest, but without asking to have force employed."[32]

Governor Clark was then allowed to return to his home in Macon where, on June 6, he was arrested and subsequently imprisoned at Fort Pulaski, Georgia.[33] Thus both the office and the mansion of Mississippi's chief executive were vacant. Although the office of the governor remained vacant only a short time, the "suitable house for the governor" remained empty much longer—a mute reminder that the war had taken an unexpected turn.

When peace returned and the fault-finding began, even the mansion and the location of the capital city were swept into the stream of controversy. Immediately after the war, newspapers in several cities advocated the relocation of the seat of government and opposed the expenditure of public funds to repair the state buildings in Jackson, especially the mansion. Faced with the massive problems of physical reconstruction and economic recovery, Mississippi's leaders did not give mansion repair high priority. And, for a time at least, all other public issues were set aside in the interest of reestablishing civil government in Mississippi and gaining the state's readmission to the Union.[34]

CHAPTER V

A Fence Around the Mansion . . . A Wall Around Mississippi

PRESIDENT ANDREW JOHNSON, anxious to restore the Union on the most liberal terms possible, appointed William L. Sharkey provisional governor of Mississippi on June 16, 1865. Johnson then ordered a convention to assemble at Jackson to nullify the Ordinance of Secession and to amend the state constitution to abolish slavery. In anticipation of the congressional demands to confer suffrage upon the freedmen, Johnson also suggested that the convention extend the right to vote to Mississippi blacks who could read and write and who owned property. However, the August convention took no action in this regard but left the matter to the Mississippi legislature which convened in October.[1]

In the fall of 1865, civil government was reestablished in Mississippi under the terms of a general presidential amnesty that restored civil rights to practically all Mississippians. High-ranking military and political officials and individuals whose wealth exceeded $20,000 were excluded from the general amnesty. They were, however, eligible for a special presidential pardon which President Johnson extended rather freely.[2]

Under the terms of the presidential amnesty, a general election was conducted in September. Since Mississippi Negroes were not yet eligible to vote, an all-white legislature composed largely of Confederate veterans was elected. Benjamin G. Humphreys, a former planter, slaveowner, and Confederate general, was elected governor and inaugurated on October 16, 1865.[3]

Within a few days after the legislature assembled, a select committee was appointed to ascertain the condition of public buildings of Jackson. The committee reported that only one public building had been completely destroyed during the war, and that all other buildings required only minor repairs to continue the functions for which they had been constructed. According to the committee's report, the governor's mansion could at that time accommodate the first family except for the fact that the interior furnishings which had been removed to Macon had not been returned. Nevertheless, the committee recommended an appropriation of $5,000 to repair the mansion. The same bill also authorized the governor to "appoint a suitable person to repair to Macon . . . to take possession of furniture he may find at that place belonging to the Governor's Mansion." Indicating some doubt that the furniture could be located, the committee also recommended an additional appropriation of $2,000 to refurnish the mansion if the trip to Macon was unproductive.[4] According to oral tradition, federal soldiers stole the furniture from Clark's residence at Macon after his arrest and imprisonment.

Since the effort to retrieve the furniture was unsuccessful, the legislature implemented the committee's recommendation and authorized the $2,000 expenditure. That amount, however, was insufficient to refurnish the mansion adequately and Mrs. Humphreys and her children did not join the governor until the spring of 1866. After the first family occupied the mansion, repair and redecoration continued through the summer.[5]

When the legislature met in special session during the fall of 1866, Governor Humphreys advised the lawmakers that both the repairing and the refurnishing of the mansion had greatly exceeded the original appropriation. The state architect, A. J. Herod, had continued the work, however, on the assumption that the legislature would honor the contracts by special appropriations. Herod's report, which Humphreys passed along to the legislature, indicated that $7,199 had already been expended for repairs and estimated that an additional $14,500 would be needed. In addition to the $2,000 appropriation, another $1,927 had been spent to furnish the mansion and $5,000 more was still needed. The total bill came to $30,626, or $23,626 in excess of the original appropriation.[6]

The House Committee on Public Buildings was asked to study the architect's estimate and report its findings. The committee later introduced a bill authorizing the expenditure of funds as requested by the architect. The bill passed the House but was defeated in the Senate. W. H. McCargo, a senator from DeSoto County, objected to the appro-

A Fence Around the Mansion . . . A Wall Around Mississippi

priation on the grounds that the repairs were not necessary. He ridiculed both the architect and his estimate. "Like the skillful physician when called to examine a patient supposed to be sick," McCargo said, "the State Architect has been able to find many diseased parts in the Public buildings, and like the physician, is likely to prescribe remedies, whether the disease be fully developed or only in its incipiency." McCargo then told his fellow lawmakers that he had personally inspected the public buildings and found "no defects . . . which will not admit the delay." There is little doubt that McCargo's opposition to the additional appropriation was a manuever to prevent the repair of the capitol and other public buildings. Strong consideration was being given to moving the capital to a more northern location and supporters realized that any substantial outlay for repairs of the existing state house would stymie that move. The bill was defeated and no additional appropriations were made to repair or refurnish the mansion until the Republican party gained control of the legislature in 1870.[7]

Although the official residence was inadequately furnished, with several rooms completely empty and still in need of many repairs, Governor Humphreys and the first lady, Mildred Maury of Port Gibson, and their children continued to occupy the governor's mansion, symbolizing the restoration of civil government in Mississippi.[8]

A wealthy planter from Claiborne County and a Whig before the war, Governor Humphreys had not favored secession during the crisis of 1861. But when the war came, like most other Whigs, he joined the Confederate army. After General William Barksdale fell at Gettysburg, Humphreys took command of Barksdale's brigade. While Governor Humphreys was away in Pennsylvania, his plantation was sacked by armies surging through the countryside living off the land. The vast dimension of the tragedy of war was measurable by his own personal loss. Unable to rebuild his plantation or restore the old way of life, Governor Humphreys became an insurance executive after leaving public office.[9]

During the first two years of Governor Humphreys' administration, Mississippi played a key role in the struggle over Reconstruction policy between President Johnson and the Radical Republicans in Congress. As the first southern legislature to meet after the war, Mississippi's refusal to ratify the Thirteenth and Fourteenth Amendments, coupled with its enactment of the Black Codes, undermined the president's position and played into the hands of the Radicals who secured a veto-proof Congress in the fall elections of 1866.[10]

In 1867, the Radical Congress assumed control over Reconstruction and reestablished military government in Mississippi, but allowed Governor Humphreys to maintain his office on a provisional basis. A new voter registration was ordered under the terms of the Reconstruction Acts of that year. Only about 2,000 white Mississippians were disfranchised under the provisions of those acts. But more importantly, 79,176 blacks were registered, a majority of 20,000 over the 58,385 white registered voters. During the summer of 1868, this newly registered electorate was in the process of voting on a new state constitution drafted by the "Black and Tan Convention" earlier that year. Simultaneously, a statewide, general election was also being held. Governor Humphreys, a candidate for reelection on the Democratic ticket, was charged with interfering in the election in an effort to defeat the constitution. Military authorities ordered his removal from office and appointed General Adelbert Ames as provisional governor.[11]

Governor Humphreys considered his removal an illegal act by military authorities and refused to vacate either his office in the capitol or the mansion.[12] The fact that both martial law and civil authority existed concurrently created a constitutional entanglement that scholars have not yet unraveled. Interestingly, one of the most dramatic confrontations between these mutually exclusive systems occurred in a contest over the occupations of the Mississippi executive mansion.

When General Ames was ordered to report to Jackson to assume the dual role of provisional and military governor, he first advised Governor Humphreys that he and his family could continue to occupy the mansion indefinitely. However, when Ames arrived at Jackson he was unable to find suitable quarters and since the headquarters of the Fourth Military District was located just across the street, he decided to move into the governor's mansion. On July 6, 1868, Ames advised Governor Humphreys of his change of plans and asked him to vacate the mansion "at as early a day as convenient." A lively correspondence between Humphreys and Ames followed that communication.[13]

Although he had by then surrendered his office in the capitol, Hum-

A Fence Around the Mansion . . . A Wall Around Mississippi

phreys declared his intention to remain in the governor's mansion. He claimed that, since the Reconstruction Acts did not allow military governors any compensation beyond their military pay, General Ames was not entitled to the use of the mansion which would in effect constitute additional compensation. Ames, who was unmarried at that time, responded that he would need only half of the residence and offered Humphreys and his family the remaining portion of the building. Humphreys replied that he found the suggestion of joint occupancy "disagreeable" to himself and his family and reiterated his resolve to remain in the mansion.[14]

During this exchange of letters, the Democratic press was quick to capitalize on the propaganda value of the removal of Governor Humphreys from the mansion by military authorities. On July 7, 1868, the Jackson *Clarion* broke the news that Governor Humphreys had received notice to vacate the executive residence, and on July 9 the editor revealed that within a few days the first family would be "forcibly ejected from their home" at the point of "bayonets." The *Vicksburg Times* headlined "The First Act of our New Despot—Shoulder Straps in the Executive Mansion." Even before it occurred, the Vicksburg paper described the encounter as "a gross, wanton, and outrageous exercise of unbridled power of brute force which is as disgraceful as it is indefensible."[15] The July 9 *Clarion* predicted that "Ole Ben Humphreys . . . will long live in the memory of his people" while those who "wrong him . . . shall be remembered only for their infamy."

At noon on July 13, a young lieutenant appeared at the mansion. Asking to see the governor, he was ushered into the right front parlor. When introduced to Humphreys, he extended his hand which was ceremoniously refused. The lieutenant handed the governor the following letter:

Headquarters, Post of Jackson
Jackson, Miss., July 13, 1868

Hon. B. G. Humphreys:

SIR: General Ames, the Provisional Governor of this state has called upon me, as the officer in command of this post, to gain possession of one-half of the mansion now occupied by you.

I send Lieutenant Bache, with a guard of men, to see that General Ames' request is carried out. Lieutenant Bache will hand you this letter.

A History of the Mississippi Governor's Mansion

> I do not desire to use force if I can help it, but he will be instructed to do so if necessary. I wish to avoid all unpleasantness to yourself and family, but if you desire, for political purposes, to have a military "pantomine," I have instructed Lieutenant Bache to carry it out with all the appearances of a reality, without actual indignity.
>
> I am sir, very respectfully, your obedient servant,
>
> JAMES BIDDLE[16]

After reading the letter, Governor Humphreys asked the young lieutenant if he intended to carry out the order to put him out by force. The officer replied that he would. The first lady described the governor's next move: "Mr. Humphreys then stepped to the door and called some of his friends in to hear what passed. He then told Lt. he would repeat his question, as he wished to have witnesses to what passed between them; the Lt. hesitated, and Mr. Humphreys insisted, so the same question was put and same reply made." Governor Humphreys then agreed to leave the mansion peacefully, thus precluding the necessity of forcible ejection at the point of bayonets. After instructing the first lady to have their personal belongings packed and ready for departure, Governor Humphreys and his friends left the mansion. A short time later, wagons were brought to the front gate and Mrs. Humphreys and her children vacated the residence.[17]

The pantomime had its effect, quite remarkably, even on an eyewitness who gave the following account of the "forcible ejection":

> The scorn she felt for . . . the tyrants themselves, who were about to perpetuate so great an outrage upon her husband, I thought I could detect in the expression of her face; but there was no demonstration, no haughty toss of the head, no dramatic sweeping by as she passed through the doors. . . . She with her distinguished husband walked out of the Governor's Mansion between files of United States soldiers. . . . I think I can sum the whole matter up by saying, that she demeaned herself upon that trying occasion, as Mississippians should have desired the mistress of the Governor's Mansion to do.[18]

This account seems to have been wishful thinking on the part of the eyewitness, differing significantly from the description given by Mrs. Humphreys herself. In a letter to her mother dated July 18, 1868, Mrs. Humphreys wrote: "I marched out with my children, through *a crowd of negroes*, who had assembled in the front yard, to see the *fun*, many of

A Fence Around the Mansion . . . A Wall Around Mississippi

them in a broad grin. The file of soldiers six in number was outside the gate." Although the first lady must have been terribly inconvenienced by the ordeal, her long, sometimes witty letter did not indicate any undue stress. "We left Lt. Bache," she told her mother, "promenading the two unfurnished parlors. He wore a red sash and sword, did not take his hat off up to the time I left." She then described the appearance of the tyrant: "He looks like Ned Ingraham at the distance I saw him. He is the young man Jennie Rowan wrote to me asking us to show him some attention, as he was a stranger and had not been engaged in the war." Finally, Mrs. Humphreys described what had been happening at the mansion since they left, also revealing some doubt in her own mind about the brutality initially attributed to General Ames: "I have heard he spends most of his time in the billiard room, and was *drunk* last Saturday. . . . Mrs. Tarpley told me she had been watching the Mansion all the week and the only visitors she had seen enter it since our departure were several detachments of *colored ladies*. . . . General Ames told Hannah's husband a cook in the Mansion that he did not wish the *vegetables in the garden disturbed, as they belonged to Governor Humphreys. I thought he was becoming* rather conscientious, considering the start he had made."[19]

Governor Humphreys' account of his "forcible ejection" must also be weighed against that of the first lady's. In his memoirs the governor described the confrontation: "He demanded and on my refusal he took possession of it . . . after expelling me and my family at the point of bayonets. I knew it was futile to disobey these orders . . . but . . . I was determined . . . to yield nothing except at the point of overpowering bayonets and that the world should know that I yielded not to civil process, but to 'stern, unrelenting military tyranny.'" The pantomime, accepted without critical evaluation by Mississippi historians and generations of journalists, has survived as fact.[20]

There is a tragic irony in the fact that Adelbert Ames was the first Republican to occupy the Mississippi governor's mansion; he was also the last. The years between his first residency in 1868-70 and his last in 1875-76 were years of bitter racial and political strife which characterized the most reckless and sustained power struggle in the state's history.

Following Humphreys' removal from the governor's mansion, Democratic voters were more determined than ever to defeat the state constitution of 1868, which they did with the aid of a large number of black voters. Consequently, Mississippi remained under military government until February 23, 1870, when the state was at last readmitted to the Union. Readmission was accomplished as a result of the general election of 1869, when James L. Alcorn fashioned a coalition of Whigs, Union Democrats, and thousands of secession Democrats who finally realized that acquiescence to political and social readjustment was the price of order and the reconstruction of the state.[21]

Despite the fact that hundreds of blacks were elected to public office at every level of state government, Alcorn's 1869 victory was hailed as the beginning of a bold new era and the end of the old order. The press in every section of the state heralded the overthrow of the political oligarchy which had dominated the Democratic party for many years. The *Grenada Sentinel* reported, "It is supposed that the Jackson ring of politicians, who, for nearly a quarter of a century, have reigned as absolute despots in Mississippi, is now dissolved. The old fogies and oligarchs, whose will was law and who appointed congressmen and governors at will, through a long series of years, have at least been crushed out. It is only to be regretted that they have perished at the hands of the blacks. But they are dead for all that." The *Columbus Democrat* announced, "The day of the Jackson clique has passed. The power it once wielded . . . has fallen from its hands forever. We are in the midst of a new order of things. The people will think and act for themselves, and the old politicians that have so long ruled and blundered must get out of the way."[22] However, as events over the next few years would indicate, the reports of the death of the Jackson clique were greatly exaggerated.

When Governor Alcorn and the first lady, the former Amelia Glover, daughter of a wealthy Alabama planter, and their children moved into the mansion in March, 1870, they found it like the state—in disarray. Like all other facets of political life in Mississippi the mansion had been caught up in the contest for power between the Republican and the Democratic party. Although the Democratic legislature originally contemplated expenditures of large sums to repair the mansion, when the Republican-controlled legislature began to implement those repairs, the Democratic press branded the expenditures as needless extravagance and positive proof that the Republicans were raiding the state treasury.

A Fence Around the Mansion . . . A Wall Around Mississippi

In January, 1870, in anticipation of Governor Alcorn's inauguration, a legislative committee examined the mansion to determine its condition and make recommendations for its repair. Chaired by Negro legislator Merrimon Howard, the committee found the mansion dilapidated. The partisan presses accused either Humphreys or Ames, respectively, of stealing the furniture. But the committee refused to be drawn into the controversy. Instead, the committee recommended an appropriation of $24,000 for the purchase of new furnishings and for extensive repair. Although the recommendations of this committee were initially rejected and no such funds were appropriated, repair contracts were let and purchases of furniture were made—as so often before—under the assumption that the legislature would later honor the contracts and pay for the furnishings.[23]

On this basis the repair was initiated under the supervision of Staunton and McKenna, general contractors. The plans called for the repair of the roof, which still leaked, the gutters, front steps, interior woodwork, and plaster, as well as painting of the mansion's exterior. The mansion proper and all the outbuildings were painted or whitewashed. The work was obviously initiated for the benefit and convenience of Governor Alcorn, but it was started in January while General Ames was still living in the residence. The *Clarion* took notice of the refurbishing activity. After objecting in broad terms to Republican extravagance and commenting specifically that the mansion furniture was being bought up North, the *Clarion* addressed a personal note to Merrimon Howard: "You may paint and whitewash the Mansion, Merryman; but you can not purify Ames with a dash of the pen. His heart is so corrupt, his little brain-pan so filled with hate for this people, and his whole system so jaundiced with meanness that a thousand coats of white wash would not disguise him."[24]

During the redecoration and repair the mansion exterior was painted yellow, "to correspond to the present complexion of affairs" according to the *Clarion*. The *Columbus Index* suggested that it would be more appropriate to paint the mansion black. The Republican legislature could insure the building against natural disasters, but it could not shield the mansion from the stormy nature of Mississippi politics.[25]

Governor Alcorn, a wealthy, ambitious, and aristocratic planter from Coahoma County, had a large family which utilized both the front portion of the mansion and the family cottage in the rear. During Alcorn's residency ceremonial functions were carried off, according to a frequent visitor, with "as much pomp and etiquette as the White House was conducted in the days of Madison." Visitors were greeted by liveried servants and pages served the governor's guests in a manner that "added to the dignity of his station."[26]

Of the many myths about the mansion which have been handed down through the years, and reiterated in the press, one such misconception is that during the Reconstruction period the mansion was occupied by scalawags who were so objectionable to the decent white people that the latter spurned all social contact with them. Alcorn was the only scalawag, that is a white Mississippian who affiliated with the Republican party, living in the mansion during Reconstruction. However, because of his great wealth and social prestige, his engaging personality and long-standing friendships, Alcorn's social relationships were largely undisturbed by the political controversies swirling around the mansion. Both the governor and the first lady were gracious, charming hosts, and Alcorn's personal wealth plus a liberal Executive Contingency Fund made frequent entertaining not only possible but also pleasant.[27]

Yet in spite of all this, Alcorn did not escape the criticism of the local Democratic press, especially when he entertained the legislature which was integrated. It was understood between Mississippi politicians and journalists of the nineteenth century that no holds were barred in such a case, no blows were too low. In a crude reference to a reception at the mansion held by Alcorn in honor of the legislature, the *Clarion* surmised that even Robert W. Flournoy, Mississippi's most despised scalawag, would have enjoyed the "mixing of the colors, and the odor was all that his olfactor could have craved."[28]

Alcorn's great ambition caused him to make a serious mistake, which many of his supporters considered a breach of faith. Alcorn resigned the office of governor in November, 1871, to accept appointment to the United States Senate. In 1869 thousands of Democrats had voted for Alcorn, trusting him as a long-time Mississippian of wealth and political prestige to lead the state through the perilous years ahead. His resignation and the subsequent elevation of a carpetbagger to the office of governor left them dismayed and divided. Alcorn's departure from the arena of state politics left a vacuum of leadership in the discordant Republican party and accelerated an already developing factionalism which the Democratic oligarchy exploited and turned to their advantage.[29]

Alcorn's successor, Ridgely C. Powers, was an Ohio carpetbagger and ex-Union officer. After the war, Powers had settled in Noxubee County where he purchased land and became involved in state politics, uniting with the conservative or Alcorn wing of the Republican party. Powers' moderate racial views and his conscientious exercise of the duties of governor enhanced his standing among conservative Republicans, and found, surprisingly, even general approval among all but the most extreme faction in the Democratic party.[30]

Powers was a bachelor during his administration, and social affairs at the mansion during his two-year residency were under the direction of his sister, Louise Powers, who acted as his hostess on formal, state occasions. For many Mississippians, and even more so for Jackson residents, a carpetbagger living in the governor's mansion added insult to injury, still another blow to the state's pride. And that insult was compounded on the occasion of an all-carpetbagger wedding held at the mansion on March 25, 1872, when the governor's sister was married to James C. McKee, a son of one of the state's most prominent carpetbaggers.[31]

As the 1873 gubernatorial election approached, Powers emerged as the first choice among conservative Republicans. In addition to the support of Alcorn, Powers also received the public endorsement of some conservative Democrats who realized the futility of nominating a Democratic ticket. Among the radical wing of the party, which included the vast majority of Negro Republicans, Adelbert Ames was the favorite. When the Republican convention nominated Ames over Powers, Alcorn bolted the party and hastily organized a rump convention of dissident Republicans and Democrats which placed his name in nomination. The Ames–Alcorn contest caused some significant shifting in the traditional party alignment. The more extreme Democrats supported Alcorn, who was touted as the white man's candidate. More moderate Democrats, fearful of the demarcation of Mississippi politics along the color line, endorsed Ames and openly campaigned for his ticket. After a bitter contest which left the Republican party permanently divided, Ames was elected along with a large number of blacks, including a lieutenant governor, whose influence over state affairs became increasingly visible.[32]

Since Ames' first residency in the governor's mansion he had married Blanche Butler, the daughter of the infamous Benjamin "Spoons" Butler. Ames had also represented Mississippi in the United States Senate during the years 1870-73. When the Ames family, including two small children, moved into the mansion in January, 1874, they found it in very good order though in need of a thorough cleaning. In letters to her mother in Massachusetts, the first lady described the mansion and its furnishings in great detail, room by room, even including diagrams of the main building, the family cottage, and the outbuildings. Mrs. Ames related the problems of adjusting to local dietary habits and cooking techniques and, as might be expected, complained of the help and the weather. She arranged for her family to occupy the second floor of the main structure since the cottage was damp and cold during the winter months and was barely furnished.[33]

Immediately upon arriving in Jackson, Mrs. Ames, a beautiful, highly educated and well-traveled New Englander, comprehended the social intricacies attached to her husband's official position. Nor was it lost on the first lady that those intricacies were further complicated by his Republican politics. Mrs. Ames went to great lengths not to offend the social conscience of the people of Mississippi. She advised her mother that she would "give but one reception this year" because integrated social affairs caused "more or less discontent, however well arranged, and we shall content ourselves with little suppers, croquet parties, etc."[34]

The lifestyle of the Ames family was circumspect and in some respects they were more like prisoners in the mansion than residents. Mrs. Ames rarely ever left the mansion and then only to return calls. "The great question which disturbs the residents here," she wrote her mother, "is shall we call upon Mrs. Ames?" Although Jacksonians were always polite and courteous to the first lady, they were "always on guard" and with the exception of a few white families, according to Mrs. Ames, "every white person in the city is inclined to be prejudiced against us." She always kept the children within the fence and cautioned them against the possibility of being kidnapped.[35]

A Fence Around the Mansion . . . A Wall Around Mississippi

Many years later Butler Ames, who was only a small boy when he lived with his father in the governor's mansion, recalled his childhood memories for Kate Markham Power when she was compiling material for her history of the first families. To refresh his memory, Miss Power reminded him of the little girl outside the fence who used to talk to him and ask him why he could not come outside and play. From Mississippi to Massachusetts their correspondence spanned a thousand miles; their memories, what must have seemed a thousand years.

Butler Ames' letter to Miss Power, dated October 29, 1937, is a documentary of those remarkable times. He wrote: "I do have very distinct recollection of Jackson days, and the fence around the Governor's Mansion. I remember distinctly the day I was shooed up the path towards the Mansion from the front gate by my father when I was running down to meet him, at the time someone commenced to shoot at him and he commenced to shoot back. . . . On one occasion, I was caught in time, just outside the gate, to prevent my going off with a man with a tame bear . . . the whole world seemed to be outside the fence."[36]

When Adelbert Ames was inaugurated in January, 1874, he too referred to an enclosure, not the fence around the mansion but the wall around Mississippi. Ames proclaimed: "Mississippi has been more fortunate than some of her sister states. The prejudiced few, who . . . would exclude the outer world, as by a Chinese wall, have failed to control her destiny."[37]

Adelbert Ames had read the reports of the death of the Democratic oligarchy; but he did not realize how exaggerated were those reports. For just over a year after his inaugural address, the *Columbus Democrat* on April 10, 1875, beheld the resurrection of the Jackson clique and expressed the forlorn hope that they would "keep away from Democratic conventions" because they had "done our state and party damage enough."

The Jackson clique's resurrection is a tribute to the survival instincts of an entrenched political organization. The clique's plan for survival was to make Reconstruction seem so calamitous that its causes—secession and war—would be obscured and to make Negro suffrage appear so injurious to good government that its discontinuation could be justified by fraud and violence. Ultimately, the color line was drawn and almost fanatical devotion to the Democratic party was required of all white Missippians.

A History of the Mississippi Governor's Mansion

The fact that Democratic strategists enrolled large numbers of blacks in their party during the "Revolution of 1875" reveals that power, not principle, was at stake. It was lost upon rank and file Mississippians that their leaders were demanding allegiance to a white man's party which numbered blacks among its membership.

The resurgence of the party elite was consummated by a Democratic landslide in the fall elections of 1875. The Democratic party captured a two-thirds majority in both houses of the legislature. Almost immediately upon its organization in January, 1876, the House instituted impeachment proceedings against several Republican officials, including Governor Ames. When his conviction became certain, Governor Ames composed a letter offering his resignation. The letter was drafted in his study at the mansion and dated March 28, 1876. The legislature accepted his resignation and dismissed the impeachment proceedings. Ames left Mississippi a few days later. His family had preceded him.[38]

Dunbar Rowland, for many years director of the Mississippi Department of Archives and History, wrote that Ames' resignation brought an end to "one of the most colossal and corrupt schemes of public robbery ever devised by a board of public plunderers." This interpretation, repeated by generations of Mississippi journalists and unchallenged by Mississippi historians, has virtually become the official record of the state's past. There have been detractors along the way, however. R. H. Thompson, a former president of the Mississippi Historical Society, perceived the impeachment of Ames in a different light and from a unique vantage point. Thompson wrote Rowland on February 15, 1929:

> I am the sole survivor of the 1876 State Senate to which articles of impeachment against Ames were presented by the House of Representatives. . . . I was then a very young man but little beyond the age required of a Senator and no doubt had imbibed to some extent the prejudice against Governor Ames then prevalent in a large majority of white people of this state. Looking backwards, it appears to me that the charges made against Governor Ames, in the newspapers of the state and in political harangues of that day, must have been exaggerated to a considerable extent.[39]

In conclusion, Thompson suggested that a history of the Ames administration written by a "friendly hand" would be welcomed because "the passions and prejudices of the past are forgotten." Thompson, like Ames,

A Fence Around the Mansion . . . A Wall Around Mississippi

was somewhat naïve. The passions and prejudices, like old times, are not forgotten.

Ames' Democratic successor was John Marshall Stone, the president pro tempore of the Senate. He occupied the mansion in the spring of 1876. When Governor William L. Waller, a Democrat, moved into the mansion in the spring of 1975, he did so under the terms of a ninety-nine-year lease entered into by the Democratic party and the people of Mississippi, for in the intervening years the Democratic party has exercised exclusive control over the political process and an unbroken succession of Democratic governors has occupied the Mississippi executive mansion.

CHAPTER VI

Of Monuments and Men

TWO DAYS AFTER he was inaugurated and a few weeks before he moved into the governor's mansion, John Marshall Stone received a letter from L. Q. C. Lamar dated March 31, 1876, and marked *Private & Confidential*. After suggesting several means by which the Democratic party leadership could implement its pledges to reduce state expenditures, Lamar reminded Stone that the "Mississippi Executive Mansion has been a great expense to the State [and] its incumbent." He then assured the governor, "if you recommend that it be sold . . . the people will hail it as a return to republican economy and simplicity of living."[1] Within a week the legislature repealed the mansion contingency fund which had originally been established in 1856. Under the headline "A Leak Stopped," the April 7 *Clarion* congratulated the lawmakers and hailed the repeal of the fund as a return to fiscal responsibility. However, neither the legislature nor Lamar, and much less the *Clarion*, realized the symbolic importance of the governor's mansion which over the next twenty-five years would become a public monument of deep historical significance.

Through the 1880s and 1890s, two movements characterized Mississippi's political and economic development. Although parallel in time, each development was in a sense exclusive of the other. First, there was the lingering temptation to return to the old order with its agrarian economy and social traditions. On the other hand, the search for a new order based on industry and commerce was considered by many of the state's leaders as the only means of full economic recovery.

The restoration of the social, economic, and political system of the Old South had wide popular support. Tradition, nostalgia, and love for the

Of Monuments and Men

Lost Cause bore heavily upon white Mississippians. Yet many others agreed with the chief justice of the Mississippi Supreme Court, Horatio F. Simrall, who advised that it was "idle and useless to grope about amid the debris and ruins of the old system." New-departure Democrats like Lamar believed that the *ancien regime* had "gone down among the dead men," but that a New South, the child and legitimate successor of the Old South, would rise like the phoenix out of the dust of its own ashes. According to one southern prophet, "Wealth and honor are in the pathway of the New South. . . . She is the coming El Dorado of American adventure."[2] This wealth, honor, and power would issue not from the farm but from the factory. The New South, according to its prophets, would be an industrial South.

But however bright the future might seem or whatever promises it held, many Mississippians were unable to break with the past, its illusions of glory, and its roll call of nearly great men. Those Mississippians whispered among themselves and to their children:

> What is that word whose sweetness brings
> Memories fraught with better things?
> Its magic echo thrills the heart
> With feelings that can ne'er depart.
> With softened voice we speak it o'er,
> Yet dearer now than e'er before—
> 'Til sacred, list! I breathe it low,
> Our cherished South in the "long ago."[3]

Though economics might have prodded Mississippians forward toward a lusty future, emotion lured them backward toward a glorious past. This deep psychological attachment for the past increased rather than diminished with the passing years. Politicians seemed to exploit rather than extricate Mississippians from this ambivalence. Their inconstant leadership marked off boundaries of incredulous dimensions. Perhaps nowhere is this better illustrated than in two speeches delivered by Governor Stone to two different audiences within a year's time. In a planned response to a toast, the MATCHLESS NAME OF MISSISSIPPI, Stone declared before the Mississippi Press Association:

> Who can read her history and dwell upon the virtues and genius of those great and brilliant men . . . without emotions . . . right or wrong, she was

A History of the Mississippi Governor's Mansion

entitled to my allegiance and affection first, last, and forever. . . . If there is one created inanimate thing upon the face of God's earth which I love above all others, that

THING IS MISSISSIPPI

. . . the brightest star that sparkles in that brilliant diadem of states, is the star which glitters to the

NAME OF MISSISSIPPI

While I shall live, I shall court no higher distinction than that of being a citizen of

MISSISSIPPI[4]

Yet while addressing a commercial convention in an effort to attract capital investment to Mississippi, Stone could say:

> Welcome . . . to the State, and to our little capital city. We come to you with but modest and simple offerings. We have no magnificent cities to commend your admiration. . . . We have here the soil and climate, but we need, for the better development of our resources, more of the energy, industry, and economy, which characterize the people of the great West. . . . They have discovered within our midst the vast mine of wealth, of which we had never dreamed, and which amazes us all. . . . We want more of the vim of northern and western men. . . . We must unlearn much that we have learned too well, but not wisely. . . . So long as we confine ourselves to the single crop of cotton . . . we can not prosper.[5]

In those two speeches Stone revealed why he succeeded as a politician and failed as a leader. As a politician he was eminently successful. During the twenty-year period from 1876 to 1896, Stone served as Mississippi's chief executive for twelve years. For political purposes he pampered the memory of the past. As governor he only nudged the people forward, he did not lead them boldly. The United States census of 1890 showed that 62.7 percent of Mississippi's farmers were sharecroppers engaged in the exclusive production of cotton.[6]

Perhaps a better illustration of Mississippi's ambivalence toward her past and her future can be noted in the Jackson *Clarion-Ledger* of May 31, 1888. Varina Anne Davis had come to Jackson to participate in the laying of the cornerstone for the Confederate monument on the old capitol green. After regaling the glorious past refreshed in memory by the visit of the "Daughter of the Confederacy," the *Clarion* asked in the very next sentence, "Why can't we organize a canning factory here?" Mississippi's leadership raised monuments to the past and praised the ghosts of great men while promising the people an even brighter future. But that bright future (which never came) paled before the luster of the past. The lure of the past canceled out the tug of the future and Mississippi stood still. And the governor's mansion, towering above the desolation of Chimneyville, grew larger in legend than in life.

When John Marshall Stone was inaugurated governor on March 29, 1876, his family was not with him and they did not move into the mansion until after the legislature adjourned in the late spring. His first residency, which extended over a period of six years from 1876 to 1882, was not a happy one and social activities at the mansion were held to an absolute minimum. Married only four years earlier in 1872, the Stones had already endured much personal sadness together when their first two children died in infancy. Additionally, Mrs. Stone, the former Mary Gillam Coman of Athens, Alabama, was an invalid who frequently suffered long periods of intense pain. Governor Stone, himself orphaned at the age of eleven, and the first lady adopted three of her brother's children. The presence of these small children enlivened the first family's otherwise unhappy circumstances. The Stones were hardly situated, however, before they were forced to evacuate the mansion during the summer of 1878 when a yellow fever epidemic threatened to decimate the population of Jackson. The first family returned to their home in Iuka where they remained for several months before returning to the mansion in the fall.[7]

Both the mansion and the governor's salary were affected by the financial retrenchment which characterized the first several years of Democratic rule following Reconstruction. Not only did the legislature repeal the mansion contingency fund, but several leading politicians and at least one newspaper objected to any expenditure of public funds on the executive residence. Throughout Stone's first six years in office, only $3,000 was appropriated for repair of the mansion. That expenditure, authorized in 1880, was designated for repair of the roof, painting, and paving; but only

$820.25 of the appropriation was actually spent because Governor Stone had asked that the major portion of the work be delayed until Mrs. Stone's condition improved.[8]

The governor's salary also became an issue of public concern. A letter to the editor appearing in the *Clarion* November 30, 1881, argued that the governor's yearly income of $4,000 could be justified only if he were responsible for the upkeep of the mansion and grounds. In no uncertain terms, the irate taxpayer disclaimed any personal liability for providing the governor such a palatial residence. It is difficult to gauge the impact of this letter and other similar expressions on the legislature. Nevertheless, in 1881 the lawmakers did reduce the chief executive's compensation to $3,000 annually.

It is also difficult to determine whether the *Clarion* reflected or was trying to influence public opinion in an article exposing what it termed the "wholesale robbery" of Ulysses S. Grant's administration, which had spent $302,345 on the White House during his term. The *Clarion* reminded its readers, "We had a miniature representation of that same sort of extravagance in Mississippi during the mongrel carpetbag era, when $40,000 for 'repair and furniture' for the Executive Mansion was considered a trifling matter by the dispensers of public plunder."[9]

Whether the expenditure $40,000 had been a matter of "public plunder" or not, Governor Stone, who had in fact introduced one of the bills authorizing part of that appropriation in 1870, became convinced that additional expenditures were necessary. In his farewell address to the legislature in January, 1882, Stone commented that, as long as the state continued to provide an executive mansion, the lawmakers were obligated to furnish the residence adequately and insure its proper care. He then catalogued the problems requiring immediate attention. Most of the furniture was more than ten years old and much of it was damaged; the carpeting was badly worn in several of the state rooms; and much of the crockery and china had been broken but not replaced during the last decade. In conclusion, he said, "almost everything in the way of furniture is needed."[10] To preclude the criticism that might otherwise result from a request for an appropriation to furnish the mansion during hard times, Governor Stone was asking that these measures be taken at the end of his term rather than at the beginning. To his political adversaries, neither the governor's hearth nor home is sacred as Tucker, Quitman, Alcorn, and Ames had found and several of their successors would also learn.

Since Stone's recommendations could not be dismissed as Republican extravagance or personal aggrandizement, the legislature accepted the legitimacy of his request. The lawmakers reestablished the mansion contingency fund and voted a $3,000 appropriation for the purchase of interior furnishings for the residence during the 1882 session.

Consequently, Stone's successor, Robert Lowry, who occupied the mansion in January, 1882, was assured that the most pressing problems would soon be remedied and that, if necessary, he could request of a more sympathetic legislature additional appropriations for repair and maintenance. After his election in 1881, Lowry sold his home in Brandon to Anselm J. McLaurin. Several years later McLaurin would also live in the governor's mansion.[11]

The circumstances surrounding Lowry's nomination in 1881 revealed a growing dissension in the Democratic ranks. Stone's renomination had been supported by a strong faction at the party's state convention. But Ethelbert Barksdale, who represented the increasingly vocal agrarians or small farmers, challenged and ultimately prevented Stone's renomination. Lowry was a compromise candidate and easily defeated his Republican opponent in the general election.[12] Even though a few Republicans continued to hold minor offices until the 1890 constitution disfranchised Mississippi Negroes, the election of 1881 was the last time the Republican party seriously challenged the Democrats until 1963.

Although Lowry was a widower when he was inaugurated on January 9, 1882, throughout his eight-year residency social activity at the governor's mansion was reminiscent of the gaiety that had characterized the mansion's hospitality in the antebellum years. At various times the governor's beautiful and popular daughters served as hostesses for both state and private functions at the mansion. Their success was measured by a prominent Jackson socialite who wrote that during the Lowry administration "the Mansion wakened to a season of gayety [sic] similar to that which had been the custom before the war came to break our spirits and take away our wealth." She also added, in explaining the long delay in the resumption of the mansion's traditional hospitality, "The Mansion had been for so many years an unknown factor in the city's social life, first because of the long Republican rule, and, second, of Mrs. Stone's invalidism, that our people were overjoyed when Governor Lowry and Mrs. Batte [Lowry's daughter, who served as hostess during his first term] threw wide open the doors and bade them enter to eat, drink, and be merry." One Jackson paper used the term "gay eighties" to describe the varied social activities at the mansion during Lowry's residency.[13]

A popular custom among young Jacksonians during the 1880s was a social affair called a "German." Young men in the various social clubs would pool their resources, hire a band, and rent a hall for ballroom dancing. When their budgets were strained they frequently called upon the Lowry family and requested the use of the mansion for their dances. From all accounts they were never turned down. Society columns in the local press gave extensive coverage to such events. One typical notice read:

> One of the most decidedly recherche and brilliant events which it has ever been the *Clarion-Ledger*'s pleasant privilege to chronicle, was the reception at the Executive Mansion on Friday night last in honor of the first anniversary of the "Ah, There" Club. The large parlors were beautifully decorated. . . . The magnificent grounds were lighted with magic lanterns; within and without all was most lovely.[14]

The reference to the "magnificent grounds" is in contrast to an account given by a visitor to Jackson who six months earlier had reported seeing stray cows grazing on the mansion square.[15]

After Lowry was reelected to a second term in 1885, virtually without opposition, the mansion's notable reputation for hospitality was enlarged even more. Under the direction of Mrs. William Henry, the governor's daughter who served as official hostess from 1886 to 1890, social life at the mansion became a "kaleidoscope of pleasure." According to a Jackson paper "those bright days continued" and young people found the mansion "a haven of delight."[16]

Through the 1880s Jackson's population was much smaller than that of Meridian, Natchez, Greenville, and Vicksburg. Consequently, legislative sessions which attracted hundreds of visitors to the capital had a measurable impact upon Jackson's economy, in addition to stimulating "an endless round of parties and receptions at the Mansion." On many occasions the governor's home overflowed with "pretty girl visitors." And as might be expected, while lawmakers dined and drank and debated under the illusion that a particular bill in which they had a vested interest could alone save mankind, young lovers caught up in such heady atmosphere plotted nightly trysts, leaving destiny and such things to their elders, unfortunately. During one particular legislative session, Lucy Pendergrast was visiting in the mansion for several days as the guest of one of the governor's daughters. She fell madly in love with Governor Lowry's son Patrick. One evening as the first family was returning to the mansion after attending a performance at the local opera house, Lucy and Patrick stopped by a minister's home. When they got back to the mansion they found a party in progress and considered the occasion appropriate to announce their marriage, to the utter surprise and quite possibly the dismay of the governor.[17]

When a similar situation occurred sometime later, the governor may have been less surprised. His son and namesake, Robert, "ran off" with Mary Foote, the granddaughter of former governor Henry Stuart Foote. When the young couple did not appear at a dinner party for several out-of-town guests, Governor Lowry apologized for their absence and insisted that dinner be served at the scheduled hour. While the guests were enjoying the governor's hospitality, Robert and Mary were at the Episcopal minister's study pledging their vows. After a private going-away party, they went to the railway station to catch a northbound train. But the young couple was startled and somewhat befuddled when they saw the governor, who had accompanied his guests to the station where they were also waiting for the same northbound train. After a preliminary survey of the threatening circumstances and the possible consequences of the discovery of their action, the newlyweds climbed over the coupling mechanism joining two cars near the end of the train and entered their pullman from the other side of the tracks. After a happy wedding night undoubtedly made even more exciting by their elopement and near discovery, the young couple telegraphed the mansion the next day and broke the news to the first family.[18]

Perhaps these two experiences with the brashness of youth prepared an indulgent father for the third and final marriage which occurred while he was governor of Mississippi. In the most unusual ceremony ever held at the executive mansion, the governor's daughter "Birdie" married James

A History of the Mississippi Governor's Mansion

L. Harris, the governor's private secretary. A guest at the wedding described the ceremony:

> One of the pretty fancies which lent beauty to the procedure was the presence, throughout the flower-decked rooms, of snow-white birds— a compliment to the bride's name. These dainty little creatures were poised wherever there was place for fluttering wings, one even finding room to spread its pinions above the snowy white shoulder of the girlish bride.[19]

One Jacksonian accurately predicted that the "Lowry's life at the Mansion will go down in social history as years of fullness and plenty with no clouds to dim the glory which were chronicled therein."

In addition to those years of fullness and plenty which characterized his residence in the mansion, there were also other important developments during Lowry's administration which affected not only the mansion but the state as a whole. Throughout his eight years in office, industrial expansion was the primary emphasis of Mississippi's political leadership. As a new-departure Democrat, Lowry envisioned an industrious and enterprising Mississippi.

Jackson in particular was imbued with the spirit of progress in the 1880s. The Jackson Board of Trade, a forerunner of the Chamber of Commerce, was organized on August 23, 1880. The board conducted an intense advertising campaign in national business journals to attract industry to Mississippi and lobbied in the legislature for special tax privileges for new industries moving to the state. State agencies also published brochures in several foreign languages in an effort to spur immigration. Although not as spectacular as industrial development on the national level, Mississippi's advancement in broadening its industrial base was significant. By the end of Lowry's administration, the mansion and its residents had benefited from the technological development spawned by the industrial revolution. Telephone service was available after 1882 and running water and electricity were added during the spring of 1888. It was also during Lowry's administration that another event occurred that is worthy of note. On January 19, 1888, the Jackson *Clarion-Ledger* was formed by the merger of the *Clarion*, established by Duncan Sneed in 1837 at Paulding, and the *Ledger*, established at Newton in 1871 by R. H. Henry. Within three months the paper proudly announced that its circulation exceeded 10,000. A notary public verified the figures. The *Clarion-Ledger*, for good

Of Monuments and Men

or bad, has for many years been the voice of Mississippi.[20] In the 1890s, the *Clarion-Ledger* raised that voice in support of industrial development and economic progress, especially in Jackson.

Much of this economic progress in Jackson was no doubt spurred by the recurring effort to relocate the capital city. In 1884, J. S. Montgomery of Oktibbeha County introduced a bill to move the capital to Meridian which at that time was larger and industrially more advanced than Jackson. The bill was presented to the House with an endorsement by a committee which had studied the proposal, but the full House rejected the measure by a vote of 46 to 33.[21]

In the midst of Mississippi's industrial boom, an event occurred at the mansion that underlined the paramount concern of most Mississippians and the devotion with which they honored their past. On March 11, 1884, Jefferson and Varina Howell Davis visited Jackson at the invitation of the state legislature. The ex-president and his wife were accorded ceremony more befitting a reigning monarch than the fallen leader of a lost cause. A state dinner at the mansion was held in Davis' honor by Governor Lowry, who twenty years earlier had been commissioned by the state of Mississippi to seek the president's release from his confinement at Fort Monroe. The dinner at the mansion was contrasted with the previous meeting of the two executives by a local journalist: "How different were the surroundings in which they found themselves then, as compared with the last visit they had together, when General Lowry was the guest and the imprisoned ex-President the host! Then instead of strolling at their ease, through the spacious apartments and about the grounds, abloom with southern flowers, they met within the forbidding walls of Fortress Monroe . . . where . . . the Southland's dethroned Chieftain was shut in, to bear his people's suffering."[22]

The 1884 visit to Jackson was one of the last joint public appearances of Jefferson and Varina Davis, and the people of Mississippi "looking upon his silver hair and bent figure, understood that it was good-by, and put their very hearts into it." There were many opportunities, however, to transfer the love and devotion for Jefferson Davis to other members of his family. Four years later, Winnie Davis, the president's daughter, represented her father at the laying of the cornerstone of the Confederate monument in Jackson. And still later the president's young grandson, whose name was legally changed from Jefferson Davis Hayes to Jefferson Hayes Davis, unveiled that monument on June 3, 1891. On both occasions the visiting dignitaries were honored at the mansion. A young Jackson woman who stood in the receiving line with the "Daughter of the Confederacy" recalled the event several years later: "It was my pleasure to receive these visitors with her . . . who was accorded all the honors that go, rightfully, to royalty. . . . A pretty incident which occurred at the Mansion closed her visit. This was the presentation by Governor Lowry, for the ladies of Jackson, of a beautiful diamond ring."[23]

Although this pretty incident may have been gratifying to those Mississippians preoccupied with past glories, it provided scant relief to small farmers bearing the burden of agricultural depression. A month before Governor Lowry presented the diamond ring to Varina Anne Davis, a newspaperman asked L. Q. C. Lamar about economic progress and the growing crime rate in Mississippi. At the time of the interview Lamar was associate justice of the United States Supreme Court. "There has been no progress in agriculture since the war," Lamar answered, "it has perhaps declined." He then explained the relationship between a depressed economy and a rising crime rate: "There is a vast army of . . . idlers, who are not essentially vicious, except that indolence is the mother of crime."[24] There were serious problems smoldering just below the surface in Mississippi.

Those problems seriously threatened Democratic solidarity during the convention of 1889. A Brookhaven paper estimated that about forty-two candidates would seek the Democratic gubernatorial nomination when the convention assembled at Jackson.[25] The prevailing issue during preconvention maneuvering was the concern for a new state constitution. Representatives of agrarian interests were demanding constitutional reform as a means of reordering the priorities of state government. For a quarter of a century the promotion of industry had so absorbed the state's political leadership that agricultural development had been neglected. Small farmers claimed that "Bourbon Democrats" maintained control over official policy through an unfair apportionment of the state legislature. Bourbon leaders had also prevented the development of independent parties by their dire predictions that the 142,000 blacks who were still registered voters would control the balance of power if whites divided over economic issues or along class lines.[26]

The only recourse considered by the small farmers was the constitutional disfranchisement of blacks, which would then make it possible for whites to divide over economic issues. By 1889 most state journals and an increasing number of Democratic leaders supported this strategy. Facing its most serious challenge since Reconstruction, the ruling elite conceded to the demand for a new constitution but did not surrender its control over the party. Not only did they nominate John Marshall Stone on the first ballot at the party convention, they also dominated the constitutional convention and prevented, except for disfranchisement of Negroes, the adoption of the major political reforms sponsored by small farmers. The final draft of the new constitution was so disappointing to Frank Burkitt, the acknowledged leader of the agrarian faction, that he and several of his supporters refused to sign the document.[27] Although it withstood this challenge, the party's power structure was placed under a thirteen-year siege and fell finally to the assault of James K. Vardaman.

Stone's nomination in 1889 was made possible when the pre-convention pretenders, including W. S. Featherston, Ethelbert Barksdale, and Stephen D. Lee, withdrew from contention. His nomination assured his election. Yet it is remarkable that, in a year when the political situation was so fraught with ominous signs of division, Stone was elected by a vote of 84,929 to 16. However, Stone was not unaccustomed to large-scale victories. He had been elected in 1877 by a vote of 97,727 to 47.

During Stone's first year in office the new constitution was adopted; it became operative in 1891. Under its provisions the governor could not succeed himself, but the terms of all incumbents were extended two years. Thus Governor Stone served a second term of six years.

When the first family, which then included only one teenaged daughter, occupied the mansion in January, 1890, they began a second residency which would prove to be much more pleasant than their first one. Mrs. Stone, who had completely recovered from her previous illness, was described by a neighbor as a "robust . . . 'French-looking person' with an active figure inclined to embonpoint [and] a round and darkly complexioned face." The first lady was also characterized as an excellent conversationalist who would preside over the mansion's social life with "real genuine hospitality" and not that "giddy show" which the uninformed mistook for hospitality.[28]

The first family was barely settled, however, before they were intruded upon by a group of ladies armed with a writ of authority from the legislature to supervise the $4,000 expenditure recently appropriated to repair and refurnish the mansion. On January 23, 1890, the *Clarion-Ledger* noted, "The ladies appointed to assist in superintending the renovation of the Executive Mansion, have been busily engaged with their duties several days." Although the legislature had intended for most of the appropriation to be used in repairing the roof, especially on the cottage in the rear of the mansion, the ladies diverted most of the funds to interior furnishings, "leaving the outside sadly in need of repairs."[29]

Apparently this experience convinced the legislature that supervision of mansion repair should be delegated to elected officials. Two years later when the lawmakers appropriated an additional $2,000 to repair, repaint, and recover the mansion, the bill also stipulated that a board consisting of the governor, the secretary of state, and the attorney general would exercise sole authority in directing the expenditure.[30] This effort was the first step toward the eventual establishment of the Capitol Commission created in 1901.

Although the law did not specify a color for the mansion's exterior, a news account in 1896 referred to the building as a gray-colored structure.[31] It may be that the building was painted white in 1892 and had by 1896 faded somewhat into an appearance of gray. There is, of course, another possible explanation. Since many Mississippians really looked upon the governor's mansion as the Mississippi White House, the residence could have been painted gray in honor of the Confederacy.

As Governor Stone would later indicate, again at the end of his term, that appropriation of $6,000 was not sufficient to repair or furnish the mansion adequately. It did, however, at least make the mansion more comfortable and attractive.[32]

The Stone family occupied the cottage annex during their second residency and reserved the front portion of the mansion almost exclusively for state occasions. The first family also made the mansion readily available for private parties and social events staged by local clubs and organizations. Although recognizing it as the official residence of the chief executive, the general public through the years have always considered the governor's mansion a public building and presumed its availability for a wide variety of social functions.

Typical of the many private parties at the mansion was the "Library" held on November 23, 1893, when the "Executive Mansion was thrown wide open . . . [and] a large number of Jackson's most cultivated people" assembled in its spacious parlors for an evening of "unique entertainment." The party format called for young ladies to disguise themselves as famous books and the young men, by correctly identifying the volume, would then have the pleasure of the lady's company for fifteen minutes. The books, in this manner, were circulated throughout the evening and "occasioned a good deal of merriment and no little rivalry for the popular novels." Surprisingly, Edward Bellamy's *Looking Backward* "had small show upon this occasion, for there was not one present who did not prefer to look forward . . . rather than at the mask that was looking backward."[33]

Generally speaking, 1893 was a good year for books in Mississippi. The legislature required by statute that Mississippi history be taught in the public schools of the state. Coincidentally, the law became operative one year after former governor Robert Lowry and prominent Democratic editor William McCardle published a history of the state. Not surprisingly, the Lowry-McCardle *School History of Mississippi* was widely used throughout the public school system.[34]

Just before Governor Stone retired from office in 1896, he again advised the legislature that the mansion's general state of repair required immediate attention. He specified the need for new linen, incidental furniture, and carpeting. He also complained of the continued problem of leakage which had plagued the first families for so many years. "The roof on the main building is slate," Stone said, "but it seems impossible to prevent it from leaking." When the roof was last repaired, payment was withheld for a period of six months or until every leak seemed to have been corrected. However, a short time after payment was made the leaks reappeared. Governor Stone further informed the legislature that the tin roof on the family quarters was "full of holes patched over with painted cloths" and also needed major repair or replacement.[35]

After detailing the need for repair at the mansion, Governor Stone brought up the subject of the governor's salary. Speaking from a "perfectly disinterested point of view," Stone assured the legislature that the governor, unless he had income from some other source, could not live on a salary less than $4,000. He also urged the lawmakers to provide an additional $500 annually for the expenses incurred in payment for fuel, electricity, and servants at the mansion. This was especially needed if the legislature did not increase the governor's salary. Finally, Stone recommended that a special committee be appointed to examine the mansion to determine its condition and make recommendations for its repair.

The legislature responded to this suggestion and the committee's report corroborated Stone's rather dismal account of the mansion's condition. The committee recommended that the roofs on both buildings be replaced and that larger gutters also be installed. Other recommendations included new and higher chimneys to reduce the danger of fires, extensive replastering, especially on the second floor of the main structure, new front steps of all-heart pine lumber, and the resetting of all fireplaces. The report contained an interesting comment on the open-range laws then current in the state. Although conceding that the "fences and gates around the grounds need[ed] repairing," the committee recommended "the least possible amount of expense in this direction, so long as the cattle range at large in the city of Jackson." "When this ceases," the report continued, "we can abondon our jail-yard fences around our public buildings." For these repairs the committee proposed an appropriation of $1,750 which was to be expended as outlined by the committee. The legislature authorized this expenditure but took no action on Governor Stone's suggestion to refurnish the mansion or his recommendation for a $500 maintenance fund.[36] Consequently, when Stone's successor, Anselm J. McLaurin, and his large family occupied the mansion in January, 1896, they did not enjoy the advantage of legislative generosity.

Governor McLaurin was elected in 1895 in one of the closest races since Reconstruction. His Populist opponent, Frank Burkitt, polled 17,466 votes from among the increasingly restive small farmers. Democratic solidarity was maintained, but only temporarily. The disparity between industrial expansion and agricultural decline had generated political unrest among the small white farmers and laborers who vocalized their discontent first through the Farmer's Alliance and then the

Of Monuments and Men

Populist party. When the poor-white masses considered Populism as an alternative to their privation, they threatened the party in power and jeopardized white supremacy. It was a revolt. But the ruling elite survived. Wilbur J. Cash described their technique:

> When our common white, our Populist . . . had come to this: The eyes of his old captains were ominous upon him. From hustings and from pulpits thousands of voices proclaimed him traitor and nigger-loving scoundrel; renegade to Southern womanhood, the Confederate dead, and the God of his fathers; Champion of the transformation of the white races into a mongrel breed.[37]

The poor whites recoiled; they were reticent but still restless. In the closing years of the nineteenth century an emerging leadership, most notably James Kimble Vardaman, both responded to and exploited that unrest.

In the meantime, Governor McLaurin presided over an unruly party splintered by conflicting and diverging interests. He found no comfort in the equally unruly elements that day of his inauguration. On inaugural night Governor McLaurin and his wife held their first reception at the executive mansion honoring the legislature, and the "very floodgates of heaven opened." According to a Jacksonian making her way to the mansion on that stormy night, "Rivers of water ran down pavements . . . while navigable streams were to be found in the low places." Nevertheless, "a large number of the beauty and chivalry of the capital city braved the elements and joined with the legislature in paying their respects to the new Chief Executive and his family at the Mansion."[38]

That local residents would in face of such conditions get out on so stormy a night is a measure of the continuing importance they attached to social life at the mansion. And no doubt it was good for business to be seen at the mansion. Jackson's population was static during the 1880s, increasing from 5,204 in 1880 to only 5,920 in 1890. A large majority of those 5,920 were blacks which meant that practically the entire white population could have been entertained at the mansion at one time.

For the McLaurin family, life at the mansion was like life in any family with several children, often hectic and always active. Family letters to a daughter not living in Jackson reflect the social customs during the 1890s, which often worked a hardship on a mother of several children who also happened to be the first lady with many official obligations. Mrs. McLaurin apologized to her daughter Mary for not having written lately but asked her indulgence due to a "spring cold and calling." "Yesterday," she told her daughter, "I took advantage of the sun and called at twelve houses, one of which is a mile and a quarter from [the mansion], and walked every step of the way." Fortunately, bad weather had reduced the number of ladies who called at the mansion and Mrs. McLaurin advised her daughter, with a sigh of relief, that she owed no more than "three or four calls now which there is no hurry about returning." Then as if to reassure her daughter that life in the mansion was not unpleasant, she added, "Still I continue to have a very nice time."[39]

The first lady's time was so consumed by "callers and so much business to attend to," that she considered appointing her sister, who was living in the mansion, her private secretary. The sister declined but did help Mrs. McLaurin with her correspondence to Mary. The "auntie" wrote on one occasion asking Mary to bring the family dinner bell with her on her next visit to the mansion. The bell was in all probability needed to assemble the smaller children, who seemed to thoroughly enjoy their life at the executive residence. On a typical afternoon a teenaged daughter came home after school and announced that she was going for a "drive," which must have meant a buggy ride in 1896. The auntie reported to Mary that no one "paid any attention to her and in about an hour in comes Willis Campbell to take her driving and your mama went in and scard [sic] him nearly to death and told Cat if she ever made an engagement without her knowing it again she would surely get her, but she did not tell her so before Willis." And like mothers through the ages, "she let her go this time."[40]

Daisy, an older daughter with more independence and privileges, was "gone the whole time." More like a boarder than a resident, Daisy was "very much admired and [had] many gentlemen friends" who called at the mansion.[41] From family correspondence, which also refers to "Little McLaurin," Louie, and Jean, it seems that at least five of McLaurin's eight children were living at the mansion during his residency. The number of children was reduced or increased by one—the records are not clear—when Daisy married Forrest Stevens of Carrollton on December 15, 1896. The marriage took place in the mansion and was the most noteworthy

Of Monuments and Men

social event which occurred during the McLaurins' four-year residency. Because the wedding notice is such a superb example of the rhythmic language and poetic license characteristic of nineteenth-century journalism, it bears repeating at length:

> The stately old building, familiarly known among all local Mississippians as the "Mansion," the gray stone walls of which have sheltered through succeeding years the old state's chief officials and the executive family, was on Tuesday, the 15th inst. the scene of a marriage, remarkable even in the high circles which the bride so royally graced for its beauty and elegant simplicity.
>
> The hour was set for high noon. . . . Throughout the rooms where the state's leading men lingered in eager expectancy, whiling away the moments with reminiscences of happy days now part of the historic past . . . the breath of dying flowers mingled with the fresh, sweet odor of the day, sweeping in through the wide, open windows. . . . The bride, Governor Anselm J. McLaurin's third daughter, is a tall and stately maiden, with eyes like the sea and hair which hides in its soft coils the glint of golden sunbeams.[42]

Life at the mansion was not always this pleasant however. One evening, not unlike the many other quiet evenings the governor enjoyed at his residence, an old friend dropped by to see McLaurin. The visitor, Judge S. R. Coleman, came to ask the governor to pardon a young man convicted of murder. After considering the case thoroughly, the governor extended executive clemency to the young man on the provision that he leave the state. When the circumstances surrounding the pardon were made public, the anti-McLaurin press exploded, and for over a year the pardon was the topic of front page news and editorial comment. Although the coverage embarrassed the governor, it did not adversely affect his political career. In 1899, when McLaurin's term expired, the Democratic convention not only praised his administration but endorsed his appointment to the United States Senate and chose as his successor a member of the McLaurin clan or "official family."[43]

The 1899 Democratic convention which passed over James K. Vardaman and nominated Andrew H. Longino was the high-water mark of the ruling elite which had dominated the Democratic party for the last quarter of a century. As a legacy of his long life in Mississippi politics, Reuben Davis bequeathed this indictment of the one-party system:

> Forty years ago, constant practice had made our public speakers so skillful in debate that every question was made clear even to men otherwise uneducated.

A History of the Mississippi Governor's Mansion

> For the last twenty years this practical union between politicians and people has not existed. Only one party is allowed to speak, and the leaders of that party no longer debate, they simply declaim and denounce. Upon this crude and windy diet, the once robust and sturdy political convictions of our people have dwindled into leanness and decay. In my judgement, this state of affairs is fatally injurious to our institutions and dangerous to our liberties. The people follow with confidence the misleading and uncontradicted assertions of their own leaders, and act upon false impressions, to their own prejudice and the injury of the common good. . . . Free government becomes an absurdity when all shades of opinion are not allowed the fullest expressions.[44]

Although Davis did not live to see it, the political process in Mississippi was once again made a public enterprise with the enactment of the popular primary in 1902. Nominations for all public offices, from justice of the peace to the chief executive, were placed in the hands of the people in primary elections. Since the primary law excluded Negroes from participation, the issue of race need not concern the rival candidates who were free to debate other issues. Yet strange as it may seem, race was the dominant theme in the first primary election held in 1903, and practice in public debate produced more cacophony than clarification. Cleverness was taken for wisdom, flamboyance for leadership, and racial brutality for racial integrity. Even though candidates were free to express all shades of opinion, Mississippi politics continued for many years to be a matter of black and white.

CHAPTER VII

The Mansion and the Myth

BY ALMOST ANY standard Governor Andrew H. Longino was a pivotal figure in Mississippi political history. He was the first governor since the Civil War who was not a Confederate veteran and the last to be chosen by the convention system. Inaugurated on January 16, 1900, Longino ushered in the century of progress and warned Mississippians to brace themselves for the inevitable changes that would follow in the wake of that progress.

Both Governor Longino and the first lady, Marion Buckley of Jackson, embraced the wave of the future and provided progressive leadership at the dawning of a new and exciting era. Mrs. Longino, who had held a clerical position in the auditor's office during the 1880s, was one of the first women in the state's history to be employed in public service. She was identified with the women's suffrage movement through her close association with Belle Kearney in the Mississippi branch of the Women's Christian Temperance Union, a movement that endorsed a wide range of political reforms in addition to temperance. Mrs. Longino was also instrumental in establishing the Old Ladies Home in Jackson, which she promoted through teas at the mansion and by direct contact with legislators.[1] Through her varied activities and visibility Mrs. Longino significantly expanded the public role of Mississippi's first lady and her involvement was a harbinger of the increasing influence women would exercise over public affairs after the passage of the Nineteenth Amendment.

The governor, even more than the first lady if controversy is the measure, was also an iconoclast. He publicly criticized Mississippians for their preoccupation with the past and their tendency to allow sentiment rather than reason to govern their lives. Although the governor was referring primarily to economic matters, Longino's political opponents distorted that criticism and accused him of repudiating the past, an act of political suicide in Mississippi.[2]

In his inaugural address Longino predicted a tidal wave of industrial development. The governor told the legislature, "I confidently hope that no more sentimental or pre-judicial opposition to . . . corporate enterprises will find favor with the Legislature." Instead, he recommended that the lawmakers offer liberal tax exemptions to attract industry to Mississippi, "so that capital hunting investment will have no just cause to pass Mississippi and go to other states offering wiser legitimate inducements."[3]

On the basis of the number of new industrial charters granted during Longino's administration, the legislature was not only liberal but highly successful in attracting new industry. Between 1900 and 1904 the number of new charters rose to 1,312, substantially above the 365 issued during the previous quadrennial. The impact of industrial expansion was especially evident in Jackson. Estimating that approximately $2.1 million in capital construction was then in progress, the *Clarion-Ledger* reported on July 29, 1902, that the city's building boom had swamped contractors with orders from all quarters and showed no signs of diminishing.

Accounting for about half of that total estimate was the construction of a new state capitol. Since architects had predicted the imminent collapse of the old capitol in 1888, much consideration had been given to the construction of a larger and more modern state house. A proposal in 1888 to restore the 1839 structure, at a cost of about $112,000, was rejected in favor of a new building to be located on larger and more spacious grounds. But for a decade the legislature could not agree upon the design or the means to finance the new capitol. Although he called a special session of the legislature in 1897 to consider the matter, Governor McLaurin vetoed the bill that provided for a new building. In justifying his veto, McLaurin criticized the design of the capitol, which he considered more appropriate for a county courthouse than a modern state house. Despite the differences over design and financing, there was general agreement among state officials that the overcrowded and dilapidated old capitol had to be replaced, and soon.[4]

The Mansion and the Myth

After his nomination by the Democratic party (which was tantamount to his election), Longino had visited Washington, D.C. and several states to study their capitol buildings. During the tour the governor-elect accumulated considerable knowledge about new building techniques and recent advances in architectural design. Shortly after his inauguration, he sent a special message to the legislature recommending the construction of a new capitol which he considered the most pressing subject that would come before the legislature during that session. Assuring the lawmakers that nothing reflected the "public spirit and state pride of the people of any commonwealth as its public buildings," he declared, "therefore . . . proud and prosperous Mississippi, can no longer afford, in these days of gigantic advancement and greatness of statehood, to be content with their present capitol building." The material he had accumulated during his recent study of other state capitols was passed on to the legislature. After wrangling over several designs, the legislature finally authorized the Capitol Commission to select a final design and advertise bids for its construction. The problem of financing a new capitol was solved when the Mississippi supreme court awarded $1 million to the state in a delinquent tax suit brought against several railroad companies.[5]

Following ground-breaking ceremonies on January 1, 1901, construction proceeded with minimal delays and difficulties. However, during the otherwise orderly and steady progress toward its completion, the new capitol was caught up in an angry dispute between Longino and the ladies of Jackson.

By 1903, Jefferson Davis was a legendary figure; his influence over public affairs through an emotional appeal to his memory was significant and growing stronger. The Jackson chapter of the United Daughters of the Confederacy asked Governor Longino to dedicate the new capitol on June 3, Jefferson Davis' birthday. In a reply that would have a bearing on his political future, Longino belittled Mississippi's devotion to the past and, as reported in the press, confessed that "he was tired of so much confederate rot." Several months later, when Longino was running for the United States Senate against H. D. Money, the *Winona Times* reported under the headline IS HE SAFE: "Governor Longino does not represent the principles and sentiment of the people of the South. He is not in sympathy with those who hold sacred the memories of a glorious past." The editor then referred to Longino's "insult" to the ladies of the state and his remark about "confederate rot." It is impossible to measure the importance of that incident upon the election results, but Longino was defeated by Money, who garnered 62.3 percent of the primary vote. In spite of the controversy, the new building was dedicated on Davis' birthday. Ceremonies were held on June 3, 1903, and state officials moved into their new quarters on September 20.[6]

The old capitol, then vacant and dilapidated, occupied a choice, downtown location. As commercial development pressed upon the borders of the capitol green, the future use of the old building became the subject of continuing debate. The free-ranging discussion was eventually widened to include the governor's mansion, which occupied an even more choice location just three blocks west on Capitol Street.

Uniquely a city of the twentieth century, Jackson was on the verge of spectacular industrial and commercial development, and the maximum utilization of real estate was basic to that growth. Following a slight increase through the last three decades of the nineteenth century, Jackson's population soared during the first thirty years of the twentieth as reflected by the following figures:

```
1880 — 5,204
1890 — 5,920
1900 — 7,866
1910 — 21,262
1920 — 22,817
1930 — 48,282
```

The first ominous sign that the blind hand of progress threatened the mansion's future was noted in 1902 when the city fathers decreed that the downtown streets be widened to accommodate the increasing demands of city traffic. That process necessitated the removal of the outer ring of oaks encircling the mansion which Mrs. Henry Stuart Foote had planted fifty years earlier. First encroaching upon the historic square, progress would soon endanger the mansion itself.[7]

However, while the future of the sixty-year-old building was being decided, Governor Longino and his family occupied the historic mansion in relative calm. Possibly because the mansion was not in good repair or well-furnished, there was a marked decline in the level of social activity

The Mansion and the Myth

during the Longino residency. Although the first family honored several distinguished visitors, including Mrs. Jefferson Davis, both state and private functions at the mansion were conducted with less ceremony and more simplicity than previously. It is quite probable that since the governor and first lady were devout Baptists and closely associated with the WCTU, their personal predilections restricted the manner of entertainment on state occasions and precluded the use of the mansion by Jackson social clubs for dances and similar festivities.[8]

Although the type of public events at the mansion might have changed during the Longino administration, the presumption of its use for public functions did not diminish. Mrs. Longino had affiliated with the Ladies Aid Society of Jackson's First Baptist Church on January 7, 1901. In addition to noting her enrollment, the minutes for that same day also recorded that the Twentieth Century Tea sponsored by the society would be held at the governor's mansion on the following Friday. The tea was postponed for some reason and subsequent minutes did not indicate that the event was ever held.[9] Nevertheless, even if the ladies were disappointed they were amply compensated for having such a distinguished member in their society, and they were usually invited to the many teas and receptions sponsored by the state and local chapters of the Mississippi WCTU, especially on those occasions when national leaders of the movement visited the capital city.

While the Longinos were living in the governor's mansion, a unique event in the residence's long and interesting history occurred. Mrs. Longino's fifth child was born at the mansion. Although there have been several other births in the executive dwelling, this was the only time that a child of a first lady was born in the governor's mansion. Mrs. Longino named her newborn daughter in honor of her sister, Gay Buckley, whose marriage to Dr. Tim Cooper also took place in the mansion.[10]

But whatever luster these events may have added to the building's history, there were other forces at work reducing the mansion's charm, especially to Jackson businessmen. By 1904 the mansion had become a luxury, a legacy of the past, which stood in the way of economic progress, and the pressure favoring its disposal mounted. Although Longino did not take a public stand on the issue of selling the mansion, he did complain of its condition. And as his predecessor McLaurin had done,

A History of the Mississippi Governor's Mansion

Longino urged the legislature to authorize emergency repairs at the residence—otherwise, he said, his successor might find the building uninhabitable. Additionally, the governor outlined the need for new furnishings to replace the old, damaged, and worn furniture, some of which was no longer usable. From 1900 to 1904, only $2,500 was expended for repair and refurnishing of the mansion. Frequent objections were raised, however, even to that small appropriation. Opponents argued against spending any state funds for emergency repair of a public building which actually needed major renovation, especially when the continued use of that building was in doubt. As a further courtesy to his successor, Governor Longino vacated the mansion shortly before the expiration of his term, allowing Governor Vardaman to occupy the residence prior to the inaugural ceremonies.[11]

James Kimble Vardaman was Mississippi's first governor to be nominated in a primary election. In the process of defeating F. A. Critz and Edmond F. Noel, Vardaman waged a blistering campaign against corporate interests. He accused Longino of selling out small farmers and workers to the banks, capitalists, and railroad companies. Vardaman also promised to break up the "Jackson ring," a political trust which he accused of subverting the democratic system through its abuse of power and wealth. Vardaman asserted that he was the only candidate who had risen from a humble background and was, consequently, the only true representative of the people. The choice was clear, he said, the people or the politicians, wealth against commonwealth. Vardaman pitched his appeal to the small farmer and laborer, but he delivered his appeal in the rhetoric of racism.[12] Vardaman's use of race was not only reckless and irresponsible but unnecessary since blacks had been eliminated from political participation by the 1890 constitution and by the "lily white" primary law of 1902. The tactic was very effective, however, and was often used by his successors.

On January 19, 1904, "the sun rose bright and clear in Jackson, but dark clouds covered the sky" as the inaugural party "emerged from the state mansion at noon." Governor-elect and Mrs. Vardaman and Dr. B. E. Ward, Vardaman's old and valued friend, entered an open carriage and drove to the new capitol. Vardaman would be the first governor to take the oath of office in the new building. For the first time in many years, neither

The Mansion and the Myth

military units nor marching bands heralded the approach. At Vardaman's insistence there was no inaugural parade, only a band of followers who walked with Vardaman to the capitol. Almost an hour later, after frequent stops to greet his admirers, Vardaman entered the legislative chamber to take the oath and deliver his inaugural address. Because the personal relationship between the incumbent and the governor-elect had been so bitter over the past few years, Governor Longino declined to make the courtesy introduction of his successor. Vardaman was introduced by one of his legislative supporters.[13]

Vardaman's inaugural address, in many respects a blueprint for reform, closed on an unexpected theme. He recommended that the official executive residence be sold or converted to some other use. The governor's mansion he said, was a "relic of aristocracy" and not in keeping with the plain, republican simplicity in which most Mississippians lived. Living in the mansion also imposed social obligations upon the governor and his family that were inconsistent with democratic government and often interfered with a constructive discharge of the governor's official duties. Finally, Vardaman asserted, the governor ought to live like other public officials who had to provide their own quarters while exercising their official duties in Jackson.[14]

This recommendation probably surprised at least some members of the legislature who, with their wives, had been so graciously entertained at the mansion only a few days earlier by the governor-elect and Mrs. Vardaman. On that evening, a cold and rainy night, Vardaman had moved among his guests with ease and charm, greeting the lawmakers with warm handshakes and flattering their wives with compliments. A representative from Lee County, J. M. Hoyle, especially enjoyed the reception and praised the governor and first lady for making the occasion "so pleasant for everyone, that it will not soon be forgotten."[15]

Essentially a gregarious and generous man, Vardaman discovered over the next four years that parties and receptions at the mansion, however much an imposition they might have been, were also an opportunity to cultivate support among lawmakers and other officials. According to his biographer, William F. Holmes, Vardaman took full advantage of the mansion's tradition of hospitality and frequently invited members of the legislature to "dinner at the mansion."[16]

A History of the Mississippi Governor's Mansion

Although Vardaman was known for his ardent and deep convictions, he was a man of plain and simple tastes. The first lady, Anna Burleson Robinson of Decatur, Alabama, also held "very pronounced views." But she, like her husband, possessed an unassuming manner completely without ostentation, which made her guests feel comfortable and at ease. A frequent visitor to the mansion who "sat at table with men of high and low degree, prominent politicians . . . and the plainest of plain people" stated that he was never able to detect in the demeanor of the first family any indication of the social or economic status of their guests.[17]

The Vardaman family retained with only slight modification their traditional lifestyle during their residence in the mansion. Social obligations notwithstanding, Vardaman kept a cow on the mansion grounds, and the children—two boys and two girls ranging in age from twelve to twenty-one—were given free run of the mansion regardless of the pressing affairs of state and the dignitaries that might be visiting their father. The first lady eventually learned to expect the unexpected dinner guests and always cooked extra servings, "usually of the home variety," because Governor Vardaman had a "way of picking up as he was on his way to dinner any friend or any other person who attracted or interested him."[18] Vardaman was genuinely fond of people, but like most politicians was an ambitious man who coveted office higher than the one he presently held. In 1907, while serving as governor, Vardaman ran for the United States Senate against Congressman John Sharp Williams. After an intense campaign distinguished for its lack of rancor and bitterness, the close count left the outcome in doubt. Believing their hero had won, a large crowd of Vardaman supporters flooded the mansion grounds in spontaneous exuberance and celebration. But a few days later, when the Democratic State Executive Committee certified the election results, Williams was declared the winner by a margin of 648 votes out of over 118,-000 cast.[19] This was only a temporary setback, however, in Vardaman's long career, which was punctuated by a series of victories and defeats. When Vardaman was elected to the Senate in 1911, he became the first of only two governors in the twentieth century elected to a higher office following a tenure as the state's chief executive. Theodore G. Bilbo was the only other ex-governor to win the race for higher office.

The Mansion and the Myth

Formal affairs, with pomp and ceremony, were almost unknown at the mansion while the Vardamans lived there, although on several occasions the circumstances might have warranted a more formal style of hospitality. Governors Charles S. Deneen of Illinois and S. W. Pennypacker of Pennsylvania, their wives, and staff members were entertained at the mansion with "plain republican simplicity" when they paid a courtesy visit to Governor Vardaman while in Mississippi to dedicate their state monuments at the Vicksburg National Park. On another occasion, when General Grant's son who was then a vice-president of the Illinois Central visited Jackson, Mrs. Vardaman refused to be in the same house with a member of the general's family. Reminding the governor that her family's plantation had been destroyed by federal soldiers during the Civil War, the first lady refused to act as hostess and went up to the family's home at Greenwood. Aletha, the Vardamans' oldest daughter, served as hostess for the reception honoring the railroad officials. Although the first lady's refusal to act as hostess was not known publicly, her obstinance "caused quite a lot of amusement among the intimate family circle at that time."[20]

Among the other prominent guests who visited the mansion during the Vardaman residency, and who were more cordially welcomed, were Alton B. Parker, the Democratic nominee for president in 1904, Miss Sophie Wright of New Orleans, a leading figure in the Kings Daughters organization, and Governor J. W. C. Beckham of Kentucky, who came to study Mississippi's new capitol building.

Perhaps the social event that sparked more ceremony than any other was the visit of William Jennings Bryan and his wife. In the two previous presidential elections, Bryan had carried Mississippi by a margin of almost ten to one. Personally and philosophically, Vardaman admired "The Great Commoner" and enthusiastically supported his bid for the presidency. For several days before Bryan's arrival, the Vardaman family turned the old mansion upside down trying to make it presentable for his visit. Arriving at Jackson in the early morning, Bryan was escorted to the mansion where he enjoyed a specially prepared breakfast that included a large quantity of vine-ripened tomatoes, one of his favorite dishes. After a full day of speeches and conferences, a formal state dinner was held at the mansion that evening.[21] Vardaman probably felt no sense of obligation on that occasion. It is likely that by the time of Bryan's visit he had already begun to modify his attitude toward the mansion and its continued use as the official executive residence.

Precisely when Vardaman changed his mind is not known, but there are indications that it was early in his administration. Governor Vardaman unexpectedly found the mansion an asset rather than a liability in his relationships with the legislature and other influential officials. His family, who thoroughly enjoyed their life at the mansion, also became sentimentally attached to the historic structure and left their personal imprint upon the mansion, especially the grounds. In celebration of his twelfth birthday, James K. Vardaman, Jr. and the first lady planted a magnolia tree at the southwest corner of the mansion and the first lady also decorated the square with several spruce trees.[22] An incident involving those and other trees might also have influenced the governor's attitude toward the mansion. The first family entertained the children from Jackson orphanages each Christmas at the mansion. At one of those parties each of the boys was given a pocket knife along with other gifts provided by Jackson merchants. After refreshments and the traditional exchange of gifts, the boys scattered throughout the grounds. They were later discovered carving their initials on various trees, some of which had been standing even before the mansion was built. When their counselors tried to discipline the boys with the threat of taking away their prized gifts, Governor Vardaman intervened in their behalf and offered his assistance to the younger boys who were having difficulty in shaping their letters.[23] The governor, who certainly left his mark on Mississippi's history, seemed to understand that young boys would want to leave some sign that they too had passed this way.

Mrs. Vardaman, an industrious and enterprising first lady, also added her personal touch to the mansion. Shortly after settling her family in the residence, she discovered several pieces of discarded antique furniture while rummaging through the basement. Since there were only limited funds with which to purchase new furniture, the first lady refinished those pieces that could be repaired and thus restored a measure of charm to the mansion's interior, drawing favorable comment from both the governor and the many guests who enjoyed their hospitality. Many years later, when she revisited the mansion, Minnie Vardaman Ratliff was delighted

The Mansion and the Myth

to see that those pieces which her mother had restored were still in use.[24]

Another occurrence, which deeply saddened Governor Vardaman, might also have contributed to his change of heart toward preserving the official executive residence. About a year after his inauguration, Governor Vardaman's mother, Mary Ann Fox Vardaman, came to visit her famous son at the governor's mansion. While the family was enjoying her visit, which had brought a special happiness to the children, she became suddenly and gravely ill. Her unexpected death on March 18, 1905, the first to occur in the mansion, shocked the Vardaman family and must have added to their feeling for that venerable old building.[25] The governor's mansion had witnessed not only the rambling course of history but now the full circle of life, and like many other Mississippians Governor Vardaman no longer considered the mansion a relic of aristocracy but a landmark rising out of the past.

In his farewell address to the legislature, Vardaman declared, "I am very much opposed to selling this property. . . . Besides being a most beautiful piece of architecture, it has a sentimental value which can not be measured in dollars and cents." The governor's mansion, Vardaman said, was a "monument to the best in the state's history . . . the only landmark left to testify of the good old days of long ago." After outlining the need for extensive repair, Vardaman concluded with a strong appeal urging the legislature to restore the mansion to a "condition becoming the dignity, power, and wealth of the State."[26]

A few days later, the first family moved out of the mansion to allow Vardaman's successor to occupy the dwelling prior to inaugural ceremonies. However, Governor Edmond F. Noel and his family startled the legislature and the local community when they declined to occupy the mansion, announcing that they would remain at the Edwards House until the legislature decided the fate of the Mississippi executive mansion. Only a few odds and ends belonging to Governor Vardaman remained in "that venerable pile of crumbling brick misnamed the Governor's 'Mansion'" when a *Clarion-Ledger* reporter interviewed Governor Noel on Janaury 22, 1908. The governor informed the reporter that his plans were indefinite and he would await the action of the legislature before arranging for permanent accommodations. The interview prompted a flurry of activity among those individuals and organizations who supported the

A History of the Mississippi Governor's Mansion

continued use of the mansion as the official residence of Mississippi's chief executive.

Various patriotic organizations throughout the state, primarily the United Daughters of the Confederacy, United Confederate Veterans, Women's Christian Temperance Union, Old Ladies Home Association, and the Daughters of 1812, began to marshall public support in favor of preserving the mansion. These organizations promoted a barrage of letters to state newspapers and to members of the state legislature protesting the sale of the mansion. Others circulated petitions and passed resolutions in support of the executive residence. Typical of these resolutions was the one passed by the UCV which stated that the mansion "should not be sacrificed to the greed of commercialism" and thus "return to oblivion the golden days of Mississippi and tear from her glorious history its brightest pages." In an effort to enlist the support of Mississippi's school children, the UDC sponsored an essay contest in the public schools on the subject "Why the Old Capitol and the Governor's Mansion Should Be Preserved."[27]

In spite of this increasing public support for the preservation of the mansion, the legislature gave every indication that its future was in jeopardy. The lawmakers asked the state attorney general to render an opinion concerning the legality of the sale of the mansion square which had been granted to Mississippi by the federal government. When the attorney general advised that the sale would be legal, local businessmen and much of the local press urged the lawmakers to act swiftly before the opposition could rally their forces.[28]

While the legislature was considering several alternatives, Governor Noel and his family decided to occupy the mansion in spite of its condition and lack of adequate furnishings. The first family supplemented the furniture in the mansion with their own possessions, which they brought to Jackson from their Lexington home. Both the governor and the first lady, Alice Tye Neilson, were fully committed to the effort to preserve the governor's mansion and felt that they could best serve that interest by occupying the residence. In a special message to the legislature dated February 26, 1908, Governor Noel made a strong plea for the mansion's preservation. Although admitting that the building brought mortification to all Mississippians who were proud of their state, Noel assured the

The Mansion and the Myth

lawmakers that the mansion's "memories and original beauty can be restored."[29]

The governor's message was widely reported, with comment, in the state press. The *Clarion-Ledger* insisted that the prevailing sentiment as reflected in the press favored the disposal of the mansion and urged the legislature not to be governed by sentiment but by good business sense. Referring to the mansion as that "dangerous old hulk, a menace to life and property," the *Clarion-Ledger* further wrote, "Let sentiment go to the winds in this day of practical thought and business." Yet only two weeks later that same paper published a special supplement entitled "Women in the War" which contained about as much sentiment as could be assembled in a single issue. But the editor was unaware of his inconsistency and repeated his suggestion to sell that "ramshackled old barn."[30]

Two weeks after his special message, Governor Noel entertained the legislature and other state officials and their wives at a reception in the mansion. During the reception the governor and first lady conducted an extensive tour of the main building and the family cottage in the rear. Although they detailed the most serious defects, especially in the family quarters, they assured their guests that the main structure itself was sound and that beautification and modernization of the historic mansion would primarily entail only redecoration. It was suggested that the family wing be replaced by a larger annex which would include the modern conveniences developed over the last twenty-five years.[31]

The reception and tour had their desired effect. Two weeks later, on March 19, 1908, a bill passed both houses of the legislature appropriating $30,000 to renovate the historic portion of the mansion and to erect a two-story annex in place of the family cottage on the north side of the main building. On April 7 the Capitol Commission, which was authorized by the legislature to supervise the renovation, appointed William S. Hull as state architect.[32] With the assistance of Mrs. Noel, who worked closely with the architect from the inception of the project to its completion, Hull modified his preliminary plans to conform to the $30,000 appropriation. During the twelve-month project, the first family occupied quarters in the Edwards House.[33]

The 1908 renovation included three phases—the beautification and improvement of the grounds, the renovation and redecoration of the original building, and the construction of a two-story annex. During the first phase, the iron fence enclosing the square, the cottage annex, and all other outbuildings were removed. The grounds were then graded and leveled, carefully avoiding damage to existing shrubs and trees. Cement sidewalks on the east, north and west sides were added according to specifications provided by the city of Jackson, and the cement walk on Capitol Street was widened. Two macadamized driveways, entering the grounds from Congress and West streets and exiting on Amite, were also added. Finally, the entire grounds were sodded with bermuda grass and several varieties of shade trees were planted.[34]

After the renovation got underway, substantially more repair was required on the original building than anticipated at first. All window and door frames were replaced by new ones of hardwood. The floors on the lower level were also replaced with hardwood and on the second story with yellow pine. All of the wallpaper and virtually all the interior woodwork was replaced, and most of the plaster molding was either repaired or removed. Throughout the interior the natural wood grain was preserved whenever possible.

Practically all of the exterior stonework was replaced by oolitic limestone and the front portico was recovered with terrazzo tile. Architect Hull originally intended to paint the mansion's exterior to correspond with the yellow-pressed brick used in the annex. However, the painters were unable to blend a color that would match the new brick. The problem was finally solved by removing one layer of the original brick from the main building and replacing it with the same kind and color used in the annex. Consequently, the mansion's exterior remained yellow until the early 1940s, when the entire building was painted white.

The only structural change in the original mansion was the removal of Nichols' grand stair which was replaced by a center flight approach leading to an interior balcony overlooking the east–west hallway connecting the family annex to the original mansion.

The annex was designed to conform to the Greek Revival style of the original structure and included all the modern conveniences available in 1908. The basement of the annex, which was built above ground level, contained a kitchen, boiler room, fuel room, storerooms, and a pantry. Family quarters were located on the second and third levels of the annex.

The Mansion and the Myth

North–south hallways which joined the two buildings provided easy access to the historic portion from the family quarters.

One important change in the mansion's exterior design was the addition of a porte-cochere at the Congress Street entrance to the east–west hallway. The porte-cochere, which was the only sheltered entrance to the mansion, was carefully designed to blend with Nichols' architectural style. The roof of the porte-cochere also served as a balcony for the family quarters on the second floor of the annex. Several years later, Governor Bilbo screened in the balcony and used it as a sitting room and occasionally for sleeping on summer nights.[35]

Only one controversy marred the orderly and steady progress of the renovation. A heated exchange between Governor Noel and a member of the Capitol Commission sparked a lively debate over the design of the two driveways leading up to the mansion. The governor complained that the extensive grading and leveling of the grounds which were necessary for the construction of the two drives would compromise the privacy the first family might otherwise enjoy if the mansion green remained elevated. Additionally, he saw no need for two thoroughfares through the grounds. For several days the *Clarion-Ledger* reported the conflict of opinions. Governor Noel lost the argument; the original plans were implemented, but the lack of privacy in the downtown residence would long remain as the chief complaint registered by succeeding first families. Except for this dispute, the renovation was greeted with general approbation and even the *Clarion-Ledger*, after praising both the architect and contractor, boasted that Mississippians could take just pride in their "very respectable Mansion."[36]

Although the major construction had been completed when the first family reoccupied the mansion in May, 1909, the interior decoration and beautification of the grounds were not finished. However, the Noels preferred the inconvenience of living in the mansion while the interior work continued to their cramped quarters in the Edwards House. Shortly after he returned to the mansion, the governor was advised that the $30,000 appropriation was exhausted. He ordered the work to continue, however, on the premise that the legislature would supplement the original sum at its next session. When the lawmakers convened in January, 1910, they did authorize an additional expenditure of $4,000 to complete the renovation; $3,200 was allocated for interior decoration and $800 for improvement of the grounds.[37]

The extensive publicity which accompanied the year-long renovation made the governor's mansion a household word among Mississippians and popularized its symbolic character. In preserving the mansion the state had saved, in Hull's words, an important landmark which even Sherman would not burn. In the flurry of rhetoric and resolutions, the mansion became a symbol of the Old South of myth and legend and, inevitably, a tourist attraction.

Conscious of the people's increasing devotion to the mansion and anxious to make it even more accessible to them, Mrs. Noel opened the executive residence to the public as often as possible. An almost endless round of public functions characterized the Noels' last two and a half years in the mansion. In addition to the "plain people," many national figures were also entertained at the mansion. The most prominent was President William Howard Taft who was honored at a luncheon on November 1, 1909.[38] Taft's visit was the only occasion when an incumbent president was entertained at the mansion. The pomp attending his visit, however, was eclipsed by the public response to Theodore Roosevelt who visited Jackson for the first and only time on March 11, 1911. Although the former president was in his own words just a plain citizen, "Colonel Roosevelt" was greeted with thunderous applause by the 7,000 people who welcomed him to the capital city. Following an early morning arrival, Roosevelt was honored at a breakfast at the mansion which was attended by a small, select group at the invitation of the governor. After breakfast Roosevelt spoke briefly from the mansion steps to a large group of Boy Scouts before going to the new capitol for his major address. Following a luncheon at the Edwards House, which highlighted his seven-hour visit, Roosevelt boarded a special train and resumed his southern tour.[39]

The visits of such prominent and illustrious personalities, as might be expected, spawned several yarns and anecdotes which eventually found their way into the stream of oral tradition. For example, it is still averred among old-timers in Jackson that Roosevelt often slept in the mansion and had his favorite room and a favorite chair. However, there is no evidence in contemporary records that the former president was ever an overnight guest in the mansion although he did come to Mississippi on several occasions.

Roosevelt was reminded of one of those previous visits after his breakfast at the mansion in 1911. Just as he was leaving the mansion for the new capitol, he was greeted by the Metcalf brothers who had accompanied Roosevelt on a 1902 bear hunt in the Mississippi Delta. The former president greeted them warmly and spoke of his recent safari in Africa. "It was great fun," he said, "but we didn't have as much trouble finding elephants there as we did finding bear in Mississippi." Roosevelt, the Metcalf brothers, and the famous Negro guide Holt Collier had spent several days in the Delta swamps without even seeing a bear. A Washington correspondent who had accompanied the presidential party filed a cartoon depicting the famous hunter face-to-face with a bear cub which he refused to shoot. After seeing the cartoon, which was reprinted in several national journals, a Brooklyn toymaker began marketing a replica of the cub which he called a "Teddy bear." According to trade journals, the teddy bear has remained the most popular toy in America over the past seven decades.[40]

Yarns, myths, and anecdotes aside, Governor Noel and the first lady did the state of Mississippi a great service in leading the effort to preserve the mansion. Even though at times theirs was an unpopular position, the continued public attachment to the historic building and the mansion's designation as a National Historic Landmark in 1975 have confirmed the Noels' belief that its preservation would be an enduring contribution to future generations.

CHAPTER VIII

A House of Glass

DURING THE BITTER infighting which characterized the Democratic party in 1910, a new term was added to the vocabulary of Mississippi politics. While campaigning against James K. Vardaman for the United States Senate, Leroy Percy, a wealthy, soft-spoken Delta planter, was heckled by Vardaman supporters at a rally at Godbold Wells. Percy retorted by calling them rednecks. For many years poor white farmers, whose quaint and sometimes crude lifestyle was often the subject of derisive anecdotes, had been called rednecks. The term may have been derived from the rough and ruddy complexion of their necks which became deeply tanned and leathery from the long hours of toil under a southern sun. But after Percy used "redneck" in a political context, the term was appropriated by the Vardaman-Bilbo faction who began wearing red neckties to dramatize their identification with the small farmers. In the 1911 Democratic primaries the red tie became symbolic of the working classes. Bilbo went a step further by adding red suspenders. When Fred Sullens, a Jackson journalist, asked why he wore both a red tie and suspenders, Bilbo replied that the suspenders "keep up my pants and the red necktie helps to keep up my courage."[1]

The redneck faction of the Democratic party virtually swept the state in the 1911 primaries. Vardaman defeated Percy in the Senate race, Theodore Bilbo was elected lieutenant governor, and the rednecks gained control of the state legislature. However, Earl Leroy Brewer, a prosperous Delta lawyer who was in no way connected with the rednecks, was elected governor without opposition. That a rich Delta lawyer would be unop-

A House of Glass

posed during such a dramatic display of political strength by the working classes is an example of the mystifying nature of Mississippi politics which continues to intrigue and confound the experts. As it turned out, Brewer's constructive leadership resulted in significant reform in a variety of areas. Perhaps the people, in their majesty, are able to perceive more than the pundits, in their wisdom, can explain.

Shortly before noon on January 16, 1912, Governor and Mrs. Edmond F. Noel left the mansion to join the governor-elect and his official party at the Edwards House, where for the past several days they had been preparing for the inaugural ceremonies. Brewer's inauguration attracted thousands to the little capital city. The Illinois Central added special cars with reduced rates for those attending the ceremonies. Others came in wagons and on horseback, a few in cars. According to a Jackson resident who had witnessed most inaugurations since 1876, it was the largest crowd in her recollection. Marching bands, military units, and the Governor's Colonels dressed in full military attire made the occasion unusually festive in spite of the chilling weather which caused a last-minute change in the inaugural plans. As originally scheduled, Brewer was to take the oath of office and deliver his inaugural address from the steps of the capitol, but a near freezing temperature forced the ceremonies inside.[2]

In Brewer's new Hudson convertible, the official party slowly made its way from the Edwards House up Capitol Street, then along State Street, and finally to the capitol. After Governor Noel introduced Brewer as both his personal and political friend, the new chief executive spoke for approximately forty-five minutes. After noting the unusual circumstances that led to his unanimous election, Governor Brewer then pledged among other things to restore party harmony and to end the "carnival of corruption" which he said had characterized Mississippi politics for the past several years. His audience applauded enthusiastically. Standing in the wings, listening intently, was young Theodore G. Bilbo, who had been sworn in as lieutenant governor the day before. The animosity between the two men would soon erupt into a bitter and public conflict. But that would not come until later, and for that day at least, Brewer, his family, and thousands of friends breathed the heady atmosphere of victory and enjoyed the inaugural festivities. Shortly after the inaugural

A History of the Mississippi Governor's Mansion

ceremony, the Noels removed their personal effects from the mansion which they had worked so hard to save and left by train for their home in Lexington.[3]

During the early evening the Brewers held their first open house at the mansion for those attending the inauguration. Following the reception the first family hurried to the inaugural ball which was held in the largest assembly hall in Jackson. But even the grand ballroom at the Stag Club could scarcely accommodate the nearly one thousand celebrants who jammed the floor and made dancing almost impossible. The first lady, the former Minnie Block of Water Valley, was exquisitely dressed in a yellow Parisian gown graced by a beaded tunic of chiffon and a long sweeping train of shimmering satin in a rich shade of yellow. The first lady's gown elicited much comment from certain elements of Jackson society and continued to be the topic of conversation for some time. The governor and his wife led the grand march to open the ball promptly at ten o'clock. The first lady did not dance during the course of the evening, but the governor did, later admitting that it was the first time in ten years though adding quickly that he enjoyed it very much. At midnight the first family retired to their rooms at the Edwards House and on the next day moved into the mansion.[4]

On their first day in the mansion, and on other special occasions afterwards, the governor assembled his family for a morning prayer before beginning the day's arduous work. The lifestyle of the Brewer family was informal, pleasant, and almost carefree in spite of a heavy social schedule and increasing official demands. Only occasionally did the machinations of Mississippi politics intrude upon their private lives at the mansion. Of the Brewers' three daughters, only Claudia, the youngest, lived in the mansion throughout their four-year residency. Earlene and Minnie, the two oldest girls, were away at school and spent only summers and holidays at home in the mansion. Yet they were there enough to enliven that historic house with all the problems and excitement of teenagers growing up in a time that was just beginning to experience the complexities of modern society. On one occasion a family dinner was interrupted by cries of desperation from a second-story bedroom. The family rushed upstairs to find Minnie pinned beneath the massive frame of a huge wardrobe which had tipped over when she stood on the bottom drawer to reach one

A House of Glass

of her favorite dresses. Fortunately, the top of the wardrobe had caught on the bed and its full weight had not fallen on the young girl. Soon after that episode Mrs. Brewer had a bench especially made for Minnie's use.[5]

The presence of two socially active young ladies and a youthfully oriented first family added a dimension to the mansion's social activity which it had not experienced since the Lowry residency. The first lady was especially generous in allowing Jackson's young people the use of "the handsome official suite of the Mansion" which, according to a local society editor, was "frequently illumined for pleasure's gay doings." After the addition of the hardwood floors in the first-floor parlors, the mansion became an even more desirable location for ballroom dances sponsored by various Jackson clubs. On many occasions the sliding doors between the west parlors were opened and the "rugs were rolled back and the furniture would be moved against the wall and the whole front half would be thrown open into a large dance floor." The Brewers found this arrangement so satisfactory for entertaining large groups that they incorporated this feature in their new home which they built at Clarksdale after the governor left office.[6]

The first lady, however, displayed no favoritism in offering the mansion to clubs, civic groups, or other organizations. She made the parlors and grounds available for a large variety of conventions, teas, receptions, book and garden clubs, and church groups. Like other first ladies, Mrs. Brewer "felt the Mansion belonged to the people and they should have an opportunity to come in and see it."[7]

The mansion's downtown location and its official, stately appearance complicated the first family's privacy as early as 1912. After the removal of the fence in 1908, the mansion was much more accessible from Capitol Street. People often misconstrued the mansion for the county courthouse, city hall, a museum; some even thought it was the public library. After several experiences with people walking in off the street, "just to look around," the Brewers resorted to the uncharacteristic habit of locking the front entrance. A member of the Brewer family wrote in 1975, "I am one ex-Governor's family that was glad to see the fence erected [in 1971] as even in 1912 there was no privacy."[8]

If strangers found the mansion's stately appearance confusing, Claudia Brewer found its interior design equally enticing to a six-year-old's imagination, especially the statuary niches in the front vestibule. Years later she remembered that she and her childhood playmates would stand in the nooks, strike a regal pose and imagine themselves to be ancient queens or perhaps a beautiful lady who struck their fancy at a recent party.

One day while Claudia was playing quietly, trying not to disturb the first lady and her guests, she was invited to come into the front parlor to play. Like the strangers, Claudia was confused, because a legislative committee was visiting the mansion at the time. The committee was there at the request of the first lady to examine the carpets in the front parlors. In 1912, Capitol Street was a busy but unpaved thoroughfare and the mansion was not air-conditioned. During the summer months, when the windows were open, layers of dust settled on the carpets in the front parlors and was then ground into the fabric by the flow of traffic through the mansion. To demonstrate to the committee the seriousness of the problem, Mrs. Brewer asked Claudia to ride her tricycle through one of the front parlors. When the legislators observed the trail of dust in her wake, they consented to the first lady's request to remove the carpets and install hardwood floors. An appropriation of $3,000 was voted for that purpose. That appropriation also included funds for the purchase of additional kitchenware.[9]

The first lady, whose green thumb was the envy of Jackson garden clubs, took a special interest in the grounds. She transformed the back half of the mansion square into one of the city's loveliest and most admired cutting gardens, which featured several varieties of roses, shasta daisies, and lilies. Mrs. Brewer also achieved a reputation as a culinary expert. Certainly one of the busiest first ladies until more recent times, Mrs. Brewer often called upon Mrs. Sam Cook, wife of the chief justice of the state supreme court, to assist her in preparing formal state dinners. Their recipes were very popular and invitations to dinner at the mansion were eagerly anticipated, eventually becoming a status symbol among Jackson's sometime sensitive social elite.

However, dinners in the mansion were not necessarily restricted to the socially sophisticated. On one occasion Governor Brewer entertained a group of men at a stag dinner. After the meal had been served in courses, finger bowls with a slice of lemon on each rim were placed in front of each guest. While the governor was telling one of his favorite stories, one of the

A House of Glass

men reached for his bowl, squeezed the lemon, added a spoonful of sugar, and drank its contents. Seeing what his guest had done, the governor then calmly squeezed the lemon in the bowl in front of him and sipped it slowly and obviously. Other guests were by then aware of what had happened. To prevent the man's embarrassment, they followed the governor's example. Apparently, the man was never made aware of his *faux pas*.[10]

Although Governor Brewer was embroiled in some of the state's most infamous political intrigue, he was a kind and generous person. He was particularly cordial and considerate toward children, as illustrated by an incident involving the boys who delivered telegrams for Western Union, located just two doors up Capitol Street. To amuse themselves between deliveries, the boys would ride their bicycles up the terraced grounds surrounding the mansion and then down the steep slopes onto Congress Street. It was great fun for the boys, but several complaints were registered with the Jackson police department. According to the complaints, the boys were wearing down the grass and causing erosion of the southeast corner of the mansion square. The police reprimanded the boys and ordered them to stop riding their bikes on the grounds. When he learned of the order, Governor Brewer exclaimed, "Jimminy Crickets!"—reportedly the strongest oath in his vocabulary. The governor advised the police, the newspapers, Western Union officials, and the general public that the boys were not seriously damaging the property. He sent word to the boys that they could continue their playful pastime. On the following Christmas, two small boys called at the mansion. Greeted at the front portico, they were escorted into the governor's study. After exchanging pleasantries with the chief magistrate, all the while standing at attention, one of the boys handed the governor a cigar wrapped in fancy paper tied with a ribbon. It was a gift from his little friends two doors up the street.[11]

During the Brewer residency the doors of the mansion were always open, especially during the week of the state fair, which usually brought celebrities to Jackson and prompted a round of social activities at the mansion. Those occasions also provided the first lady an opportunity to demonstrate her gracious charm and on at least one occasion an opportunity to play the role of peacemaker. When Ty Cobb and Louis Disbrough, a nationally known racing driver, were both attending the state fair they were invited to a reception at the mansion. Although they had been close friends at one time, for the last few years the two men had not been on speaking terms. Unaware of that strained relationship or that they had previously been well acquainted, the first lady introduced them to each other as though they were perfect strangers. Prompted by such charming surroundings and the honest mistake of the hostess, the two men "grabbed one another in a bear hug" and revived their dormant friendship.[12]

Although the mansion may have worked its charm on visiting celebrities, the fractious nature of Mississippi politics lay beyond its healing power. During the sensational bribery trial stemming from charges against Theodore Bilbo and his law partner, G. A. Hobbs, a series of anonymous threats against Governor Brewer and his family forced the governor to take special precautions to protect his family. Henry Trott, one of the trusties on duty at the governor's mansion, was assigned to guard little Claudia against the possibility of kidnapping. For several weeks Henry accompanied the small child whenever she left the mansion. During those anxious weeks Claudia developed a fond attachment for her protector. Sometime later, Governor Brewer discovered a note under his dinner plate. In his young daughter's scribbled hand the note read simply: "Please set Henry free."[13]

Henry Trott and another prisoner from the state penitentiary had been assigned as domestic servants to the governor's mansion. The use of prison labor in such a capacity at the mansion had been recommended by Governor Noel in 1908, but the practice was not implemented until 1912. By a joint resolution the legislature authorized the governor and first lady, in consultation with the prison superintendent, to select several men and women prisoners who were then transferred to the governor's mansion where special living quarters were provided on the basement floor.[14] Customarily, only Negro prisoners who had been convicted of murder committed in passion were selected. The number of prisoners assigned to the mansion varied over the years, from as few as two to as many as thirteen. A monthly allowance for food and clothing, which was often insufficient to cover their actual cost, was appropriated by the legislature, but the first family sometimes found it necessary to supplement the appropriation.

Although convict labor had been employed infrequently throughout

A House of Glass

the mansion's history, the 1912 resolution established the practice as a permanent means of providing domestic service for the first family. In addition to relieving the governor's family of an added expense, the system also eliminated the problem of finding suitable persons for the many varied tasks required at the mansion. Over the years the system worked to the general satisfaction of the first family and to the personal benefit of the inmates selected for the assignment. Beginning with Governor Brewer and continuing through his successors, the inmates received an executive pardon following their service at the mansion. Partly due to the new pattern of race relations in Mississippi and in part due to general prison reform, and in spite of its record of success, the practice was discontinued during the Waller administration.

On his last day in the mansion, which he vacated several days before the expiration of his term, Governor Brewer asked Claudia to come to the east parlor which he used as an office and library. Henry Trott and the other inmate who had served the governor as a domestic were then brought to the room. The governor handed Claudia some very official-looking papers and asked her to give them to Henry and the other man. Unable to read the document, Henry did not comprehend its importance until the younger man said, "Henry, don't you know what it is? Little Missy done set us free!" After his term expired, Governor Brewer returned to Clarksdale and resumed his law practice. Henry Trott also moved to Clarksdale and continued in the employ of the Brewer family for many years after his pardon.[15]

Earl Brewer and his family did not remain in Jackson for the inauguration of his successor, Theodore G. Bilbo, who had been nominated in the 1915 primary. Enmity between them had become so intense that Brewer refused to participate in the ceremony elevating Bilbo to the governorship. Governor Brewer had been instrumental in securing an indictment against Bilbo and had publicly favored his impeachment. Bilbo countercharged that Brewer was squandering the state's funds and was guilty of sexual improprieties.[16] Undoubtedly one of the state's most sordid campaigns, the crude and intemperate rhetoric that characterized the 1915 election is epitomized by a remark Fred Sullens printed in the August 5, 1915 *Jackson Daily News*. Sullens suggested that, if Bilbo were elected, the great golden eagle atop the capitol dome should be taken down and

A History of the Mississippi Governor's Mansion

replaced by a "puking buzzard." Nevertheless, "The Man," as he was called by friends and foes alike, won the election over four opponents in the first primary.

Although unsightly short at 5'2" but resplendent in a white Palm Beach and the ever-present red necktie, Governor-elect Bilbo triumphantly led the inaugural parade on January 18, 1916. He was not accompanied by the incumbent, but there were bands, marching units, and the "Colonels," which he had increased from the usual number of twelve to forty-five. Like Vardaman, Theodore Bilbo was introduced by a legislative supporter because the governor refused to make the customary presentation of his successor.[17]

Throughout the campaign Bilbo had sneered at Brewer's opulence and his "high-falutin" life style at the mansion. In his inaugural address he reiterated a similar disdain. Referring to the mansion as a "pretentious residence, to be maintained on a certain scale of luxury, inconsistent with the simple tastes and habits that are characteristic of the great body of the people," Bilbo averred, "I frankly confess that I have no sympathy with this scheme of isolation. . . . I come to the Governor's office a plain citizen of simple tastes and inclinations, and do not like to surrender that identity nor the dignity that goes with it for any official pomp and circumstances." In conclusion he said, "I would suggest that the Mansion be sold and other simpler provision be made for a residence for the Executive more in harmony with democratic standards of simplicity and unpretentious dignity."[18] To the rednecks, and in the rhetoric of their diminutive leader, the governor's mansion which Nichols had designed in republican simplicity was no longer a "suitable house for the Governor." It was more a relic of aristocracy, a reminder of privilege, a house of glass and class.

It is not known precisely what Bilbo meant by the "scheme of isolation." It is evident, however, that he often felt isolated, if not confined, in the governor's mansion. Even on his inauguration Governor Bilbo and the first lady, Linda Gaddy Bedgood, spent a lonely night at the mansion with their two children. As a devout Baptist, Bilbo refused to take part in the inaugural ball or allow the first lady to attend, even though she wished to do so. They spent their first night trying to get the mansion in order and rearranging some of the furniture to make room for the things they brought from their home in Poplarville.

A House of Glass

Several rooms were actually vacant and the west parlors, across from the family dining room, remained empty during Bilbo's first residency. The simple furniture which they brought from Poplarville did not complement the mansion's spacious parlors and high ceilings. The first family was somewhat dismayed by the size of the executive residence and, according to Bilbo's biographer, they often felt as though they were sentenced to "confinement at the Mansion." In an effort to make the residence more accommodating to his simple tastes, Bilbo built a screen porch on the roof of the porte-cochere at the Congress Street entrance. The addition was used primarily for a sitting room, but he occasionally slept on the porch on cool, summer nights.[19] Bilbo, both in life and legend, is a lonely, restless figure stalking across the pages of Mississippi's past. No doubt, on sleepless nights after the children were in bed and the city was still, and while his enemies plotted, Bilbo would lie awake on that porch and scheme. Perhaps he sometimes reflected.

In his inaugural address Bilbo also complained that the governor's salary of $5,000 was not sufficient to maintain the mansion. Fuel alone cost over $600 a year. And, as he later discovered, the ten-dollar monthly food allowance for inmates at the mansion was not enough to cover the actual cost. As he so often did, Bilbo compounded his own problems by increasing the number of servants from two to four. Although the use of convict labor at the mansion continued to provide capable domestic service through Bilbo's first administration, the system became the subject of controversy for one of the very few times during its use. On one of his summer vacations, which he usually spent on the Mississippi Gulf Coast, Bilbo took the servants from the mansion to his summer home. This action prompted a "riotous objection" in the anti-Bilbo press.[20] The outcry lasted only a short time and was probably more a result of his opponents' relentless efforts to discredit him personally than any real objection to the first family's use of mansion servants even during their vacation period.

However, there was another controversy, about another mansion, that did not wane and proved costly to The Man's political fortunes, at least in the short run. Bilbo's "Dream House" at Juniper Grove in Pearl River County became the focus of an angry dispute between the governor and several organizations throughout the state. Although not completed until

A History of the Mississippi Governor's Mansion

the 1930s, the plans for the Dream House were laid shortly after his first inauguration. While the old capitol was being restored in 1918, Bilbo suggested that the columns from that building be sold to the highest bidder. Sometime later, the Capitol Commission announced that the governor's bid of one dollar was the highest and awarded the columns to Bilbo, who transferred them to Poplarville for use at his Dream House. Through the summer of 1918, the United Daughters of the Confederacy and the Daughters of the American Revolution protested the purchase and even questioned its legality since Bilbo, as a member of the Capitol Commission, was prevented by statute from doing business with the state. Their objections did not prevail, however, and the columns adorned the Dream House which included twenty-three rooms, twelve fireplaces, and five bathrooms. The Dream House was considered by many, "for that time and place," a symbol of luxury.[21] Although it is not possible to assess the impact of that controversy on the congressional election in 1918, Bilbo was defeated by Paul B. Johnson, Sr., in the Sixth Congressional District, on August 20.

But Bilbo would become accustomed to both controversy and defeat during his illustrious career, which spanned the years from 1907 to 1947. Bilbo outlived and seemed enlivened by controversy. Yet the strain would eventually become too great for his family. From the vantage point of thirty years' experience, a former first lady of Mississippi admitted, "If I ever thought ——— would have gotten into politics I never would have married him." Another first lady explained, "It's a hard life being married to a politician. Politics is their life, their vitality. Without campaign speeches, endless hours of handshaking and their never-ending ambitions to climb the political ladder higher and higher, they would surely die inside."[22] Bilbo was like that. The handshakes and the cheers renewed him, the climb energized him. And in those early years, down around the bottom rungs, when the ladder was leaning but not yet straight-up, Mrs. Bilbo accompanied The Man on the hustings, occasionally taking the stump herself as she did in the 1915 campaign. Mrs. Bilbo was probably the first woman in the state's history to campaign with and for her husband running for a statewide office.[23]

During Bilbo's first residency in the mansion, the first family included a daughter by the governor's previous marriage and a son, Theodore Bilbo,

Governor and Mrs. H. L. White celebrate their Golden Wedding Anniversary in the Mansion with (left to right) Mrs. J. Tubb, Gov. White, Mrs. White, John Bell Williams, Mrs. John Bell Williams and J. Tubb.

Dinner was served in the Gold Room.

Paul Johnson Jr. & Dorothy Power in the west parlor on their wedding day, February 8, 1941.

Elaine Wright on her wedding day, January 5, 1952.

Governor Paul Johnson escorting his daughter, Patricia, to the west parlor on April 4, 1965.

Mrs. Edmond F. Noel—her efforts helped preserve the Mansion in 1908.

Reviewing stand at the Mansion during a 1937 parade of United Confederate veterans—one of the many organizations that helped save the Mansion in 1908.

Southwest view of the Mansion shortly after the renovation in 1908.

Among the Mansion's most notable visitors were Jefferson and Varina Davis in 1884.

William Jennings Bryan visited Governor James K. Vardaman in 1906.

Earl Leroy Brewer and his Colonels.

Theodore G. Bilbo and his Colonels.

Governor Thomas Bailey and friends at west entrance to Mansion.

Lt. Gov. Dennis Murphree, Governor Paul Johnson, Sr. (mounted) & unidentified man on west lawn.

Governor J. P. Coleman and the silent sentry.

Fielding L. Wright inaugural ceremony.

John Bell Williams inaugural ceremony.

Reviewing stand in front of Mansion—1964, Governors Paul Johnson, Orval Faubus, Ross Barnett, Jimmie Davis, and George Wallace.

A House of Glass

Jr. Although their personal lives may have been active as a result of the two small children, social life at the mansion was dull in comparison with the busy schedule maintained by the Brewers. The Bilbos rarely entertained large groups at formal receptions, and there never was "a really big wing-ding" during their first residency. Social functions were usually restricted to small groups and then only when necessary. One of the governor's few concessions to the first lady's sociability was his grudging permission for her bridge parties, which may have revealed something of Bilbo's growing amenability to worldly pleasures so foreign to his Baptist sensitivity.[24]

However, Bilbo's farewell address to the legislature indicated that he had not changed his mind about the governor's mansion. "After four years' service in the Governor's office and occupancy of the Governor's Mansion," he said, "I desire to repeat . . . my convictions upon the proposition to sell this relic of royalty." Even if the legislature found it expedient to maintain the building for economic reasons, he would still recommend that the mansion be converted into a state library or a supreme court building and that the official executive residence be relocated.[25]

This recommendation was only one of many sweeping reforms Bilbo urged upon the legislature in January, 1920. His address embraced such a wide range of suggestions that he left his successor, Lee M. Russell, with little to say. A lawyer from Lafayette County, Russell had been lieutenant governor under Bilbo and was elected with Bilbo's active support. Ironically, the only substantial difference in Bilbo's farewell and Russell's inaugural address concerned the governor's mansion. Russell admitted that the mansion's disrepair and general appearance were "a source of mortification to all our people," but he urged the legislature to repair rather than dispose of that historic building.[26] Russell's disagreement with Bilbo on the continued use of the mansion as the official executive residence was the first step toward a complete break between the two men which would culminate in still another public scandal.

Russell's disclosure of the mansion's condition did not come as a surprise to the legislature. Shortly before his inauguration a joint committee had inspected the mansion and found that a great deal of work was necessary to prepare both the interior and the grounds for the new first family. At the request of this committee, about a dozen convicts from the Rankin County jail were assigned to "clean up the Mansion and grounds." The committee also discovered to their surprise that the mansion was not only poorly furnished, but that much of the furniture had been damaged by smoke rising from the furnace in the basement. There was also ample evidence on both the walls and draperies that the leaking roof remained not only a source of inconvenience to the first family but a continued source of damage to the mansion's interior.[27]

Consequently, when Governor Russell recommended a special appropriation for the mansion most legislators were convinced that substantial repair was necessary to prevent even further deterioration. In addition to a general face-lifting, Russell also recommended the purchase of a "modern vacuum cleaner" and the construction of a state-owned power plant to provide electricity for the mansion and other public buildings in Jackson. Although the legislature did not heed his suggestion to build a power plant (which had also been recommended by Bilbo), the lawmakers did appropriate $5,000 for repair and furnishing of the mansion. The law authorized the governor to expend the funds largely at his own discretion.[28]

During his administration Russell was in many ways a beleaguered man, and the mansion became more a fortress than a residence. The four years that he and the first lady, Ethelmary Day of Hastings, Montana, spent in the mansion were rather lonely and largely private. They were one of only two first families to occupy the residence without children. During Russell's administration the state experienced four consecutive and disastrous years of agricultural depression. Like other farm belts, Mississippi witnessed the nadir of American agriculture in the 1920s, and as farm tenancy and rural poverty increased racial violence showed a corresponding rise. Far from being unified as Brewer had hoped, the Democratic party splintered even further during the two tumultuous terms of Brewer and Bilbo. Even the Vardaman-Bilbo faction disintegrated during the 1918 congressional elections when Vardaman was defeated for the Senate by Byron Patton Harrison and Bilbo lost to Paul Johnson, Sr. The formation of new cliques factionalized the party, just as the reorganization of the old Klan terrorized the countryside. In the

A House of Glass

gubernatorial campaign of 1919, Democratic politicians vented themselves in crude and reckless innuendoes. Cliques, rings, and factions, each accusing the others of dealing for power, disgraced the state. This orgy of accusation culminated in the $100,000 seduction and breach of promise suit filed against Governor Russell by Frances Birkhead, his former secretary. Charging the governor with seducing her repeatedly on the promise of marriage, Miss Birkhead also alleged that an abortion arranged by the governor left her an invalid for life. Disclaiming any culpability, Governor Russell said the suit was "the most damnable blackmail conspiracy in the history of Mississippi." He attributed the scurrilous charges to his political enemies. Specifically, he identified the conspirators as the agents of several fire insurance companies against which he had filed an anti-trust suit the year before. However, a legislative investigation of Russell's charges produced no evidence that the insurance companies were in any way connected with the suit. After the first trial was dismissed on a technicality, a second trial date was set for December, 1922, in the federal court at Oxford, Russell's hometown. During the trial, Miss Birkhead's testimony was thoroughly discredited and a jury took only twenty-five minutes to declare the governor innocent of the charges.[29]

While the trial was in progress, Theodore Bilbo was called as a material witness. When he refused to honor the summons, he was held in contempt of court and sentenced to thirty days in the Oxford jail. Later, the sentence was shortened to ten days, and from the steps of the Oxford jail Bilbo announced that he would again run for governor in the 1923 election.[30]

In spite of his acquittal, Russell's integrity was compromised and both he and the office he held were ridiculed in the state press. Some journals compared Mississippi's recent chief executives, unfavorably, with Nero, Claudius, and Caligula. The *Natchez Democrat* proclaimed that it was "time for all Mississippians to get together," call "a halt on such horrible conditions," and bring "the ship of state back to the moorings of honor and common decency." A Jackson paper, noting that Governor Russell was vacationing on the Gulf Coast, suggested that another executive mansion be constructed on the seashore. "The truth is," the paper

A History of the Mississippi Governor's Mansion

asserted, the governor "means nothing whatever to our gay and festive lives."[31] For the first time in many years the mansion's charm seemed, to some at least, an empty and unnecessary tradition.

Twice during the twenties, in 1923 and again in 1926, efforts were made to dispose of the mansion or at least convert it to some use other than the official executive residence. Ironically, both proposals came from one of the state's most famous women. While campaigning for office in 1923, Belle Kearney, one of the first women elected to public office in Mississippi, suggested that the mansion be converted into a museum or a public shrine. Later, as a member of the state Senate in 1926, she introduced a bill to relocate the executive residence to the home of the superintendent of the state hospital for the insane which was then vacant. The bill also provided for the remodeling of the mansion to accommodate the supreme court and the state library.[32] It is not known if Ms. Kearney was motivated to relocate the executive residence at the state mental institution by any consideration other than the fact that the spacious home was then vacant. The record does indicate, however, that the bill was defeated. It is worthy of note that two men who would later occupy the mansion, Martin Sennett Conner and Thomas L. Bailey, were serving in the House of Representatives when Belle Kearney introduced this bill. There is no indication of their position toward the bill, because it was never voted on by the House, having failed to pass the Senate. There is evidence, however, that Henry Lewis Whitfield who succeeded Lee Russell was instrumental in preserving the house on Capitol Street as the official executive residence.

Soon after Governor Whitfield occupied the mansion in January, 1924, fresh from his triumph over Bilbo in the 1923 election, the first lady, Mary Dampeer White of Steens Creek, set about restoring some damaged furniture she found in the basement. Her project was not as crucial, however, as the challenge facing the governor, who would attempt to repair the sullied reputation of the executive branch of state government which had bottomed out under the three previous administrations. Both Whitfields enjoyed a large measure of success.[33]

Governor Whitfield, a former state superintendent of education and president of Mississippi State College for Women, was slightly rotund and

A House of Glass

soft-spoken. On the campaign trail he presented quite a contrast to the bantam and bombastic Bilbo. Throughout the campaign, Whitfield addressed himself to the problem of rural unemployment and the alarming increase in racial violence. The people responded to his positive and constructive approach to these problems. In 1923, Mississippi women exercised the suffrage in a statewide election for the first time. Their vote undoubtedly provided Whitfield his narrow margin of victory.

Once in office, Whitfield embraced a broad legislative program including better mental health care, the extension of vocational training, tax reform, and improvement of the quality of life for Mississippi Negroes. Whitfield's position on race elicited a generally favorable response and even praise from some of the state's leading newspapers. In commending Whitfield for his pledge to be the governor of *all* the people, including Mississippi blacks, the *Jackson Daily News* admitted, "We all know . . . that we have not been giving the Negro a square deal, and it is gratifying to know that we have a Governor endowed with the courage to speak out and tell the truth about it."[34]

There was, of course, some criticism and opposition. But in two important areas Governor Whitfield was successful in improving the Negro's condition in the state. Through his years in office, 1924–27, there was a marked decline in racial violence and a substantial increase in state appropriations for Negro education. The black exodus slowed and the Committee of One Hundred, an organization of prominent Mississippi blacks, praised the governor for his concern. "Certainly," proclaimed a committee spokesman, "when the highest official of the commonwealth speaks thus, the Negro has another big reason for not losing faith."[35]

Whitfield's achievements in race relations were only one facet of his effort to reorder the state's priorities. In his inaugural address, Whitfield referred to the prejudice against business corporations and outside investment which had dominated the state's economic climate since the days of Vardaman. To counteract this prejudice and offset the state's declining personal income, Whitfield recommended a state-sponsored program to attract industry to Mississippi as a means of providing employment opportunities to the increasing number of small farmers who were unable to exact a living income from their exhausted and eroded farms. Though his success was modest, a later administration would revive and expand upon Whitfield's initial efforts to balance agriculture with industry.[36]

Of all Whitfield's achievements, the most significant was the restoration of credibility and prestige to the office of governor. The various activities at the mansion reflected his personal character, and the lifestyle of the first family mirrored his integrity. Since Whitfield was a deeply religious man like many of his predecessors, there were very few elaborate social events, and at no time would the governor permit ballroom dancing or allow intoxicants to be served in the mansion. For the first family, which included only one of the Whitfields' four sons, "life at the Mansion was really a quiet home life."[37] Although the Whitfields' personal entertaining was limited, the use of the mansion for a variety of public functions continued during their residency.

In the 1920s, Jackson was rapidly becoming the major convention center for various state organizations. Consequently, as the number of tourists through the mansion increased and their presence became more taxing upon the first lady, the role of mansion hostess began to take shape. Mrs. Whitfield was assisted by her sister, Mrs. Paul Gaston, Sr., during her first busy year in the mansion. The inconvenience stemming from the mansion's dual character as both a public building and a private residence that would later plague the first families was becoming evident in the 1920s.

Governor Whitfield often preferred to work at the mansion rather than at his office in the capitol, especially at night. While a special commission which he appointed to evaluate the curriculum and teaching methods of the public school system was drafting its final report, Governor Whitfield met with them each night at the mansion. Later, when several northern educators visited Mississippi on a tour of southern schools, Whitfield brought them to the mansion for working sessions. The governor also entertained many northern investors at the mansion while they were in the state seeking new plant locations.[38]

In spite of the inconveniences that might have been caused by the flow of tourists or club meetings and public receptions, Whitfield's congeniality made the visitors feel more like honored guests than intruders upon his privacy. This aspect of his personality is well illustrated by an incident

A House of Glass

involving some schoolboys who paid the governor an unexpected call at the mansion. It seems that several boys were sitting around with nothing much to do during the lunch hour one day at Central High School, just a few blocks from the mansion. On a dare, three of them left the school grounds, walked through Smith Park, then up to the back door of the mansion. When a servant greeted them, they told a sad story of being poor and hungry and asked for food. An unexpected turn of events caught them by surprise. Just as they were telling their story, Governor Whitfield walked by and heard of their plight. Realizing the hoax they were playing, the governor announced that he was about to have lunch and insisted that the boys join him in the family dining room. Unable to talk themselves out of what they had talked themselves into, the boys sheepishly joined the governor for lunch. Through the pleasant ordeal, Whitfield played the gracious host. But the governor was accustomed to young people, and their presence was always a source of special pleasure to him. His girls at the "W" were accorded more than a perfunctory standing invitation to visit him at the mansion whenever they were in Jackson, and the young students frequently called upon Whitfield, who had done so much for the college during his presidency of that institution.[39]

Of the many guests who were honored at the mansion during their residency, the Whitfields probably most enjoyed America's sagacious wit Will Rogers, who visited Jackson during Whitfield's administration. Rogers later praised the first family for their hospitality and admitted that he felt very much at home in that historic and spacious mansion.[40]

During the fall of 1926, Governor Whitfield began experiencing intense pain in his hip and knee. Upon the advice of his physician, he spent a brief time in Hot Springs, Arkansas. After the pain continued, further diagnosis revealed the ailment as bone cancer. An operation to remove Whitfield's leg just above the knee was performed at a Memphis hospital in December. On January 6, 1927, the governor returned to Jackson. A marching band and large crowd of well-wishers greeted him at the train station to escort him to the mansion. Upon his arrival at the residence, the Negro servants formed a file between Congress Street and the portecochere entrance and cheered his return.[41]

Over the next two months, Governor Whitfield learned to walk with the aid of crutches and went to his office in the capitol almost every day until

A History of the Mississippi Governor's Mansion

his worsening condition further reduced his mobility. He then set up an office in the mansion and conducted the affairs of state from there. State officials conferred with the governor almost daily at the mansion until early in March , when the doctors advised the family that the governor's condition was critical and offered little hope for his recovery. Throughout the night before the governor's demise there rose from the mansion grounds the haunting wails of chants and prayers. The black servants, who "were passionately devoted to Governor Whitfield," kept an all-night vigil. Periodically, they were advised of his condition, and each report was followed by their haunting refrain offered up in his behalf. Henry Whitfield died at 4:41 A.M. on March 18, 1927.[42]

After a brief memorial service at the capitol, the governor's body was returned to Columbus for interment. When Lieutenant Governor Dennis Murphree was subsequently elevated to the office of governor, he graciously offered Mrs. Whitfield the continued use of the executive residence until the expiration of her husband's term. She declined and with her son moved out of the mansion shortly after the governor's death. At his own request, Governor Murphree was not sworn in as the state's chief executive until after the burial of the former governor; and his family did not experience the excitement normally associated with occupying the governor's mansion.[43]

Dennis Murphree had served in the state legislature for twelve years prior to his election as lieutenant governor in 1923. His family had lived with him in Jackson during most of that time, and after the 1923 campaign they bought a farm just outside the city. Both the governor and first lady, the former Clara Martin, were from Calhoun County, and the strong ties of a closely knit family characterized their eleven-month residency in the mansion. The most festive social occasion at the mansion during the Murphrees' brief residency was the wedding of the governor's cousin, Ruth Scott, to William Fox on June 15, 1927. The governor's trusting nature predisposed him to an open door policy during his term that extended even to the executive residence. The doors at the mansion were seldom locked during the daytime and people frequently walked in just to look around. Since the first family occupied the living area in the annex and one of the second-floor bedrooms in the historical portion, their privacy was intruded upon when visitors went upstairs, which they often

A House of Glass

did. On one occasion, the governor's oldest daughter met an unknown couple walking up the main staircase. When she asked if she could be of assistance to the strangers, the young man asked the location of the office which issued marriage licenses. He was surprised to learn that he was in the governor's mansion, not in the county courthouse.[44]

In the absence of an official hostess, Mrs. Murphree's responsibilities as first lady were multiplied to include, in addition to caring for her own family, the planning of meals and receptions for state occasions, the ordering of supplies and food, and the supervision of the domestic servants and groundskeepers. Yet the artistically inclined first lady managed to find time for her ceramics and needlepoint.

Social activity at the mansion was not as demanding as it might have been, because the disastrous flood of 1927 consumed much of the governor's attention and he spent long periods of time in the Mississippi Delta. Additionally, the summer months were devoted to a vigorous political campaign. Prior to the death of Governor Whitfield, Murphree had announced his intention to seek reelection as lieutenant governor. But after his elevation to the governorship, he decided to run for that office against Theodore Bilbo, who had already announced. Just before the campaign began in earnest, Governor Murphree called his children together in the mansion and tried to explain to them the nature of Mississippi politics. He warned them that during such a campaign as he was entering, they would hear many things about their father and about others. They were to judge those statements on the basis of what they knew personally about the people and about those making such statements.[45] It is likely that many similar scenes have occurred either at the governor's mansion or in private homes throughout Mississippi. In the campaign of 1927, Bilbo was reelected by a margin of 16,000 votes.

When The Man moved into the mansion for the second time in January, 1928, many things had changed. He did not feel the same about the pretentions of high station as he had four years earlier. He drove from the mansion to his inaugural ceremony in a new, custom-built, $6,000 Cadillac, a gift from his supporters. In his inaugural address he did not repeat his earlier suggestion to sell the governor's mansion; instead, a short time later, he recommended that a garage be built for his Cadillac. Bilbo also asked that a birdbath and pergola be built on the mansion grounds, and that the lawn be resodded and terraced. At the crest of his popularity, The Man got everything he asked for, including additional furniture for the mansion purchased at state expense. During Bilbo's second residency, a total of $15,000 was spent on the mansion, about half as much as the 1908 renovation and more than the total expenditures for the previous twenty years. A Vicksburg supporter also donated an ornate bedroom suite which has in tradition become known as the "Bilbo bed." After Bilbo left office, the state purchased the bedroom furniture at a cost of $500.[46] Regardless of the controversy and even scandal which periodically surfaced during his long and tumultuous career, Bilbo's supporters developed a tenacious loyalty to The Man. They excused his exploits and reveled in his achievements. On one occasion some of his supporters came to visit him at the mansion, but the first family was away for the weekend. The disappointed visitors decided not to waste the trip so they camped on the front portico and awaited the return of their idol.

As a measure of change in Bilbo's value system, he allowed the first lady to attend the second inaugural ball, although he did not attend himself.[47] For the first two years, especially after he resolved a problem involving his son and namesake, Bilbo's second residency in the mansion was much happier than his first. The governor wrote of his son's unfortunate confrontation with some schoolboys who taunted him and often physically accosted him as he walked home to the mansion after school. "I shall never forget this boy," he wrote, "crying as though his heart would break because . . . some boy hurled at him the statement, 'Your daddy is nothing but a jailbird.'" The young son explained how he resolved the situation:

> While coming home a gang jumped on me . . . just because I was the Governor's kid. . . . I came home looking pitiful. . . . When Dad got home he . . . asked me if I had some friends. I told him some. He said to get the gang together and have them trail me until the trouble started. Well, the next afternoon . . . the same gang which whipped me the afternoon before lit into me again. But that time help arrived. It was short but good.[48]

After this incident the first lady, his daughter and son were happy in the mansion. With his family now comfortable and content, The Man turned to his "real children," the voters of Mississippi.

During his last two years in office, Bilbo was absorbed in an effort to revitalize the state's economy, which was reeling under the disastrous consequences of the stock market crash of 1929 and the depression which followed. Economic problems were compounded when the state's colleges and universities lost their accreditation following Bilbo's dismissal of several college presidents and faculty members. Under the constant threat of impeachment, Bilbo was reluctant to call the lawmakers into special session to deal with these and other problems. After gaining the legislature's assurance that he would not be impeached, Bilbo finally called a special session.[49] But when the legislature issued bonds to gain operating revenue, no purchasers could be found. The state languished in debt and depression.

Bilbo's all-absorbing love for the machinations of politics eventually led to an estangement with his wife, who had through the more recent years "remained in the background socially and officially." During the political fury generated by the election of 1931, "all the rumors about The Man as a ladies' man were revived" and, no doubt, amplified. The strain and pressure became unbearable to Mrs. Bilbo; she and the two children left the mansion in October, 1931. When she asked Bilbo to let her live in the Dream House, he refused. She remained in Jackson and sparked intense but temporary excitement by announcing that she would run for governor. However, she did no more than announce and made no effort to seek the office.[50]

Bilbo remained in the mansion for several weeks after his family left. His last night in the executive residence was sadder even than his first night sixteen years earlier. The Man, according to his biographer, "retired from the Executive Mansion to a hotel room, without wife, without daughter or son, without prospect, without glory." When he left office he was disheartened and many believed defeated. Fred Sullens recorded his political epitaph:

> Beneath this stone old Theo lies;
> Nobody laughs and nobody cries;
> Where he's gone, or how he fares,
> Nobody knows and nobody cares.[51]

But like the sea which gives life and is unruly, Mississippi politics is unpredictable. Two years later The Man was elected to the United States Senate, then reelected in 1940, and again elected in 1946.

CHAPTER IX

All the Changing Life of Mississippi

IN HIS INAUGURAL address delivered on January 19, 1932, Martin Sennett Conner issued a somber declaration. "We assume our duties," he said, "at a time when the whole world is sick, when men are shaken with doubt and with fear, and many are wondering if our very civilization is about to crumble." The governor needed no flurry of rhetoric to convince his audience of the grave situation facing not only Mississippi but the entire nation. Conner was inheriting a bankrupt state treasury against which $13 million in outstanding obligations had accumulated. Among these unpaid debts were a light bill at the governor's mansion totaling $1,258.54 (which had been carried since 1928), a fuel bill of $233.08, a grocery bill of over $400, and a $416 bill for a refrigerator which had recently been installed at the executive residence.[1]

At forty-one, Mike Conner was among the youngest of the forty-five men who have served as Mississippi's chief executive. Yet few of them have entered the office better trained or with more experience in public service. At twenty-four, the Yale-trained lawyer was elected to the legislature. After serving five terms as Speaker of the House of Representatives, Conner ran unsuccessfully for governor in 1923 and 1927. Fred Sullens, whose inordinate enmity for Bilbo sometimes bordered on the irrational, hailed Conner's success in 1931 as an overwhelming repudiation of Bilbo's "four year orgy of graft, corruption, extravagance, political trickery, demagoguery and scandal in high places."[2]

Conner's election was the fulfillment of a lifelong dream and his family eagerly anticipated occupying the governor's mansion. Sensitive to the recurring criticism that some governors had removed state-owned furnishings from the executive residence, the first lady, Alma Lucille Graham of Seminary, asked the secretary of state to make an inventory of the mansion property before they moved in and again when they vacated the dwelling. The first family, which included a young daughter, Lady Rachel, and Mrs. Conner's mother, occupied the family quarters in the 1908 annex, reserving the historic portion exclusively for guests and state occasions.[3]

The excitement and thrill of living in the historic mansion was diminished, however, as the winter rains brought the realization that living in an almost century-old building had its special problems. The mansion continued to leak so badly that buckets were scattered throughout the downstairs areas where the problem was most serious. The heating system in the basement also continued to plague the first family, smoke escaped through the worn and leaking pipes, soiling both furnishings and interior walls.[4]

The legislature was already aware that these and other problems existed at the mansion. Just prior to Conner's inauguration a select committee had inspected the building to ascertain its condition. For the first time a legislative committee had the benefit of a "woman's touch" in recommending an appropriation for the repair and refurnishing of the mansion. Mrs. Nellie Nugent Somerville, who had been elected to the legislature in 1923, was a member of that special committee. On the basis of the committee's recommendations the legislature authorized an appropriation of $11,000 to redecorate the family quarters and to make minor repairs throughout the mansion. Most of the money was spent for repairs of a cosmetic nature, however, and the more serious problems remained for many years. The legislature also increased the maintenance fund to $2,500 annually.[5]

This increase was certainly warranted, because Governor Conner used the mansion for official business perhaps more than any of his predecessors. The general economic circumstances and rising unemployment lengthened that ever-present line of office-seekers which even under normal circumstances require so much of the governor's time. As both the number and the persistence of callers at his capitol office became increasingly disruptive, Conner extended his working hours at the mansion. His private secretary practically moved her files to the mansion, and key legislators were more than happy to confer with the governor in those relatively calm surroundings.[6]

The governor's inaccessibility, at least at his capitol office, prompted a great deal of criticism, much of it unfair. He was often referred to as "Closed Door Conner." His political opponents accused him of being aloof, remote, and insensitive to the suffering of the people. But R. H. Singleton, a gifted craftsman who was employed to repair some of the cornices in the mansion during Conner's administration, remembered the governor as a friendly and very cordial man. Singleton, who has worked at the mansion at various times over the past forty years, testified that Conner's reputation for aloofness was not justified. A former employee of a Jackson radio station also remembered seeing the governor display deep emotions, even weeping at times, during his impassioned broadcasts in support of the sales tax measure which Conner considered the only means of bringing order to the state's financial chaos.[7]

Conner's proposal to enact a 3 percent sales tax was met with a torrent of opposition and criticism. At a meeting in Jackson, 5,000 people gathered to protest its enactment. After a spirited rally, the crowd marched upon the capitol and a contingent called at the governor's office. So alarming were the prospects that the governor's secretary locked the door. Conner ordered the door opened, however, and allowed the crowd to enter his private office. During the heated exchange which followed, a man drew a pistol and pointed it at the governor. A scuffle ensued and the man was disarmed. Finally the office was cleared.[8]

Following a more rational discussion of the economic advantages of the tax over the next few weeks, a surprisingly strong support for the measure developed. Among the most vocal advocates of the new tax were the public school teachers, the state's largest block vote. The teachers' support was based on the realization that the state would be unable to maintain the school system without additional revenues. Years later, Alfred H. Stone, the first tax commissioner to administer the law, credited teachers and other friends of public schools with passage of the bill. When finally passed, the law established a 2 percent tax rather than the 3 percent Conner had recommended.[9]

The tax measure was only one aspect of Conner's new economic policy. As an immediate remedy he slashed the state's budget by cutting back on

All the Changing Life of Mississippi

salaries, jobs, and government services; as a basis of full recovery he recommended a broad program of industrial development and agricultural diversification. Though highly controversial, Conner's legislative program was enacted. It was also highly successful. When he retired from office in 1936, Conner left a $3 million surplus in the state treasury.[10]

Conner was convinced that Mississippi's vast industrial potential would never be realized until the state's national image was improved. Throughout his four years in office, he often spoke of a "new politics" for Mississippi. The new politics would be characterized by a business-like approach to state government. Demagoguery would have no place in Mississippi's promising future. Conner's intention to disassociate himself from the "old politics" was practical as well as theoretical. Perhaps the only time in the mansion's history when its traditional hospitality was not extended to a visiting dignitary occurred on November 17, 1934. On that Saturday afternoon the annual Ole Miss–LSU football game was played at the fairgrounds in Jackson. Senator Huey P. Long of Louisiana and a host of supporters accompanied the team to Jackson. Long was met at the train station by a motorcycle escort from the Jackson police department. As his entourage paraded up Capitol Street and approached the mansion, Long motioned to his escorts to stop. He dispatched an aide to the mansion with an invitation for Governor Conner to accompany him to the fairgrounds. After ringing the bell several times but to no avail, the aide returned to inform the illustrious senator that nobody was home. The motorcade resumed its noisy, winding course to the fairgrounds. LSU won, 14–0. Undoubtedly, Governor Conner attended the game because he had an intense interest in collegiate sports. Following his term as governor, he was appointed commissioner of athletics for the Southeastern Conference.[11]

By 1935 the success of Conner's economic policy could be measured by the decline in unemployment. Convinced that industrial development was the only remedy for continued depression and the only means of full economic recovery, Mississippi voters elected Hugh Lawson White, a millionaire industrialist, in a narrow run-off over Paul B. Johnson, Sr., in the Democratic primary of 1935.

While serving two terms as mayor of Columbia, White had implemented an industrial recruitment program which greatly increased job opportunities and lessened the impact of depression on that small community in Marion County. Pledging to do for the state what he had done in Columbia, White campaigned on a platform of industrial development which would balance agriculture with industry. His program was not new, but rather an expanded and enlarged version of policies already initiated by Whitfield and Conner. The major achievements of White's first administration were the creation of an apparatus to direct and coordinate the state's industrial development program and the enactment of tax measures specifically designed to attract industry. The most important industry brought to the state under the Balance Agriculture With Industry program was the Ingalls Corporation at Pascagoula.[12]

When Governor White and the first lady, the former Judith Weir Sugg of Providence, Kentucky, moved into the executive mansion in January, 1936, its interior was in the best condition it had been for several years. The private family quarters, which the Whites used during their residency, had recently been redecorated and new furniture had been purchased during the Conner administration. Most of the leaks had been stopped, temporarily at least. And other than the continuing problem of smoke rising from the basement, the physical condition of the mansion was very good. However, the first family would soon realize that the physical arrangement of the mansion created several problems. By 1936 the schedule of public functions at the executive residence had so increased that family privacy was becoming almost impossible. There was no means of closing off the upstairs family quarters from the state rooms in the historic portion. During the hours when the mansion was open to public tours, the family quarters were often as public as the main building. Since the increasing flow of traffic through the dwelling also put an added strain on the servants, the number of inmates assigned to the mansion increased during White's administration.[13]

The problem of privacy in the mansion became especially significant after Governor White suffered a heart attack and was confined to his bed for almost a year. During that year, after he was allowed to resume a limited work schedule, most of the governor's official duties were performed at the mansion. His correspondence and other paper work, his conferences with legislative leaders and state officials, plus a variety of other responsibilities, kept the level of activity at the mansion at an

All the Changing Life of Mississippi

all-time high. After White resumed a more active schedule, an elevator was installed in the annex, facilitating his access to the family quarters on the second story.[14]

Although the first family did not have any children, they took advantage of every opportunity to entertain small children at the mansion. They were also especially generous in making the mansion available to young people for a variety of functions. The executive residence became headquarters or rendezvous point for high school and college students from Columbia when they came to Jackson.[15]

Although most governors since the Civil War had entertained northern industrialists, it was during White's administration that they became such frequent guests at the mansion. Both Mrs. White, the epitome of a southern lady and a talented musician, and the governor, who was well known for his hearty appetite, were ideally suited for this kind of entertainment. The governor was a successful businessman who could talk the industrialists' language and understand their problems during a period of economic uncertainty. With sufficient encouragement, the first lady often provided additional entertainment on the mansion's piano. Resplendent with history and reminiscent of the Old South, the governor's mansion was an ideal setting for the display of traditional southern hospitality. Many decisions to locate new plants in Mississippi, although certainly based on economic considerations, were made in those pleasant and charming surroundings which undoubtedly put the decision-makers in a positive frame of mind. There would be many similar decisions and other visitors over the next forty years.

In the late 1930s, the Mississippi Federal Writers Project began compiling material for a souvenir volume on the history of Mississippi's first ladies entitled "Mistresses of the Mansion." The project was under the direction of Kate Markham Power, whose family had been closely associated with the mansion and its occupants since 1842. Mrs. White enthusiastically endorsed the project and offered her assistance to Miss Power. Although a great deal of material was assembled, the book was never published. However, the extensive correspondence between Miss Power and the descendants of several first families, dating from Tilghman Tucker to Hugh White, has been preserved in the Mississippi Department of Archives and History. To read her correspondence is to admire her persistence and dedication to the project. In a letter to the granddaughter of Mrs. Benjamin Humphreys, Miss Power admitted that some of the material she had collected would have to be handled delicately but added proudly that "none of the First Ladies brought discredit" to the state.[16]

During the last two years of Governor White's term, the nation in general—and the rural South in particular—experienced a recurrence of hard times similar to though not as severe as those of the early thirties. When Mississippi's economy took a downward turn in 1938 and 1939, critics of White's policy of a balanced budget and financial retrenchment became increasingly vocal.

The new economic policies of Conner and White became the central issue in the gubernatorial election of 1939. The most outspoken critic of the BAWI program was Paul B. Johnson, Sr., who ran on the pledge, "I will never balance the budget of this state at the expense of suffering humanity." Evincing "more interest in people than in treasury surpluses," Johnson also pointed out that the turn-around in the state's economy predicted by the BAWI advocates had not materialized. Since Governor White was not eligible to succeed himself, Mike Conner announced for governor and campaigned in defense of the state's new economic departure. In the second primary, which revived some of the bitterness of earlier campaigns, Johnson defeated Conner by almost 30,000 votes.[17]

Johnson's margin of victory, which came in his third bid for office, was the largest majority a gubernatorial candidate had received up to that time. A former judge and United States congressman, Governor Johnson was a self-styled representative of the "runt hog people," or the common man. And like Conner, his election to the governorship was the fulfillment of a life-long dream. Shortly before his inauguration on January 16, 1940, Johnson and his family occupied the governor's mansion with anticipation and great excitement.[18]

The first family, which included three children—Paul, Jr., Patrick, and Peggy—utilized the family quarters in the annex. Both of the boys were away at school or working, and Peggy was the only one of the three who lived at the mansion during the Johnson residency. The first family frequently returned to their home at Hattiesburg during Johnson's administration, because the governor was ill through most of his term and the trips back home rested him from the pressure of public life. An avid horseman, the governor also relished the open air and riding which had always been a source of pleasure for him and his family.[19]

For a combination of reasons, entertainment and social activity at the mansion during the Johnson residency were considerably diminished in comparison with former years. First of all, the governor's health required a judicious use and conservation of his energy. Continuing hard times, which lingered until the outbreak of World War II, also placed an added strain on the first family's limited budget. However, the gregarious and charming first lady, Corinne Venable of McComb, like all her predecessors, understood that although the executive residence was the governor's home, it was also the governor's mansion with a rich history and sentimental value to the people. In spite of the fact that she had only four servants and a maintenance fund which was seldom adequate to meet the necessary expenses, Mrs. Johnson opened the mansion as often as possible and allowed its continued use for public functions.

Shortly after his inauguration, Governor Johnson and his wife honored his "colonels," their wives, and other supporters at an open house at the mansion. Very few Mississippi politicians have enjoyed the enduring loyalty of supporters over so long a period of time as did Governor Paul Johnson, Sr. His ability to sustain that relationship with his supporters, whose commitment remained undiminished even in defeat, may be unique in Mississippi's political history. His first reception in the mansion was more like a love feast than a victory celebration. Mrs. Johnson would remember it, twenty years later, as the most splendid social event at the mansion during their residency.[20]

Among the other notable occasions during the Johnson, Sr. administration was the marriage of his older son. On February 8, 1941, Paul Johnson, Jr., and Dorothy Power were married in the elegant west parlor. Traditional wedding vows were exchanged before the lofty mantelpiece banked with bridal greens and white flowers. The ceremony was attended by approximately four hundred people, including some of the governor's best and oldest friends as well as some political enemies of long standing. One of the guests was Senator Bilbo, whose 5'2" frame provided a poor view of the festivities. The Man pulled up a chair, stood on it, peered over the heads of those in front, obscured the view of those behind, and

A History of the Mississippi Governor's Mansion

watched the ceremony. Twenty-four years later, Governor Paul Johnson, Jr., would escort his daughter down the grand staircase into the same west parlor where her wedding also would be solemnized.[21]

Yet another social highlight during Governor Johnson's residency was the visit of a future queen. During World War II, a Dutch Air Force Training School was located at Jackson, and on two occasions members of the Dutch royal family came to the capital city to review the troops at the air base. Prince Bernhard zu Lippe-Biesterfield was in Jackson on July 24, 1942, and Princess Juliana on October 30, 1943. Both Prince Bernhard and Princess Juliana (later Queen Juliana of the Netherlands) were received at the mansion. Their visits mark the only occasions when members of a royal family were honored at the mansion.[22]

The war also brought other distinguished callers to the mansion. On one occasion Governor Johnson was awakened in the middle of the night by a phone call. On the other end of the line a voice said, "The President is calling." Governor Johnson took the phone to talk with President Franklin D. Roosevelt, as he had done many times before. The president asked Governor Johnson to accompany him on an inspection tour of Camp Shelby but cautioned him not to disclose the fact of his visit to anyone outside his immediate family. A few days later, on September 29, 1942, Governor Johnson met President Roosevelt at Hattiesburg and together they toured that sprawling installation of 300,000 acres, where at its peak period over 75,000 men were in training.[23]

Like millions of other homes throughout America during World War II, the Mississippi executive mansion displayed in a front window a double-starred banner indicating that two of its sons had gone to war. Both of the Johnson boys, Paul, Jr., and Patrick, volunteered for military duty and were sworn into service in the governor's capitol office. The war which took two sons from the mansion left a wife and child in their place. When Paul, Jr., was transferred to a California Marine base, his wife Dorothy and their daughter, Patricia, moved into the mansion until she could join her husband on the West Coast. One afternoon while Patricia was sleeping in one of the upstairs bedrooms in the historic portion of the mansion, a piece of plaster fell from the ceiling near the sleeping child. Besides frightening the family, the incident also revealed that the long series of cosmetic repairs to the mansion had not corrected the structural damage

All the Changing Life of Mississippi

which over the years had become increasingly serious and possibly dangerous.[24]

Although the mansion was one hundred years old in 1942, there is no evidence that any special recognition was given to that fact or that any celebration was held to honor its centennial. A couple of years earlier, a Jackson columnist who noted the one hundredth anniversary of the old capitol was also prompted to review the "glorious history" of the governor's mansion. There had been no official efforts to relocate the mansion recently, but there had been some general discussion in favor of such action. Continued growth of downtown Jackson and the building's aging condition renewed the hopes of Jackson businessmen that the mansion square would eventually become available for commercial development. In this regard the reporter surmised that "as an official residence of the governor of the state . . . the Old Mansion has about outlived its usefulness." "Even the newer structure," he said, "is now antiquated, by comparison with modern residences." But after recounting the previous efforts to relocate the executive residence, the journalist seemed to be convinced by his own argument over the next few paragraphs that maybe the mansion should be preserved after all. Anyway, he concluded, "the pecan trees usually provide [the governor] with plenty of nuts."[25] Disposing of the governor's mansion seemed the logical thing to do, but this reporter could not bring himself to the point of endorsing it.

Surviving the latest threat, the mansion was given a new lease on life as well as a facelift. The yellow brick exterior which had been added in the 1908 renovation was painted white during the residency of Paul Johnson, Sr. The similarity between the mansion's front portico and the south portico at the White House became more perceptible after the color change and prompted an occasional reference to the governor's mansion as the Mississippi White House.[26]

During the Thanksgiving holidays of 1943, the mansion was the scene of a very special dinner—one of the first family's sons was home on leave. It was a timely visit, because a few days later Governor Johnson suffered a heart attack while at home in Hattiesburg.[27]

For almost forty years Paul Johnson, Sr., had been a central figure in Mississippi politics. He was a veteran of many battles and campaigns and had known defeat as well as victories. His latest victory, and some con-

A History of the Mississippi Governor's Mansion

sidered it his greatest, had been won at a heavy cost. During his first two years in office, Governor Johnson was involved in a bitter struggle to enact a law providing free textbooks in the public schools. Surprisingly, his proposal met fierce opposition. Its opponents considered the measure socialistic and its author radical. In the waning weeks of the bitter struggle the measure appeared to be defeated. But on the day of the final roll call, the law was passed by a margin of one vote. It was a singular triumph for the school children of Mississippi and for Governor Johnson. But the years of rigorous public life had taken their toll, and the governor's health declined. On December 26, 1943, Paul Johnson, Sr., died at his home in Hattiesburg.[28]

For the second time in less than twenty years, Lieutenant Governor Dennis Murphree was elevated to the office of chief executive. During the three-week interval between Governor Johnson's death and the inauguration of Thomas L. Bailey, Governor Murphree exercised the duties of the office but did not occupy the executive mansion, which remained vacant until January, 1944.

By force of circumstances that must have kept Murphree awake for most of those twenty-one nights, Bailey rather than he would take the oath of office on January 18, 1944. By a margin of only 435 votes, Bailey had won a spot in the run-off primary the previous August and then had gone on to defeat Martin S. Conner for the Democratic nomination. It is probable that Murphree, who ran third, would also have defeated Conner. It is something of a tradition in Mississippi politics that the candidate who wins the the first primary loses the second which is the only one that really counts. Murphree was making his third and last race for the office and Bailey his second.

When Governor and Mrs. Bailey, the former Nella Massey of Birmingham, Alabama, occupied the mansion, they chose to live in the historic portion rather than the family annex. The first family, which included two children, Nellah and Harold—both of whom were young adults, was very active, energetic, and industrious. Both the tempo and variety of activities at the mansion quickened during the Baileys' residency.

The mansion also continued to display the double-starred banner, as both the son and son-in-law of the first family were in military service. And like millions of others in wartime America, Governor Bailey had a

All the Changing Life of Mississippi

victory garden on the mansion grounds. Mrs. Bailey was also an avid gardener, though she experienced the same problems other first ladies had encountered in cultivating a lawn under the large trees shading the mansion grounds.[29]

Through the last two years of war, Mrs. Bailey held bond drives and other patriotic meetings at the mansion. When national figures visited Jackson in support of the war effort, she always opened the mansion for public receptions. Some of those distinguished visitors included General Claire Chennault, who was an overnight guest, General Lewis Hershey, national director of the Selective Service, and his wife, and Lord and Lady Halifax of Great Britain who came to Jackson during their American tour.[30]

Both Governor Bailey and the first lady were conscious of the symbolic importance of the executive mansion to the people of Mississippi, and they contributed significantly to the enrichment of its historic character. At the request of the first family in the spring of 1944, the legislature authorized the purchase of antique furnishings "in keeping with the Mansion's tradition, period, and design."[31] Unfortunately, detailed records of those purchases were not maintained, and it is not known precisely which antiques now used in the mansion were among those secured by the Baileys.

During the Baileys' abbreviated residency, the mansion witnessed the full cycle of life, birth, marriage, and death. Nellah Bailey, the first lady's namesake, was married to Hunter C. Webb in the mansion's beautiful music room. The scene was a familiar one throughout America—the bride wore white and the groom wore GI green. The Webbs' first child was also born in the mansion, an event which occasioned a celebration among the inmates working at the mansion. Unfortunately, the celebration took place during the absence of Otis Goodwin, the governor's valued bodyguard and chauffeur, who was responsible for keeping order among the other prisoners. The enthusiastic fête, enlivened by the discovery of the location of spiritous beverages, got out of hand, and an altercation between two prisoners resulted. During the fight, one of the male servants received a knife wound. Following this incident, all the inmates were returned to Parchman prison except Goodwin, who remained with the governor and was at his bedside when he died. During the interim required to select and train new servants, the first family moved to the Heidelberg Hotel.[32]

While a jubilant world celebrated the end of mankind's most costly war, the mansion was twice draped in mourning. In August, 1945, the governor's aging mother, Mrs. Rosa Powell Bailey, died after a prolonged illness. And just over a year later, Governor Bailey himself succumbed, the victim of spinal malignancy. Through the long ordeal the governor was often confined to his bed, though he continued to direct the affairs of state as best he could from the mansion. On July 11, 1946, Governor Bailey had designated Lieutenant Governor Fielding L. Wright as acting governor, but as his condition improved in early September, Bailey again resumed the duties of his office.[33]

A few months before Governor Bailey's death, an incident occurred in the mansion which illustrates that special kind of camaraderie that exists between old political adversaries and which perhaps only they can fully understand. Sometime after his Democratic primary victory of July 2, 1946, Senator Bilbo came to see Governor Bailey at the mansion. For the first few minutes the old warriors, who had battled each other for so many years, were very formal, addressing each other as "Governor" and "Senator." Bilbo advised the governor of the attempt that would be made to deny him his seat in the United States Senate. On the basis that large numbers of Mississippi Negroes had been denied the right to vote in the Democratic primary, a movement was underway to challenge Bilbo's election and his right to represent Mississippi. Both men were suffering from the physical infirmities that would claim their lives within a year. Bailey was paralyzed from the waist down and Bilbo, whose speech was frequently interrupted by an ugly cough, was even then showing the signs of debilitating throat cancer.

Bilbo asked the governor if he would support his effort to retain his seat in the Senate. Governor Bailey looked at Bilbo intently and silently for a minute or two. The governor reminded the senator that he had never supported him in any election, that he had always been on the other side in every political struggle over the last thirty years. But the governor continued that he had been elected by all the people and that those same people had also elected Bilbo to the United States Senate. Bilbo was therefore, said the governor, the senator of the people of Mississippi.

All the Changing Life of Mississippi

Bailey then assured Bilbo that if he were denied his seat in the Senate, The Man would have it the next day by appointment, and the next day, and every day thereafter as long as he was alive and governor. Bilbo was deeply touched by Bailey's response. The embattled little warrior was weakened under the stress of time—he was almost seventy—and the agony of an incurable illness. He wept at the promise of his reprieve. Soon the conversation between them warmed and they dropped the formal titles, each calling the other Tom and Theo. They joked and spoke of old times, refought some of the old battles but without the bitterness. A few moments later Senator Bilbo again thanked Governor Bailey for his support, apologized for taking his time, encouraged him to rest, and then left the mansion.[34] As circumstances developed, Governor Bailey did not have to fulfill his promise. Death came to the governor before the issue of Bilbo's status came before the Senate; and before the Senate came to a decision, death came to Bilbo.

Through the fall of 1946, Governor Bailey's condition worsened. After October 14, his doctors would not permit visitors to the mansion. Through the weeks of pain the governor was comforted by his family and friends. He must also have found solace in the very surroundings in which his suffering occurred. Shortly after he occupied the executive residence, Governor Bailey reflected on the mansion's history. "In all the changing life of Mississippi," he wrote, "it has stood as a symbol of the sturdy faith of Mississippians. . . . It has witnessed the transition . . . of a great state and a great people from near frontierhood to high levels of social, economic, and spiritual development. . . . It looks to a future full of promise."

Bailey's reflection may have been prompted by his awareness that, as Mississippi emerged from World War II, she faced a precarious but promising future. In his last message to the legislature on January 15, 1946, Bailey anticipated the sweeping changes that would follow the world's most unsettling war. The *Jackson Daily News* headlined his address "Build Now For 25 Years, Bailey Urges!" But unfortunately, the state would be deprived of Bailey's innovative and constructive leadership. The governor died on November 2, 1946, in the mansion which he loved and had long admired as "a monument of deepest historical significance."[35]

Bailey's successor, Fielding L. Wright, an old and valued friend, was at

A History of the Mississippi Governor's Mansion

his bedside when the governor died. A few moments later, the former lieutenant governor took the oath of office in the southeast parlor in the mansion. Both the new governor and his first lady, Nan Kelly Wright of Rolling Fork, were close personal friends of Mrs. Bailey and they encouraged her to remain at the mansion as long as she desired. She declined their generous offer and stayed only until she could find suitable accommodations in Jackson. Although the inmates who had served as domestics had been pardoned by Governor Wright, they stayed with the former first lady until she left the mansion in early December. Following her husband's death, Mrs. Bailey continued to serve her adopted state for many years. She was the first woman in Mississippi's history elected to a statewide office. After first serving by appointment, Mrs. Bailey was elected state tax collector in 1947 and continued in office until her death in 1956.[36]

Within a few days after Mrs. Bailey had vacated the mansion, the new first family and their thirteen-year-old daughter, Elaine, occupied the executive residence. Their son, Fielding, Jr., remained at Rolling Fork to manage the family law firm. By December 12, the first family was comfortably settled in time for the entire family to celebrate Christmas in the mansion.[37] The Fielding Wright family shares with that of John Marshall Stone the longest continuous residence in the mansion's history. After serving the remaining two years of Bailey's unexpired term, Governor Wright was elected to a full four-year term embracing the years 1948-52.

For the first few weeks following his inauguration Governor Wright was engaged in the transition of authority from the previous administration to his own. The first lady, Elaine, and Eula Poole, the new hostess at the mansion, were also busy during those first weeks in the residence. They were redecorating the mansion for a reception honoring members and officers of the Debutante Club of Mississippi. Invitations were sent to debs and their parents in twenty-three cities over the state. After the success of the first reception, which was held on December 27, 1946, the event became an annual affair through the Wrights' six-year residency.[38]

The frequency of public activity at the mansion greatly increased during the postwar years, as the Wrights always consented to the use of the mansion for meetings and receptions of local and state organizations. Although they occupied the family quarters in the annex, the first family

All the Changing Life of Mississippi

found the increased level of activity in the public part of the mansion a constant source of inconvenience and a frequent invasion of their family privacy. With a teenage daughter and a stream of youthful visitors, the Wrights soon learned that even the family quarters could provide only a small measure of privacy.

Although the family area in the annex was comfortably furnished, some of the carpeting and draperies were worn and needed replacing. The molding in several rooms needed repair, and the first family also experienced problems with the mansion's heating and plumbing system. The age of the building was beginning to tell and structural damage was becoming more readily discernible.

After Governor Wright extended the executive pardon to the inmates who had served under Governor Bailey, the first family selected a new group of thirteen servants, the largest number to work at the mansion at one time. As always, the inmates' service was entirely satisfactory to the first family and they received the traditional pardon at the end of Wright's term.

Governor Wright, a prosperous Delta lawyer, was reserved and soft-spoken and often accused by his political opponents of lacking the common touch. But those who knew him well, while conceding his reserve, often referred to his dry sense of humor and his fondness for practical jokes as illustrated by an incident involving the upstairs maids at the mansion. For some time after Thomas Bailey's demise, an old floor model radio was left in the east bedroom where the governor's death had occurred. Its circuitry was shorted and the radio would often begin playing with only a slight touch or vibration. Rumors of a ghost in the mansion circulated among the servants. One afternoon while the maids were preparing the room for guests, Governor Wright—who had concealed himself in the shower—rustled the curtain as the maids entered the room. Having attracted their attention, the governor then rushed past them through the open door with the curtain draped over his body, concealing his identity. The women fled the room and for quite some time afterwards would not venture back upstairs.[39]

If that hoax was not sufficient to produce a mansion ghost story, a late night incident involving some rather prominent visitors probably was. The president of Sears and an assistant named Brooks were overnight

A History of the Mississippi Governor's Mansion

guests of Governor Wright. After a full day of meetings and conferences which extended to a late hour, they finally retired for a needed rest. While the mansion was draped in silence and the sounds of a busy city were stilled, Brooks enjoyed a deep sleep. Without warning, the slats of the half-tester on which he was sleeping fell. The bed and then Brooks crashed to the floor. Amplified by the stillness of night, the sound careered through the mansion, startling the first family and guests, as well as the servants who were already suspicious.[40]

Through the years, first families have kept a great variety of pets at the mansion, but Governor Wright probably had the most unusual. Some friends had given the governor two live turkeys for a holiday feast. The fowls were placed in a makeshift pen in the rear of the mansion grounds. In the process of feeding the birds to fatten them for the feast, Governor Wright developed an attachment for the birds. When the time came, he refused their bounty to be exacted at so great a cost. Finally he gave them away on the condition that they be spared.

Probably as much as any other occupant, Governor Wright enjoyed living in the downtown mansion and, like his predecessors, he often brought work home with him. He used the front east parlor as a study, usually finding the mansion less hectic than his office in the capitol. But even there he was sometimes interrupted. Four days before his second inauguration he was visited by a young reporter from *Tiger Talks*, the Central High School paper. The governor could hardly refuse this exclusive interview since the reporter was his lovely daughter, Elaine, who was then a senior at Central. He did, however, begin the interview with a very paternalistic "Hurry up, you're holding up a meeting of the Building Commission." The members of the commission were sitting, probably impatiently, in the parlor across the hall. After what must have been the easiest interview any Mississippi governor ever had, the reporter concluded, "Thanks, I didn't know you could be so cooperative and if you need any help explaining to the B.C., I'll be glad to help." Graciously declining her offer, the governor quipped, "That's okay, squirt, you've gotten me in enough trouble already."[41]

The Building Commission was waiting to confer with Governor Wright about the general condition of the executive mansion, to determine the

All the Changing Life of Mississippi

extent of repairs that might be necessary. The commission's findings resulted in an expenditure of $3,000 for "emergency repair" and a more extensive investigation by engineers and architects. Over the next four years the mansion underwent a "little White House repair job." The entire plumbing and electrical systems were reworked or replaced. Some load-bearing walls were strengthened and new carpets and draperies were purchased for several rooms. An effort was also made to resod the lawn with grass varieties known to flourish under shady conditions. However, that attempt proved unsuccessful and the grounds continued to suffer from erosion. The original estimate for the project was $71,000, but the final cost was slightly higher.[42]

While the major repair work was underway, the first family entertained a group of Venezuelan diplomats at a buffet in the mansion. The South Americans were in Mississippi to participate in christening ceremonies for a cargo ship which had been built by the Ingalls Corporation in Pascagoula. The first lady had been asked to christen the ship but an attack of influenza prevented her acceptance. The honor was then accorded to Elaine.[43]

The most important social affair which occurred during the Wrights' entire six-year residency took place just a few days before the family vacated the executive mansion. Elaine Wright had scheduled a summer wedding shortly after her graduation from college. But when her fiancé's employer assigned him to one of its foreign offices, the couple was forced to reschedule their wedding. The governor decided to remain in the historic mansion through early January to allow his daughter to be married in the elegant parlor where she made her debut only a month earlier. The wedding was planned for January 5, 1952, to coincide with the first lady's birthday. On the day of the nuptials the mansion overflowed with guests and friends of the first family. The Wrights' last few days in the mansion proved to be as exciting and busy as their first days had been. On January 9, Governor and Mrs. Wright left the mansion and returned to their home in Rolling Fork.

A few days later Governor and Mrs. Hugh Lawson White returned to the mansion which they had occupied twenty years earlier. They found that the dwelling had undergone many changes during that interval. The

A History of the Mississippi Governor's Mansion

family quarters had been redecorated and many antique pieces had been secured for the state rooms in the historic portion. The grounds had been beautified and the entire mechanical system had been overhauled.

Change could be seen not only at the mansion—it was omnipresent in the postwar world; it revolutionized Mississippi's economy and modified its political climate. The wartime boom which spurred industrial expansion showed no signs of diminishing. Through the 1950s, the number of industrial workers steadily increased and the number of agricultural workers correspondingly declined. Governor White's immediate predecessors had not only restored a measure of respectability to the office, they had also abandoned rhetoric in favor of a rational approach to the state's economic and social problems. But the impact of economic development following World War II combined with a series of Supreme Court decisions to ignite the civil rights movement, which, like a fire bell in the night, aroused the Old Guard politicians who rushed out to extinguish the flames of change which threatened Mississippi's long-standing traditions and customs.

During Governor Wright's administration, Mississippi felt the first wave of that movement. In 1948, southern Democrats withdrew from the national convention and organized the Democratic States' Rights party at a convention in Birmingham. As the vice-presidential nominee for the new party, Governor Wright and other Mississippi leaders campaigned for the "Dixiecrats" who carried only four southern states. Although failing to throw the election into the House of Representatives as they had hoped, Mississippi's leadership counseled a continued opposition to civil rights legislation and federal policies that would alter the state's system of racial segregation.[44] Through the 1950s, as in the 1850s, in the mansion's parlors national resolve and southern resistance were weighed, one against the other. Resistance, acting as a countervailing force, increased rather than diminished the movement. Some things, however, did not change. The mansion's tradition of hospitality continued undisturbed, for a while at least.

In a *Clarion Ledger* interview on January 20, 1952, the first lady admitted that she was more excited about living in the mansion the second time than she had been in 1936. But she would soon discover that the ever-lengthening line of tourists through the mansion would complicate family privacy much more than she had anticipated. The fact that the first family did not have children simplified the situation somewhat, but the governor's age and health presented special problems. At the time of his second inauguration Governor White was seventy years old and weighed about 280 pounds. He was also bothered by the lingering effects of the heart attack experienced during his first term in office. To make matters still worse, while on a trip to the Gulf Coast the governor suffered an unfortunate fall which resulted in a broken leg. The elevator installed at the mansion during his first residency was in heavy use until White, to the dismay of the security men, got stuck between floors. After that experience the governor made scarce use of the device, preferring the slower, less convenient, but more certain stairs leading to the family quarters on the second floor annex.[45]

When the Whites returned to the mansion in 1952, their historical curiosity, still strong, was turned toward the dwelling's furnishings. The first lady initiated a long-range project to identify the origin of the mansion's notable collection of beds, mirrors, tables, chairs, piano, and in particular a portrait of a distinguished looking but unknown southern gentleman. For several weeks Jackson papers carried feature stories and pictures about the mansion's furnishings. Readers were asked to provide Mrs. White with any information they might have about the "mystery beds and other furnishings."[46]

Those articles and pictures not only turned up many "experts" who volunteered to identify various antique pieces in the mansion, but also revived several stories about the executive furnishings which had become oral tradition over the years. There was the time, according to recollections, when tester bedposts were used for kindling during an unusually cold winter. Memories of Sherman's raid included one tale of Union horses eating oats from the mansion's grand piano. Another told of a famous mirror donated to the mansion by a wealthy Vicksburg family who had buried the piece during the war to prevent Yankees from stealing it. Many antiques were "positively" identified by older Jacksonians who recalled seeing them "many, many years ago." The first lady soon learned to accept with caution such positive identification of very old pieces which she knew to have been secured only recently.[47]

Perhaps the most interesting response to the first lady's campaign to

A History of the Mississippi Governor's Mansion

discover the origin of the mansion's furnishings was the identification of the "mystery bed" located in one of the state rooms on the second floor. This particular bed was known to be of antebellum origin and was thought to have been used during the McWillie administration. The possibility that it was the very bed in which the first birth in the executive residence occurred was not even suspected. However, Mrs. Henrietta Mitchell, a granddaughter of Governor McWillie, positively identified the bed as the one in which her sister was born while their parents were living at the mansion. Her identification raised several intriguing questions—how did the furniture survive Sherman's raid? If it was taken to Macon by Governor Pettus, how and when was it returned to the mansion? Unfortunately, Mrs. Henry could not provide the answers to these questions, and in spite of her certainty the authenticity of the bedroom suite has not yet been fully established.[48] Although many of the mysteries surrounding the mansion's furnishings were not solved, Mrs. White's interest and the information she accumulated was the beginning of a systematic inventory of the historical property in the mansion which, by a 1974 statute, is now under the supervision of the Mississippi Department of Archives and History.

In 1955 one of the mansion's most beautiful parlors was the elegant gold room. The silk damask draperies were specially dyed for this room and imported from Italy, while the lace curtains were imported from Switzerland. The magnificent mirror above the mantel, originally on loan to the mansion from the Stewart family of Natchez, was later purchased by the state. Over the years, the mirror has reflected the images of dignitaries and plain citizens alike—equally welcome in the mansion. It was in this room, so appropriately appointed, that Governor and Mrs. White celebrated their golden wedding anniversary on June 14, 1955.[49] In that crowded, gilded room, overflowing with the governor's old friends and well-wishers, he undoubtedly glanced up to see mirrored above the mantel the halcyon days of his youth, the years of his hopes, his time of dreams. Probably to Governor White, who was then seventy-three years old and in his last year of public life, recollections prevailed over expectations.

But in 1955 Anne Moody was only fifteen, still in high school and dreaming. James Meredith was twenty-two, in the Air Force, and had not yet decided to apply for admission to the University of Mississippi. Charles Evers was thirty-three and had been out of college, Alcorn University, only four years. Aaron Henry, also thirty-three, was the current secretary of the Mississippi Pharmaceutical Association. Fannie Lou Hamer was thirty-eight, the youngest of twenty children and the wife of a sharecropper in Sunflower County. Two weeks before the governor's wedding anniversary the U.S. Supreme Court had issued its "all deliberate speed" ruling in the second Brown vs Board of Education decision. Moody, Meredith, Evers, Henry, Hamer, and other black Mississippians were stirred by the court's historic mandate. Expectations, not recollections, prevailed in Mississippi's black community of 1955.

The Brown decision and the national Democratic party's commitment to the implementation of that decision greatly complicated Mississippi's relationship with the national organization. Following the 1948 presidential election and the Dixiecrat movement, Governor White had pursued a cautious policy carefully designed to prevent a complete and irreparable breach between the state and the national party. With the exception of evangelist Billy Graham, who visited the mansion during his Jackson crusade in 1954, and General Douglas MacArthur, who came to Mississippi at the invitation of the state legislature following his dismissal by President Truman, the mansion's most prominent visitors during White's second term were national Democratic leaders who shuttled in and out of Mississippi from 1952 to 1956 in their continued effort to assuage the state's leadership and keep Mississippi within the party. The mansion's guest list during those years reads like a Who's Who in the national Democratic party. Lyndon B. Johnson, Governor Frank Clement of Tennessee, Stephen Mitchell and Paul M. Butler, the latter both national chairmen of the Democratic party, came to Mississippi at various times to promote party unity. Adlai Stevenson, the Democratic presidential nominee in 1952 and 1956 and a personal friend of Governor White, was an overnight guest of the first family during a campaign trip to the state.[50] Stevenson carried the state in both the 1952 and 1956 elections.

Alben Barkley, a former vice-president and senator from Kentucky, was also an overnight guest at the mansion when he came to Jackson to address the Jefferson-Jackson Day dinner. A great orator, Barkley thrilled his audience with old-time rhetoric, recalling the days when elocution was a requisite for public success. Following the dinner, Barkley was coaxed into joining the festivities on the roof of the Heidelberg, a popular Jackson custom for many years. Under the pretext that such conviviality might afford more conducive surroundings for a discussion of the philosophical ramifications of states' rights, he cheerfully accepted. The governor and first lady declined the gracious offer to join the discussion on the roof and returned to the mansion. After waiting up for their famous guest until about midnight, the Whites retired. Sometime later, about 3:00 A.M., the former vice-president of the United States slipped in the back door all the while cautioning the security men not to disturb the first family. A notoriously early riser, Governor White dispatched his servants to Barkley's room the next morning to arouse the vice-president and announce an early breakfast.[51]

Largely through the efforts of Governor White and his successor, J. P. Coleman, Mississippi maintained its traditional loyalty to the Democratic party through the 1950s. But the signs of party unrest among Mississippi Democrats became increasingly ominous and their resistance to the implementation of the desegregation decision continued unwavering. Only fifteen days after Governor White's golden wedding anniversary, Mississippi Democrats went to the polls to nominate a candidate for governor and other state officers. Paul Johnson, Jr. and James P. Coleman emerged as first primary winners from a formidable field of five candidates including Ross Barnett, Mary D. Cain, and Fielding L. Wright. Overcoming a deficit of almost 20,000 votes, Coleman was nominated in the run-off primary.

CHAPTER X

And the Walls Came Tumbling Down

FOLLOWING THE 1954 school desegregation decision, race again became the dominant and inescapable theme in Mississippi politics. And in spite of his effort to inject constitutional reform, school consolidation, industrial development, and other issues in the 1955 campaign, James P. Coleman found, as did other candidates, that a firm commitment to segregation was a necessary preface to the discussion of all other issues.[1] Coleman, who was one of only five men in the twentieth century to be elected the first time he ran for governor of Mississippi, had previously served in all three branches of state government. No governor since John Anthony Quitman had brought more experience to his office than did Coleman.

Like most Mississippians, Coleman came from a rural background. But perhaps more than most of his predecessors, he retained his identification with the soil. In his capitol office a Georgia stock stood silently and almost arrogantly in the corner, a proud reminder not only of Coleman's personal origins but also of the rural heritage of the state of Mississippi over whose destiny he now presided. The first family brought only their personal effects to the mansion. Whenever the press of public affairs permitted, on weekends and holidays, the Colemans returned to the family farm in Choctaw County. One summer after the legislature adjourned, Governor Coleman moved the capitol to Ackerman for several weeks, preferring the old home place to the stately mansion in downtown Jackson. To newsmen who visited the summer capitol, Governor Coleman extended his best Choctaw County "horsepitality" and a personally conducted tour of the family farm, pointing out the route Grant's army had taken as it moved toward Chattanooga.²

Governor Coleman's enduring interest and love for his native Choctaw County, reflected in his history entitled *Choctaw County Chronicles*, was also evident throughout his term in office and his residency in the Mississippi executive mansion. His childhood friends and teachers were proud of his achievements, and the governor equally proud to acknowledge his obligations to those who molded his early life, especially to those teachers under whose tutelage the first spark of intellectual curiosity was ignited. To honor them and his friends from childhood, Coleman invited his high school graduating class to hold its 1959 reunion at the governor's mansion in Jackson. All but one of the surviving members of his senior class and most of the teachers attended the reunion.³

When Governor Coleman and the first lady, Margaret Dennis of Williamsport, Indiana, and their fourteen-year-old son moved into the private family quarters they had mixed feelings about living in the downtown residence. As a historian, Coleman appreciated the traditional symbolism of the governor's mansion, and as a congenial and gregarious host both he and the first lady enjoyed the opportunities for hospitality the mansion afforded its residents. But the Coleman family was living in the mansion at a time of tremendous economic and social change. During this period, the rising level of activity in downtown Jackson with its blaring sirens and heavy nighttime traffic greatly complicated life at the mansion. The ever-present tourists and public meetings created a hotel-like atmosphere at the executive residence. From 1956 to 1960, tourists from all fifty states and at least eighteen countries signed the mansion's guest register. Unaware that the rear section of the building was occupied as family living quarters, tourists often strolled through the open corridors leading from the state rooms on the second floor to the private chambers in the annex. Consequently, as the frequency of public tours increased and the range of other public functions at the mansion widened, the first family's privacy diminished. It had become an inconvenience of crisis proportions.

Shortly after Governor and Mrs. Coleman moved into the mansion, a reporter interviewed the first family. Among his many questions he asked how they liked living in the middle of downtown Jackson. The Colemans

And the Walls Came Tumbling Down

admitted that, although they were comfortable and enjoyed living in the mansion, they did miss the neighborly visits occasioned by the need to borrow, for example, a dozen eggs. Several days after the interview appeared in a local paper, the first family received a surprise visit *from* Anabel Power, who lived in one of the few remaining downtown residences across the street from the mansion. Miss Power's father had acquired the Amite Street property in 1842, the same year the "suitable house for the Governor" was first occupied. Six generations of her family had lived across the street from the mansion. She brought the first family a dozen eggs and welcomed them to the neighborhood.[4]

The Colemans found the mansion, especially the family quarters, in need of extensive repair and redecoration. It had been almost ten years since the "little White House" project of the mid-forties was completed. Governor Coleman suggested a major renovation of the mansion shortly after taking office but did not press the issue, preferring instead to direct the restoration of the old capitol. Largely through his encouragement and personal interest in the project, the 1839 structure was fully restored both to the acclaim of architectural historians and to the pleasure of thousands of tourists who have visited this historic shrine in the intervening years.[5]

Governor Coleman often found the daily rush of visitors to his capitol office so pressing that he sometimes used the mansion for official duties. He redecorated the northwest parlor as an office and frequently used it for small conferences.[6] One of the most important conferences held in this mansion office occurred on February 25, 1957, when Governor James E. Folsom of Alabama and several key legislators from Alabama and Mississippi met with Governor Coleman to plan the Tombigbee River inland waterways project. Both governors and the legislators present at that meeting agreed that the cost of the project, originally estimated at $234 million, should be federally funded. But they also agreed that the two states should pursue the project if federal funds did not become available. The construction of the Tenn-Tom inland waterway, which ultimately will connect the Tennessee and Tombigbee rivers to the Gulf of Mexico, is now underway.

The impending break between the southern states and the national Democratic party, which had been temporarily mended though not healed since the 1948 walkout, brought many prominent national Demo-

A History of the Mississippi Governor's Mansion

crats to Jackson in their continuing effort to keep Mississippi within party ranks, especially in presidential elections. Speaker Sam Rayburn spent three days in Jackson and was Governor Coleman's guest for two nights in the governor's mansion. Senator Richard Russell of Georgia and Governor Buford Ellington of Tennessee, a native Mississippian, were also overnight guests of Governor Coleman. On October 17, 1957, Senator John F. Kennedy spoke in Jackson and was honored at a reception at the Heidelberg Hotel with senatorial colleagues James O. Eastland and John C. Stennis, and many other state officials. Senator Kennedy, then only three years away from the presidency, spent that night at the governor's mansion. He slept in the famous Bilbo bed.[7]

All visitors to the mansion during Governor Coleman's residency were obviously not of such national prominence. Nor were the circumstances always as pleasant. As social tensions and racial unrest became more pronounced during the late 1950s, security problems at the mansion became more serious. One afternoon, an elderly and deranged woman burst through the main entrance and announced that she had come to see the governor. Before the mansion hostess could secure either her name or the purpose for which she wished to see the governor, the woman barged into Coleman's office in the front parlor. After the governor patiently and cordially discussed her personal problems, she left his office. Only one highway patrolman was assigned to mansion security during Coleman's residency but in succeeding administrations security concerns heightened and additional agents were assigned to the mansion.

Throughout Coleman's residency, the practice of using convict labor at the mansion continued. But, possibly reflecting the generally unsettled conditions of race relations in the 1950s, there were indications that this long established tradition would feel the repercussions of the civil rights movement. Dissension and fighting among the inmates caused the return of several prisoners to Parchman. Only one of the mansion servants remained in Jackson through Governor Coleman's four years in office. At the end of his term, Coleman pardoned the inmates who were then serving at the mansion. Significantly, the local press noted that those traditional pardons were the only ones granted during his entire administration.[8] The civil rights movement often prompted a comparison be-

And the Walls Came Tumbling Down

tween the system of segregation and the antebellum system of slavery. Although there were occasional references to the use of Negro convict labor in the mansion as a relic of the old system when blacks worked in the "big house," it is significant and somewhat surprising that more was not made of the situation. That the practice did not attract more criticism than it did is an indication that the system worked so well and to the special benefit of the prisoners.

There were other indications that the volatile fifties would resurrect the passions of earlier years. During Coleman's residency, one of the mansion's most famous occupants again became the focus of controversy. After the *Clarion Ledger-Jackson Daily News* ran a feature article on General Adelbert Ames, whose portrait hung in the Hall of Governors in the capitol building, a "76-year-old unreconstructed Rebel" wrote a blistering letter to the secretary of state. He was "shocked beyond words" that the general's portrait, decked in Union blue and adorned with medals and ribbons "earned by blood of Confederate soldier boys," was so prominently displayed, and demanded its removal. The aging rebel was probably unaware that one of the decorations adorning the general's uniform was the Congressional Medal of Honor won for gallantry on the plain of Manassas. When a local reporter called on the secretary of state for his comments, he found the office closed for a state holiday—it was Robert E. Lee's birthday. For several days, the press carried reports of the controversy. The state president of the United Daughters of the Confederacy, Helen Wamble, was interviewed. However, Mrs. Wamble provided little encouragement to the unreconstructed rebel's effort to have the portrait removed. In response to an inquiry about the UDC's position on the matter, she replied that it was a historical fact that Adelbert Ames had been governor and, since the UDC was dedicated to the preservation of historical facts, she felt the picture should remain in the Hall of Governors. When Governor Coleman was asked about it at a press conference, he pointed out that there were a number of people in Mississippi who would like to see the portraits of Vardaman and Bilbo removed. The Governor explained further that the Hall of Governors should not be confused with the Hall of Fame, which was located in the Department of Archives and History. The Hall of Fame contained the portraits of out-

A History of the Mississippi Governor's Mansion

standing Mississippians who had made valuable contributions to the state and nation in law, politics, art, education, and business. The Hall of Governors included only the pictures of the state's chief executives who had served in that capacity since 1817.[9]

Although this incident seems trivial and almost comical on the surface, the unreconstructed rebel's response at seeing a Yankee general's picture in the state capitol was not unlike Mississippi's gut reaction to the impending crisis of change. As Governor Coleman's four-year term neared its end, plans were already underway to commemorate the centennial of the Civil War. Such famous old and almost forgotten battlefields as Brice's Crossroads, Champion's Hill, and Newton Station would be refurbished and revisited in the early 1960s. But there would also be new battlefields—like Oxford, Meridian, and Canton. Few people were aware that the Civil War centennial and the civil rights movement were on a collision course. It certainly did not seem that way during the gubernatorial campaign of 1959. Making his third consecutive bid for the state's highest office, Ross R. Barnett defeated Carroll Gartin in a run-off election by a margin of almost 40,000 votes.

Throughout the campaign Ross Barnett promised to keep the door of his capitol office open and the door to white schools closed to Negroes. He kept the first promise but not the other. During the first four months of his administration, Barnett's receptionist logged over 18,000 visitors to the governor's office in the capitol. But during his last summer in office, a Mississippi Negro graduated from the University of Mississippi.[10] The racial barrier to Mississippi's traditionally all-white public school system had been broken.

Although not a campaign promise, but more as a result of his congenial and gregarious nature, Governor Barnett maintained a similar though statistically less astounding policy of open house at the mansion. During his four-year residency, approximately 35,000 visitors toured the executive residence.[11]

Governor Barnett and the first lady, the former Pearl Crawford of Jackson, anticipated living in the mansion and occupied the downtown residence with eagerness. The Barnett family had lived in Jackson for many years, and the governor recalled with fondness the excitement his family experienced when, after three strenuous campaigns, they finally

And the Walls Came Tumbling Down

realized their life-long dream of "living in the big white house on Capitol Street." The Barnett family occupied the state rooms in the historic portion of the mansion, reserving the bedrooms in the family quarters for guests or family members who often visited in the mansion.[12]

Extensive preparation for the inaugural reception made it one of the most elaborate in recent years. Governor and Mrs. Barnett, along with Lieutenant Governor and Mrs. Paul B. Johnson, Jr., received over 3,000 visitors who filed through the gold room, then into the Music Room, the state dining room, and finally overflowed onto the mansion grounds.

Although the Barnetts' children, a son and two daughters, were married and did not permanently reside in the executive residence, they frequently visited the mansion for Sunday dinner and holidays. Sundays were always special days at the mansion and often attracted prominent guests, including such diverse and distinguished visitors as Governor Elbert Carvel of Delaware, Alabama Governor George C. Wallace, and Edward Teller. When the legislature was in session, Governor Barnett usually held Sunday afternoon conferences with key House and Senate leaders to discuss the legislation that would be considered during the coming week. Sundays were also special days for less famous guests who visited the mansion. On the fourth Sunday in April, 1960, the governor invited a sacred harp association to hold its regular fourth Sunday "all day singing and dinner on the ground" at the historical Mississippi executive mansion. A Barnett family reunion, held on Sunday, August 7, 1960, brought more than 300 of the first family's relatives to the mansion for a picnic on the very grounds where Grant's soldiers had bivouacked almost one hundred years earlier.[13]

Perhaps more than any of his predecessors, certainly in the twentieth century, Barnett's residency illustrated the public character of the executive mansion. While the Barnetts lived there it was truly the "people's mansion." Within the same week the governor and first lady might entertain wealthy northern industrialists and local taxi drivers, each with equal ease. When the governor's son brought home several of his college friends who had found themselves snowed-in and unable to leave Jackson, they were cordially and openly received by the governor and first lady. That some of them may have had to sleep on the floor did not detract from their excitement at spending the night in the governor's mansion.

A History of the Mississippi Governor's Mansion

As one of the last great stump orators on the Mississippi political scene, Governor Barnett was in great demand and often seemed at his best when addressing a hostile audience. He often found such audiences on various speaking tours, which took him to forty-seven colleges and universities throughout the country. To the student audiences he always issued a standing invitation to visit him at the governor's mansion in Jackson. Barnett was as genuine as he was controversial, as a college student from Utah discovered on a hitch-hiking trip across the country. Appearing at the mansion's front steps one day with his pack and camping gear, the student announced that Governor Barnett had invited him to the mansion when the Governor spoke in Utah sometime earlier—he received the traditional mansion welcome. After spending a week at the mansion as the official guest of the governor of Mississippi, the young man resumed his cross-country jaunt.[14]

Perhaps the most unusual, and certainly the shortest, residency in the mansion's history occurred during the Barnett administration. When both the governor and lieutenant governor are out of the state, the president pro tempore of the Senate serves as acting governor. In June, 1961, Governor Barnett and Lieutenant Governor Paul Johnson were attending the National Governors' Conference in Honolulu. During their absence, Senator George Yarborough and his family, with the prior agreement and encouragement of Governor Barnett, occupied the governor's mansion for a few days. Although short, the residency was a special delight to the senator's twin sons.[15]

There also occurred during the Barnett residency the most extensive renovation since 1908 and the sharpest controversy in the building's history. The renovation, costing approximately $302,724.80, included both interior redecoration and beautification of the grounds. For several years the first families had complained of leaking pipes, falling plaster, cracking walls, sagging doors, outmoded appliances, broken furniture, soiled drapes, and worn carpets. Although considerable funds had been expended for mansion repair, especially during the Fielding Wright residency, most of the work was largely of an emergency nature and did not resolve the most serious problems which had increasingly made the mansion less accommodating. Shortly after Barnett's inauguration, the

And the Walls Came Tumbling Down

first lady requested the Building Committee to inspect the mansion to assess its overall condition and to consider a major renovation. A subcommittee of the commission responded to Mrs. Barnett's request, and over the next several months plans were formulated to correct the most serious defects in the building which was then almost one-hundred-twenty years old.[16]

Part of the 1961 project included the installation of an outdoor lighting system designed to minimize glare while highlighting the beauty of the natural setting in which the mansion was located. The system and its effects were acclaimed by a Keep Jackson Beautiful Workshop which was held in the capital city on May 5, 1961. In addition to the outdoor lighting system, grounds improvement also included resodding, landscaping, and resurfacing of all driveways and sidewalks on the grounds. That perennial item, repair of the roof, also appeared in the contract specifications, as did the repainting of the exterior walls.[17]

The most costly feature of the 1961 renovation was interior redecoration, which included some repair of every room in the mansion. Several rooms were recarpeted or repainted. Moldings and cornices were repaired in practically every room, and many of the mansion's antique furnishings were restored. One of the largest single expenditures was the installation of a new kitchen with all the modern appliances. The old kitchen equipment was retained and moved into the basement. The only structural changes which affected the physical appearance of the building was the removal of the screen porch from the porte-cochere which Governor Bilbo had added during his first residency.[18]

The large expenditure for mansion renovation prompted considerable comment from Governor Barnett's political opponents and from the press in general. Objections were raised first to the amount of the expenditure and then to the fact that no itemized account was made available. Only $24,683 of the $302,724 appropriation had been done on a contract basis, with the remaining portion allocated on a cost plus basis. Several newsmen and at least one prominent legislator complained that their efforts to secure detailed information from the Building Commission proved futile. They were told that all records and accounts for the mansion project had been transferred to the governor's office. But when they sought the information from the governor's office they were told that the records were not in that office.[19]

After the controversy had raged for some time, Governor Barnett and the first lady invited newsmen to tour the mansion on Saturday, September 15, 1961, to see the work that had been done. With representatives of the various contractors on hand, the first family led the newsmen from room to room explaining in detail the improvements and repairs that had been made.[20] When the group inspected the new $28,750 kitchen, Governor Barnett opened the sparsely stocked refrigerator and jokingly remarked to the reporters, "See, we haven't got very much to eat." As the entourage moved gradually and slowly from one room to another, a sense of anticipation swelled as they neared the single most publicized aspect of the renovation project—the gold bathroom.

The disclosure of an expenditure of $10,000 for a new bathroom with gold fixtures had unleashed a torrent of comment and provoked a controversy unparalleled in the mansion's history. An article in the Jackson *State Times* was typical of the press reaction to the news about the bathroom. According to "reliable sources," the paper reported, the states of Louisiana and Alabama had secret agents in Mississippi trying to pirate the plans for the mansion's gold bathroom. Rumors were circulating, said the *Jackson Daily News*, that when the president of Standard Oil had recently visited the governor's mansion he "had occasion to use the new facility and a few minutes later a commitment was made to 'Ole Ross' to build a $125 million oil refinery in the state."[21] Both Louisiana and Alabama had been hopeful of landing the new industry.

The glamorous gold bathroom proved a disappointment to the newsmen. One reporter confessed that he had anticipated, on the basis of all the publicity, a scene of opulence that would excite the envy of a Byzantine monarch. Instead, he found that the rather small room was tastefully decorated with gold-plated fixtures and marble floors. The faucets on the lavatory and the tub-shower combination were not, as he expected, solid gold. The marble dressing table was trimmed in gold and the mirror above the table was edged in gold leaf. Governor Barnett, after admonishing the reporters, "I wish you fellows would quit saying it is *my* bathroom," pointed out the gold bathroom was not for his personal use since it was located about one hundred feet from his bedroom. The governor used the

And the Walls Came Tumbling Down

famous Bilbo suite and showed newsmen the less conspicuous facility adjacent to his room.

Although the controversy over the gold bathroom and the renovation of the mansion waned, there were other matters of concern, more pressing and perilous, that did not subside. On March 28, 1961, Governor Barnett, dressed in a Confederate uniform and standing in front of Mississippi's antebellum governor's mansion, reviewed 6,000 Confederate-clad marchers in a reenactment of a typical Civil War parade of troops. The two-hour parade drew thousands of excited and cheering onlookers who in the midst of the most serious and dramatic challenge to the state's racial and social customs since the 1860s paused to recall the glories of former times.[22]

Only the day before and just a block away, there had been another parade, but in the language of the sixties it was called a demonstration. A group of Jackson State University students were demonstrating against the jailing of several black Tougaloo students who had been arrested for attempting to use the Jackson public library. Among the students then enrolled at Jackson State was James Howard Meredith. A month after Governor Barnett "reviewed the troops," Meredith filed suit in federal court seeking admission to the University of Mississippi.

Throughout the long legal battle which the state of Mississippi waged in 1961 and 1962 to prevent James Meredith's admission to the University of Mississippi, the governor's mansion often became a command post in which the strategy of resistance was conceived and from which orders were issued to carry out that strategy. The socio-political climate which produced this resistance was described by a federal judge as an "eerie atmosphere of never-never land."

Even after the United States Supreme Court had ordered the University to admit Meredith and even after Governor Ross Barnett had yielded to that inevitability, the antebellum mansion again became the focus of resistance.

Following the Supreme Court's decree dated September 10, 1962, Governor Barnett and his advisors began negotiations with Attorney General Robert F. Kennedy for the admission of Meredith in a manner that would be the most palatable to the majority of Mississippians and in a manner not to provoke violence. It was finally agreed that Meredith would be brought to the Oxford campus and registered on Monday morning, September 31. However, at the last minute those plans were slightly but significantly altered.

During the early morning hours of Sunday, September 30, plans were already underway to bring Meredith to the campus the following day. However, by mid-morning a small crowd began gathering at the mansion in Jackson. Cars were driving aimlessly around the mansion square—blaring their horns as directed by a Jackson radio station. Inside, Governor Barnett huddled with a four-man task force he would later send to Oxford. Across the street from the mansion, occupants of the Citizens' Council office appeared at the windows waving Confederate flags to the crowd below. Excitement, like the crowd, was building.

Alarmed by the intensity of the demonstration, Governor Barnett placed a call to Robert Kennedy urging him to postpone Meredith's enrollment. When Kennedy refused, Barnett then suggested that it might be better to bring Meredith to the campus later that afternoon rather than the next day since the campus would be practically deserted following a football weekend in Jackson. Finally, this plan was agreed upon and orders were issued to the contingent of federal marshals at Memphis to accompany Meredith to Oxford that afternoon.

As the transport planes were preparing for the short flight to Oxford, the ominous news was flashed to Jackson—"Planes full of marshals heading South!" It had already been rumored through the crowd at the mansion that marshals would soon appear to arrest Governor Barnett. This latest news prompted a Jackson radio station to interrupt its regular program with a bulletin from the Citizens' Council urging the station's listeners to go to the mansion. Simultaneously, an official in the Citizens' Council headquarters used a hand-held amplifier to direct the crowd: "Take your places around the sidewalks of the Governor's Mansion. Don't let anyone through." Soon, a wall of flesh numbering more than 2,000 people ranging from carpenters to college professors ringed the mansion and shouted defiance.

Inside the mansion, it occurred to Tom Watkins, one of the governor's advisors, that university officials should be advised that Meredith would arrive on the campus that afternoon rather than Monday morning. At 3:30 the telephone rang in Chancellor John D. Williams' study where he

And the Walls Came Tumbling Down

and several other university officials were planning for Meredith's enrollment which, according to their latest information, was scheduled for the next morning.

Following this phone call, the focal point of the Meredith crisis shifted swiftly and dramatically from the mansion in Jackson to the Lyceum at Oxford. The university's administration building, the Lyceum was designed in the grand style of Greek Revival architecture and built during the late 1840s. Like the mansion, the Lyceum was designed by William Nichols and was symbolic of Mississippi's past—"a past that would not die."

The marshals who had been expected at the mansion, began appearing at the Lyceum in late afternoon. An angry crowd soon surrounded that historic building. By nightfall, the crowd had become a mob. Following a night of rioting, James Meredith enrolled at the University of Mississippi early the next morning.[23]

In August, 1963, James Meredith climaxed his "three years in Mississippi" by graduating from Ole Miss. In that same month Paul B. Johnson, Jr., erased the disappointment of three previous defeats by winning a run-off election against former governor J. P. Coleman and then defeating his Republican opponent, Rubel Phillips, in the general election. Except for the 1947 Republican candidate, who received only 4,102 votes, it was the first time since 1881 that a Republican gubernatorial candidate had entered the state's general election.

As a courtesy to his successor, Governor Barnett vacated the executive residence before the end of his term to allow the governor-elect and his family to settle themselves in the mansion before the inaugural ceremonies.

When Paul B. Johnson, Jr. took the oath of office on January 21, 1964, he became the only son of a former chief executive to succeed his father to the state's highest office. He also became governor during Mississippi's most difficult years, at least in the twentieth century. The mansion's guest list over the next four years reflected the tenor of those times. The winds of change which had buffeted the mansion during the forties were prevailing in the sixties. Mississippi would either seek shelter in its past as it had done so often before, or it would weather the storm.

In his inaugural address, Governor Johnson advised Mississippians of their only viable option. "You and I are part of this world," he said, "whether we like it or not. . . . We are Americans as well as Mississippians." After assuring his audience that "hate, prejudice, and ignorance will not lead Mississippi," Johnson offered an alternative. "If I must fight, it will not be a rear guard defense of yesterday. It will be an all out assault of our share of tomorrow." He concluded, "God bless everyone of you, all Mississippians, black and white, here and away from home."[24] Over the next four years Governor Johnson led the ship of state through some rather stormy seas; but proving herself seaworthy, Mississippi adjusted to change and continues the assault on her share of the future, with enthusiasm.

When Governor Johnson and the first lady, Dorothy Power of Red Banks, and their three children returned to the governor's mansion in 1964 it was like a homecoming. That historic mansion had already played an important part in their lives. The governor and first lady were married in the mansion in 1941 and had lived there for a short time during Governor Johnson, Sr.'s administration. Their oldest daughter, Patricia, had lived in the mansion while her father was in basic training at a Marine base on the West Coast. In February, 1966, Paul and Dorothy Johnson celebrated their twenty-fifth wedding anniversary in the same room in which they had been married.[25]

The Johnson children and the first lady's mother, who also lived in the mansion, occupied the family quarters in the annex. The governor and his wife used the bedrooms in the historical portion. The Johnsons were a closely knit family and reactivated the use of the patio in the rear of the mansion for barbecues and family cookouts on those rare occasions when the governor enjoyed a night at home. Christmas and Thanksgiving at the mansion were special days which were often enlivened by the presence of the former first lady, Mrs. Paul Johnson, Sr., who frequently visited her son during the early years of his administration. On one of those visits the former first lady was greeted by an excited granddaughter who showed her a baby bed she had found in the attic. It was the one Patricia had used many years earlier when living with her grandmother in the mansion.[26]

For the first time in many years, the first family consisted of several teenagers, and the mansion's social calendar reflected that fact. Patricia was then a student at Belhaven College in Jackson and frequently brought

And the Walls Came Tumbling Down

her friends home from school. On one occasion when the Belhaven baseball team got in a jam, she and a few volunteers brought the team's uniforms to the mansion for emergency cleaning. They were washed in the mansion's famous gold bathroom. On several other occasions, two in particular, "Tish" was the focus of gala social affairs at the mansion. Tish's formal presentation was made at a debutante ball at the mansion, and on April 4, 1965, she was married in the same west parlor which had been the scene of her parents' wedding almost twenty-five years earlier.[27]

Through its 125-year history, the mansion had been the scene of many gala social affairs—levees, soirees, Germans, receptions, and formal state dinners. The mansion's social history has been an index to the changing customs and traditions of a hospitable people. So it was only natural that the traditions of the sixties would be reflected by social events at the mansion. The Johnsons' two sons, Shelby and Chipper (Paul B., III), students at Central High School, organized and carried off a highly successful "sock hop" complete with drums, guitars, organ, and amplifiers (which according to Governor Johnson was, next to television, modern technology's worst achievement). About forty students and three teachers attended the dance which was conducted under the students' own system of crowd control. Each person invited to the dance was given a slip of paper which gained admission to the mansion and which must be surrendered to the doorkeeper upon leaving the party. Several "crashers" were turned away. While the teenagers were enjoying their sock hop at the mansion, a few blocks down the street at the city auditorium Guy Lombardo was entertaining a much larger audience but with much less volume.[28]

Like most first families before them, the Johnsons had the usual menagerie of pets, including several blue tick hounds for which special kennels were built in the rear of the mansion, a poodle named Superdog, a Heinz variety pooch named Billy Sunday Harper but known affectionately to the family as Sunday, and a German shepherd named Max. The governor and Chipper were also quite fond of riding and often slipped out to a Jackson stable to enjoy an early morning or late afternoon ride in solitude and quiet.

By the mid-1960s family privacy at the mansion was virtually nonexistent. For several years first families had observed clerks and secretaries in neighboring high-rise office buildings using binoculars to observe the activities of mansion residents. As the city's population leaped from 98,271 in 1950 to 144,442 in 1960, there was a corresponding rise in the noise level in downtown Jackson. Since the mansion is located in the heart of the downtown banking district, the first family was sometimes aroused in the middle of the night by the sound of burglar alarms. When an amateur thief activated an alarm at a jewelry store a few doors down Capitol Street, he ran through the mansion grounds in hurried escape. No doubt he was as startled as he was disappointed when he was intercepted by a security agent assigned to the mansion.[29]

After the Old Capitol Museum became a favorite of school children throughout the state, busloads of sightseers ranging from first-graders to graduate students daily tromped through its corridors. They frequently added a tour of the mansion to their agenda after arriving at Jackson. To the credit of all of Mississippi's first families, there is no evidence on record that any group has been denied the opportunity of seeing and touring the mansion. However, beyond the matter of privacy, tourists posed another and possibly more serious problem. Mrs. Gladys Seeley, who served as official mansion hostess for three first families, became acutely aware of the security problem at the mansion during the 1960s as sightseers also became souvenir seekers. In spite of all she could do to prevent it, many visitors acted upon the compulsion to take some memento or reminder of their visit and many small articles disappeared over the years. Even some dinner guests were not averse to taking an ash tray, a butter knife, or other small articles which could be easily concealed.[30]

Dinner at the mansion has always been a special treat to many Mississippians. Its famous dinners are usually conducted with an apparent charm that belies the sometimes frantic activity that occurs behind the scene. The use of convict labor as domestic servants has frequently elicited comment from distinguished visitors to the executive mansion, who have unfailingly commended the dignified and graceful manner in which the inmates performed their duties. But as most first ladies had learned, sometimes the hard way, there was a learning period to be endured before that expertise could be developed. The Johnsons' first family dinner at the mansion came during such a period. Dorothy Johnson, a culinarian in her own right and an author of the well-known

And the Walls Came Tumbling Down

cookbook *Dinner With Dot*, ordered oyster stew for the family's first private dinner after occupying the mansion. To her dismay and the impatience of her family, the dish was prepared in the manner of beef stew. After cutting the oysters, the cook chopped onion and carrots, added potatoes, boiled the stew and shortly served the family in the state dining room. Graciously, the first lady suggested the proper steps for preparing the fresh Gulf oysters. While the family reminisced, probably about the long road to victory, the cook prepared a second serving according to Mrs. Johnson's instructions. After dinner, the gardener, who had been pressed into domestic service due to illness of one of the other cooks, appeared at the door and announced, "We's got banana pudden' for dessert; how many ya'll wants it?"[31]

Despite the small problems endemic to the use of inmates as domestic servants and after the trial period had passed, the first family found the system highly satisfactory. During the Johnson residency all but two of the nine inmates initially assigned to the mansion remained for the full four years, and all of them were pardoned at the expiration of the governor's term. One of the servants working at the mansion when the Johnsons left office was asked to remain with the family and moved to Hattiesburg where she continued in the employ of the Johnson family for many years. Whatever the problems of using prison labor at the mansion may have been, recidivism among those inmates was practically zero. According to Martin Fraley, chairman of the Mississippi Probation and Parole Board, no inmate who had served at the governor's mansion and received an executive pardon had returned to Parchman.[32]

After the initial period of adjustment the servants become much more confident and secure, which is fortunate because their skills were often tested. As an example, the governor telephoned the mansion at six o'clock one evening to advise the first lady that Allen Dulles and several other guests would stay over for dinner. At seven-thirty a formal dinner for eighteen in the state dining room was carried off without a hitch—all this in spite of the crisis occasioned by the birth of puppies occurring simultaneously in a more remote part of the mansion.[33]

The most formal dinner during the Johnsons' residency, and a unique one in the long list of notable dinners in the mansion's history, was the state dinner held in honor of the governor and first lady of Yucatan on

A History of the Mississippi Governor's Mansion

May 27, 1964. Governor Luis Torres y Mesias was visiting Jackson on a trade mission in May, 1964. He also was honored at a public reception attended by 100 of Mississippi's most prominent political and business leaders. The state dinner for the governor and first lady of Yucatan marked the only occasion when a chief executive of a foreign territory visited the mansion.[34]

Among the other distinguished visitors to the mansion during the Johnson residency were Governors Jimmie Davis and John McKeithen of Louisiana, Governor and Mrs. George Wallace, and Governor Orval Faubus of Arkansas. In addition, J. Edgar Hoover, who was in Jackson to formally open a new FBI office in the city, was also honored at a reception in the mansion.[35]

After the renovation of the mansion under the previous administration, the Johnson family found the building in rather good condition. Some structural problems remained, however, and additional work was done during their occupancy. On the day of Johnson's inaugural reception, which attracted several thousand visitors, someone noticed that the chandelier in the west parlor occasionally shimmered, sometimes enough to rattle the glass ornaments. It was later discovered that the massive fixture was suspended by a badly worn cord and chain which could have broken at any time. That problem was no sooner corrected, however, than still another one developed. A pipe in an upstairs bathroom burst, causing extensive water damage. Because of the notoriety attached to the redecoration of the gold bathroom, both the first family and the Building Commission were inclined to repair the break rather than replace the faulty pipe. It was finally decided, however, that the short-term repair would not be wise, so the plumbing system in the bath was replaced and a clothes closet was also added. The linen closet down the hall, which the first lady had been using as a clothes closet, was then reconverted to its original use. Other than this redecoration, very little was done to the mansion while the Johnsons were in residence. A few pieces of furniture, mainly tables and chairs and a rug for the second floor sitting room, were purchased and several antique pieces were refinished.[36]

The only structural addition during the Johnson residency was the construction of a garage apartment for the security personnel stationed at the mansion. Prior to this addition, the highway patrolmen lived in cramped quarters on the lower floor of the annex. Their quarters did not include kitchen facilities, a sitting room, or shower facilities. As the number of security men increased, this additional space became imperative.

The growing concern for security at the mansion and the increase of the personnel assigned for that purpose were a response to the turbulence taking place in the streets of American cities. Paul Johnson's administration coincided with a crescendo in civil rights activity and its spin-off of violence. Although violence and even death often attended the struggle of Mississippi Negroes to achieve equality of opportunity, Governor Paul Johnson provided a constructive leadership which enabled Mississippi to adjust to the sweeping changes of the 1960s. But unlike the state, which had the worst behind it by 1968, the mansion would face a crisis in the late 1960s which threatened its very existence. Though the turbulence of racial readjustment was diminishing, the controversy about the mansion was mounting.

Early in 1967, when the political climate was heating up in anticipation of the summer primaries, the executive mansion was "deluged with a flood of letters, telegrams and telephone calls" urging the first lady to announce as a candidate for governor in the primary elections. For what must have been the mansion's most unusual press conference, Dorothy Johnson invited the state press to the mansion on February 9, 1967. She read a statement in response to the requests that she become a surrogate candidate for her husband, as Mrs. George Wallace had recently done with success. In her statement to the press she said, "I am realistic enough, however, to know that the enthusiasm for my candidacy constitutes a tribute to my husband's administration as governor during the crucial three years just passed." She then confessed that she was anxious to return to Hattiesburg and private life after the expiration of the governor's term.[37]

Even if Mrs. Johnson did not relish the idea of running for governor, there were others who certainly did. The Democratic campaign of 1967 attracted a field of seven candidates including one former governor and one future governor, Ross Barnett and Bill Waller. The eventual winner was John Bell Williams, who had for the last twenty years represented the Fourth Congressional District in the United States Congress.

A History of the Mississippi Governor's Mansion

Shortly after his inauguration in January, 1968, Governor Williams occupied the executive mansion; but his family did not join him until his two young sons completed their school year in Washington. After his family joined him in the summer of 1968, the Williams family moved into the private quarters in the 1908 annex. From the very beginning of their residency, the first family experienced the inconvenience of living in the sixty-year-old annex. Governor Williams, however, was concerned more about his family's safety than the inconvenience posed by the mansion's antiquated living arrangement.[38]

The governor and the first lady, the former Elizabeth Ann Wells, occupied the bedrooms on the east side of the annex and their sons used the ones across the wide hallway dividing the annex. Although a sprinkler system had been installed during Governor Johnson's term, there was no fire alarm and no outside fire escape in the family section of the mansion. The potential dangers confronting the first family in an emergency evacuation of the mansion induced the governor to add those safety mechanisms during the first few months of his residency. The addition of those systems, however, only reduced but did not eliminate the dangers of living in a 130-year-old structure which, as later investigation revealed, was in need of substantial repair.

Like their predecessors, the Williams family had their favorite pets, including cats and dogs. But an unusual addition to the mansion's menagerie was made during their occupancy. Someone, in a practical joke directed against one of the patrolmen assigned to the mansion, left two rabbits at the security apartment. Soon thereafter, the governor was forced to seek approval of the State Building Commission to construct additional facilities to accommodate the burgeoning population. Eventually, to the delight of several of the governor's young friends, new homes were found for the mansion's rabbit population.[39]

There also occurred during the Williams residency an incident significant in its rarity. During an altercation between two of the servants, a male prisoner received a knife wound which resulted in his death. This was the only incident of its kind in the mansion's history.[40]

Like most of her predecessors, the first lady had her favorite projects and interests. Mrs. Williams gave a great deal of her time and energy to promoting the improvement of mental health care in Mississippi. Considering herself more a dreamer than a reformer, the first lady toured most of the health care institutions throughout the state and advocated the modernization of both the physical facilities and rehabilitation techniques. The state has profited significantly from her interest. The establishment of regional health care centers and the emphasis upon preventive techniques which are now characteristic of the state's mental health program bear the mark of her efforts.[41]

Although having abandoned an earlier inclination to pursue a theatrical career, the first lady maintained a lively interest in both the performing and creative arts. Her close association with the Mississippi Arts Festival accounts for the large number of celebrities appearing on the mansion's guest list during her residency. The list included such premier performers as Jack Benny, Joan Crawford, Hal Holbrook, Ernie Ford, Harry James, Phil Harris, the Lennon Sisters, Celeste Holm, and many others.[42]

These distinguished guests, as well as other visitors to the mansion, were greeted by the first family at the back door on rainy days since there was no drive to the mansion's main entrance. The guests' rain apparel was then placed in the mansion's most famous closet, a metal pipe extended between wooden frames built of two-by-fours. These embarrassing circumstances prompted Governor Williams to recommend the construction of a paved driveway fronting the mansion. However, when those plans were disclosed to the public in April of 1968, there was such vocal opposition that the project was delayed for almost two years. The state president of the Garden Clubs of Mississippi declared that the proposed driveway would "ruin the looks" of the "beautiful grounds." Going one step further, the president of the local garden club protested that the drive would "ruin the appearance of the Mansion" itself. Letters, telegrams, telephone calls, and personal pleas were sufficient to forestall the implementation of the proposal.[43]

During the general debate over the addition of the drive, other issues were also injected into the controversy. The long-standing consideration of relocating the mansion in a Jackson residential section resurfaced. Since the 1940s the proposal had been periodically advanced, but always met resistance. Governor Williams revived the proposal on August 8, 1969, at a meeting of the State Building Commission. After pointing out the security problems associated with the downtown residence and re-

A History of the Mississippi Governor's Mansion

viewing a long list of needed repairs to the existing structure, he asked the commission to consider the feasibility of building a new executive residence and redesignating the mansion as a historical museum. The first lady had several months earlier noted the condition of the mansion in an interview with a local reporter. On February 6, 1969, Mrs. Williams answered questions cautiously about her plans to redecorate the historical mansion. Pointing out that the residence was a very old building which required constant attention and upkeep, the first lady disclosed that many problems existed in the structure but that she had no definite plans at that time nor would she make specific recommendations for repair or redecoration until the mansion's future was decided.[44]

The possibility of disposing of the historic mansion prompted extensive comment in the state press, particularly in the Jackson papers. The reaction in 1969 was remarkably similar to that of 1908. A columnist for the *Clarion-Ledger* confessed that she was "assailed by a sense of history . . . [and] once upon a time" whenever she entered the mansion. She urged all of those who loved history and revered the past to vocalize their objections to turning the mansion into a museum. The writer even compared the disposal of the mansion with the "federal government's tendency to give away our strategic holdings around the world," which she confessed was a "mystery to most common sense Americans."[45]

The approbation the Building Commission may have gained by its decision to preserve the mansion as the official executive residence was soon lost in the public uproar which greeted its decision to build a fence around the mansion square. Following a study of the security arrangements at the Texas and Georgia governor's mansions, the commission authorized the construction of an enclosure similar to the wrought iron fence that had been added to the mansion in 1855. Garden clubs, civic groups, newspapers, and especially those on the other side of the fence politically, were even more vocal in their opposition to the fence than they had been to the driveway. Despite the uproar, security considerations prevailed and a low bid contract of $125,775 was awarded to a Jackson firm on July 8, 1970. Construction began shortly afterwards.[46]

When the enclosure was completed in February, 1971, the public was generally pleased, and even some of the project's major detractors admit-

And the Walls Came Tumbling Down

ted that the fence was an attractive addition. Their change of sentiment followed a tea which the first lady held in November, 1970, for the board members of the Keep Jackson Beautiful organization and for representatives of other local clubs. At that time construction was well underway, and Mrs. Williams was able to show the visitors how the enclosure would complement the architectural style of the mansion. She also pointed out that the driveway, which had become one phase of the new construction, would be unobtrusive and would not require the removal of any trees or shrubbery.[47]

The first lady had not invited the group to the mansion to review the progress of the fence, however. They were there for another purpose, a much more significant one. Two months before their tour of the mansion and grounds, Mrs. Williams had addressed a board meeting of Keep Jackson Beautiful. At that meeting she disclosed the fact that the mansion was in a serious state of disrepair and required major structural renovation. Her address provoked a great deal of interest and some skepticism. The tendency toward cosmetic repair since 1908 had allowed structural deterioration to go unnoticed and thus uncorrected. However, this fact was not generally known and visitors to the mansion did not observe the structural damage since the first ladies had usually gone to great lengths to make the mansion attractive.

To allay any skepticism, Mrs. Williams conducted her visitors on a room-by-room tour during which she carefully pointed out the most serious defects. Most of the group were convinced that the mansion's condition did in fact require an immediate and major renovation. Shortly after this tour, the Building Commission authorized an architectural firm to prepare plans for renovation of the original structure and an addition to the 1908 annex. The specifications estimated that at least $1.2 million would be needed for the renovation and addition.[48]

However, the disclosure of these plans sparked still more debate. A consensus on what to do about the mansion seemed more remote than ever. After several articles of conflicting assessments appeared in the local press, Carl McIntyre, Sunday editor of the *Clarion Ledger-Jackson Daily News*, toured the building and reported his findings in a February 3, 1971, article under the title "Mansion Crumbling." McIntyre indicated that most reports about the condition of the mansion were understatements rather than exaggerations. He considered the $1.2 million expenditure a small sum to preserve one of the city's outstanding landmarks.

Since there were several prominent political figures and even some members of the press who were still not convinced that the condition of the building required such a large outlay, the Building Commission authorized a Jackson engineering firm to conduct a safety inspection of the mansion. The inspection was made at the suggestion of Governor Williams, who was becoming even more concerned for the safety of his family, servants, and the hundreds of visitors who were touring the mansion daily. On July 8, 1971, the results of that inspection were presented to the Building Commission. The findings shocked both the commission and the general public. The safety report indicated that the mansion's structural condition was unsound and its continued occupancy unsafe. The governor and his family were advised to evacuate the mansion. A week after the report was made, Governor Williams invited the state press to tour the building. During this tour, which lasted for several hours, he pointed out the major findings of the safety engineers. He showed the faulty wiring which the report had singled out as a special safety hazard. He noted the open stairwells which could funnel a fire from the main floor to the second story in a matter of seconds. Additionally, Governor Williams pointed to the exposed and leaking pipes, loose and crumbling mortar, leaking gas lines, sagging and leaning walls. He invited the press to hang their hats in the mansion's famous closet.[49]

A few days after this tour, which was conducted on July 15, 1971, Governor Williams and his family vacated the Mississippi executive mansion. This action was taken during the heat of summer primaries. As might be expected, the mansion and its future use as an official residence were injected into the campaign.

CHAPTER XI

Home of Our Heritage

MISSISSIPPI GUBERNATORIAL campaigns are generally over by August since, for the last hundred years or so, the Democratic party has experienced only token opposition in the general elections. However, in 1971 (as in 1963 and 1967) opposition candidates stretched the campaign into the fall. In this respect the 1971 governor's race was not unusual; but what did make the contest unique was one of the entrants. For the first time in Mississippi's often tumultuous political history, a Negro ran for the state's highest office. Charles Evers, mayor of Fayette and brother of the slain civil rights activist Medgar Evers, conducted an active though losing campaign against William L. Waller. During that historic contest, the fate of the governor's mansion became a minor although persistent issue.

Both William Waller and the future first lady, Carroll Waller, promised not only to preserve the governor's mansion as one of the state's oldest and most admired landmarks, but also to restore it to its past splendor. At a speech in Prentiss on October 12, 1971, Mrs. Waller briefly outlined the mansion's history and called upon Mississippi women to "come to the rescue of the Governor's Mansion and help secure the . . . restoration that is befitting this historic and rich home of our heritage."[1] The future of Mississippi's most famous home, then vacant and dilapidated, was again in jeopardy as it had been several times before. Bill Waller, fully endorsing his wife's effort to save the mansion, also promised during the campaign that his family would live in the official executive residence if he were elected governor.

A month after his election, Governor-elect Waller met with the members of the State Building Commission on December 16 at a special

A History of the Mississippi Governor's Mansion

meeting called by Governor Williams. During that meeting, Governor Williams detailed the condition of the 130-year-old residence which he had vacated five months earlier, and outlined the alternatives available to the Building Commission. The choices were basically the same as those discussed by Governor Noel over sixty years earlier, when he had urged the legislature not to dispose of the mansion. Governor Williams first suggested that a new mansion could be constructed in a residential area. But he did not consider that action a likely alternative since a similar proposal had met such strong public opposition when it was raised earlier in his administration. Secondly, the mansion could be made livable by correcting its major structural defects. Some of the safety hazards could be eliminated by installing a new mechanical system. Again, however, Governor Williams discounted this proposal because such stop-gap measures would merely delay the major repairs that must be done eventually. Finally, Williams advised the commission that the wisest course of action, and the only one he could conscientiously endorse, was a major renovation of the existing structure.[2]

Governor-elect Waller concurred in that recommendation and assured the Building Commission that he would do everything he could to support its effort to secure legislative authorization for the mansion project. The commission agreed unanimously to submit a request to the legislature seeking approval and allocation of funds to restore the Mississippi executive mansion. A subcommittee was appointed to locate a temporary residence to be used by the first family while the restoration was in progress. At the same meeting, Waller noted the lack of any standard procedure for the identification and preservation of the furnishings in the mansion. He reminded the commission that there had often been some confusion about mansion furnishings. Especially in times of political strife, various governors had been accused of taking state property from the executive residence when they left office. Waller suggested that a catalog of the furnishings be taken at the beginning and at the end of each new administration to eliminate this problem. The commission readily agreed, and in its request for authorization to restore the mansion also asked the legislature to establish such a procedure. Subsequently, a law was passed which placed the original mansion and its historical furnishings under the administration of the Mississippi Department of Archives

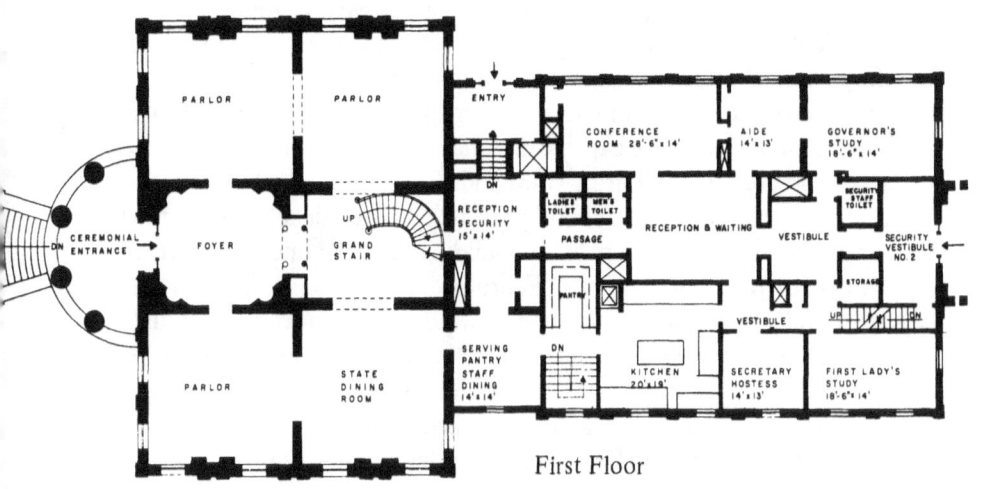

First Floor

Second Floor

A History of the Mississippi Governor's Mansion

and History.[3] Throughout the three-and-a-half-year restoration, this department worked closely with the architects and contractors to maintain the historical integrity of the original mansion.

In preparation for its initial request for legislative approval, the Building Commission, under the capable direction of James Chastain, authorized a Jackson architectural firm, Ware and Lewis, to conduct a preliminary evaluation of the mansion's condition and prepare a detailed cost estimate for a complete restoration of the building. The architect's report, presented to the commission on February 7, 1972, outlined the general deterioration and structural fatigue which had rendered the building unsafe. Interior walls showed a differential settlement in the order of 1-½ inches, and the bond in several foundation walls was lost. Bricks and mortar could easily be separated or raked with no more than a pocket knife. Floor framing and joists had also deteriorated considerably, both from wet and dry rot.[4]

In addition to noting structural damage, the report also detailed the lack of storage space and the inconvenient arrangement of the kitchen facilities which were located some distance from the food storage areas. The family quarters were considered functionally inadequate to accommodate an average family of four. Exposed pipes and loosely hanging electrical wiring were found throughout the 1908 annex. It was also determined that the spacious hallways connecting the state rooms in the historic portion with the upstairs family rooms seriously compromised the first family's privacy.[5]

The mechanical system, barely meeting minimum standards, was judged antiquated, dilapidated, and inadequate. The most serious deficiencies, other than structural deterioration, were found in the electrical, heating, and plumbing systems which required almost complete replacement.[6] This preliminary evaluation was made in consultation with Dr. R. A. McLemore, director of the Department of Archives and History, Miss Charlotte Capers, chief executor for the Mansion Project at the Department of Archives and History, and Mississippi's first lady.

After studying the preliminary report, the Building Commission on February 17, 1972, officially appointed Ware and Lewis architects for the restoration of the mansion and authorized the firm to prepare full-scale specifications for the project. On the same day the Department of Archives was given the responsibility for acquisition and disposition of period furnishings and other collections relating to the restoration. Soon after the appointment of the architectural firm, arrangements were made by that department to transfer all the interior furnishings from the mansion to a local storage warehouse for safekeeping. Prior to the transfer, Mississippi Educational Television—at the request of Governor Waller—made a thorough pictorial inventory of the articles to be stored. By early April, the mansion was cleared. More detailed excavations were then possible.[7]

To conduct the architectural excavations, the Building Commission secured the services of Charles Peterson, FAIA, an internationally known restorationist and consultant. During the early stages of the restoration, Peterson spent several days in Jackson working with the project architects. Working with a small group of skilled craftsmen and relying on Miss Capers' special knowledge of the mansion's history and interior design, which made her a valued consultant throughout the project, Peterson removed outer layers of paint and wallpaper in an effort to locate doors, passages, stairwells, and other original construction details which had been altered over the years, especially during the extensive renovation in 1908. He was successful in solving many of the mysteries of the mansion's original design. Perhaps his most significant discovery was the location of the original grand staircase which had graced the mansion's main entrance until it was removed by William Hull in 1908. The integrity of the design was reestablished during the 1975 restoration. The basic objective of Peterson and the Department of Archives, with the enthusiastic support of the first lady, was to reconstruct the historic portion of the mansion as nearly as possible to the original interior design of William Nichols. While these excavations were in progress, the legislature in May, 1972, authorized the expenditure of $1.5 million for the mansion project.[8]

Over the next two months the architects continued their study of the mansion's structural design, and in early July they presented their plans for restoration to the State Building Commission. Initially, the project called for a major renovation of the 1908 annex, which also included the construction of a twenty-foot extension to the existing structure and the complete restoration of the front or historic portion of the mansion.

A History of the Mississippi Governor's Mansion

However, commission members were advised that upon further determination the 1908 addition might be found so seriously damaged that a new structure would be necessary to replace the annex. About a month later, on August 10, 1972, the Building Commission decided that it would be less costly to demolish the annex and construct a modern townhouse addition. New plans were then designed for the addition and the commission began preparing specifications prior to the acceptance of bids for the construction and restoration.[9]

Since the basic objective of the entire project was to restore the mansion to the historical period of its construction, it would also be necessary to secure furnishings, draperies, chandeliers, floor coverings, and other incidental pieces dating from the 1840s. Much of the furniture in the mansion at the time of its restoration was of a much later period and, although some of it could be used, most of it was not suitable for an 1840 decor. Because of their historical value, however, such pieces as the Bilbo bed and the Claiborne bed were used in the historic mansion. The remainder, including the famous gold bathroom (part of which is in the first lady's suite), were placed in various rooms throughout the family quarters.

To direct the search for period furnishings, to guarantee their authenticity, and more specifically to design the decor throughout the mansion, the Building Commission and the Archives obtained the services of Edward Jones of Albany, Georgia, one of America's outstanding restorationists and designers. Jones' distinguished career included restoration of several rooms in the White House, the Thomas Jefferson and John Quincy Adams diplomatic reception rooms at the U.S. State Department, and the selection and acquisition of furnishings for the Nineteenth Century American Wing of New York's Metropolitan Museum. A gifted and temperamental artist, Jones conceived the interior decor for the Mississippi mansion and then literally went around the world collecting chandeliers from India, fabrics from England, and antiques from all across America. After locating antiques of the precise period, he selected fabrics of the texture, color, and design to match them. Then, to achieve the ultimate blend and to unify each room, he hand-mixed the final coat of wall coloring for the state rooms in the original mansion. Those historic parlors, breathtakingly beautiful, bear the mark of his genius. Through-

Home of Our Heritage

out the two-year period necessary to complete the decor, Jones worked closely with Mrs. Waller, Berle Smith, a Jackson interior designer and consultant for the restoration, Elbert Hilliard, McLemore's successor as director of the Department of Archives and History, Miss Capers, and James Wooldridge, curator of historical properties in the mansion representing the Department of Archives.[10]

Following months of painstaking research by an ever-increasing number of consultants and staff members of the Department of Archives, actual construction began soon after the bids were awarded on February 27, 1973. The general contract was awarded to Wise Construction Company of Jackson.[11] Over the next two years feature stories highlighting various aspects of the restoration appeared in the Jackson press almost weekly. One article featured three generations of craftsmen working at the mansion. Another announced that construction workers had found a Civil War surrender document dated 8 May 1865 and countersigned by General and later Governor Benjamin G. Humphreys. On the yellowed sheet a penciled message instructed the Confederate troops in the Trans-Mississippi Department to accept the surrender terms agreed upon by General Richard Taylor, C.S.A., and General Edward Canby, U.S.A. The document had apparently been tucked away and covered up during the redecoration of the mansion right after the war. Such experiences, plus the frequent visits of the governor and first lady, gave the construction workers an appreciation of the historic character of the building they were restoring. According to the general contractor, Terrell Wise, they had such an appreciation and derived from it an added incentive.[12] A little over two years and many change orders later, their work was done. Many have praised its quality.

Original construction schedules anticipated the completion of the project in much less than two and a half years. But many problems, which could not have been anticipated before construction began and a more detailed study of the stress condition of the original framework made, extended the period of construction. Change orders arising from those unexpected contingencies necessitated several revisions in the construction schedule and increased the final cost. The low bid of $1.8 million did not include the acquisition of period antiques, which required another $400,000. Consequently, the legislature supplemented the original appropriation in 1973 by an additional allocation of $1 million.[13] The location of period furnishings and the delicate negotiations leading to the purchase of those expensive items could not be fitted into a predetermined time table. Despite all those problems, however, the temptation to meet schedules at the expense of historical integrity was avoided. The results are obvious even to the untrained eye. The structural unison between the older building and the modern addition is an achievement of style and form that enhances the timeless beauty of the Mississippi mansion.

During the final stages of construction, while the classic furnishings were being shipped to the mansion in preparation for the reopening, a problem of special concern to the first lady developed. Because the legislative appropriation had been exhausted, there remained virtually no funds for the restoration of the mansion grounds. But largely through her efforts, the beautification of the grounds became something of a public crusade. Mrs. Waller launched an extensive campaign to secure through private sources the funds necessary to transform the downtown square into a setting of natural beauty equal to the mansion's imposing and stately dignity. By means of a rigorous speaking tour that carried her to every part of the state, and through her column "News From Your Mansion" which appeared in papers statewide, the first lady offered garden clubs, historical societies, civic groups, and private businesses a challenge to underwrite the beautification of the mansion grounds. She also initiated a program called "Dimes for the Mansion," through which Mississippi schoolchildren contributed to the project.

During the early months of 1975, Mrs. Waller received numerous pledges of support, and monetary gifts began pouring into a special fund established at a local bank. Many individuals made not only cash donations but also offered goods and services. Others among the growing list of mansion patrons contributed furnishings, portraits, books, and personal articles which had belonged to former first families. A bedroom suite valued at $15,000 was donated to the mansion by Mrs. Ferdinand Herff of San Antonio, Texas. The furniture had earlier been offered to the White House but was not of the period to which that residence was being restored. Subsequently, Jones requested the suite for use in the Mississippi mansion, since it did belong to the period of the mansion's restora-

Home of Our Heritage

tion. The Mississippi Library Commission sponsored a drive to collect autographed books by Mississippi authors to be placed in the mansion's library. At the request of the first lady, the Griggsville Wildlife Society of Illinois contributed a set of prints depicting Mississippi wildlife. These reproductions included all the official state animals which, at the request of Governor Waller, had been designated as such by the legislature.[14] This spontaneous reaction to the first lady's campaign was gratifying to her personally. It was also typical of the public's response to the restoration, which was almost unanimously favorable.

There was, of course, some objection to the expenditure of $2.5 million for the restoration and $400,000 for antique furnishings. But those objections were countered by the enthusiastic endorsement of a wide variety of organizations over the state. Typical of that endorsement was a resolution passed by the Mississippi Society, Sons of Confederate Veterans, which referred to the mansion as one of the state's most "revered landmarks."[15] In the mansion's long history there had been few times when so large an expenditure evoked so little criticism.

Only a few weeks before the dedication, which had been scheduled for June 8, 1975, the mansion's east lawn was an ugly display of noxious weeds and naked earth. Scarred and rutted by heavy equipment during construction and badly eroded by winter rains, the mansion's spacious lawn was almost barren of decorative flora. But through those last weeks an almost magical transformation occurred. A formal garden of natural beauty and graceful symmetry was fashioned from the creative design of Bill Garbo, a landscape architect associated with the Mississippi Research and Development Center. In consultation with Mrs. Waller and after a great deal of research, Bill Garbo designed the garden in a neo-classical style featuring Mississippi flora popular during the period of the mansion's construction.[16]

The east garden includes a classical period gazebo fronted by symmetrical turfs with boxwood borders and a fountain surrounded by perennials and also bordered by boxwood. Walks of crushed and raked clamshells from the Mississippi Gulf Coast criss-cross the formal gardens. On the north lawn is a rose garden featuring the "Mississippi Rose," which was specially hybridized for the mansion at the request of the first lady by J. Benjamin Williams, a noted horticulturist of Silver Springs, Maryland.

A History of the Mississippi Governor's Mansion

The rose garden is bordered by a replica of the wrought iron fence that enclosed the mansion square from 1855 until its removal in 1908. The fence was designed and donated by Harper's Foundry of Jackson. The Mississippi Garden Clubs which donated the fountain also adopted the care and maintenance of the rose garden as a bicentennial project.[17]

Spaced through the grounds are casual benches specially designed for the mansion and built from the historic Manship House cedars. A matching gazebo, in a less formal setting, is located on the west lawn and provides a unifying symmetry to the grounds. The Mississippi Federated Women's Club provided funds for one gazebo and the other was made possible by Mississippi schoolchildren through their "Dimes for the Mansion" program. To maintain maximum year-round beauty, selected grasses and shrubbery hybridized by Mississippi State University were planted over the mansion's tree-shaded lawn. To the mansion's forty trees, some of which were standing before it was built, several new ones— including two bicentennial trees and a magnolia—were added during the restoration of the grounds. As part of the national organization's "Liberty Tree" project designed to provide a living memorial to America's bicentennial, the Garden Clubs of Mississippi planted a beautiful American holly at the mansion. The United States Marine Corps, with the cooperation of the Mississippi Forestry Association, also planted a tulip poplar in commemoration of the bicentennial.[18]

The magnolia was transplanted from the temporary executive residence on Eastover Drive to replace the one which had been removed in the early stages of the restoration. It had been planted by Mrs. Vardaman and James K. Vardaman, Jr., in 1905, but its root system was damaging the mansion's foundation. Mrs. Waller, a naturalist and conservationist by instinct, disdained to see the tree destroyed. She suggested instead that a desk for the governor's study be constructed from its stock. She was advised, however, that there was not sufficient material to build a desk large enough to complement the governor's spacious study. Determined to save the tree in some form, she then proposed a smaller desk for the first lady's study. When Mrs. Vardaman planted the magnolia in 1905 she did so after her illustrious husband had recommended that the mansion be disposed of as an official executive residence. Her faith in the mansion's future, perhaps exemplified by the planting of the magnolia, was justified.

Home of Our Heritage

Four years later, in his farewell address to the legislature, Governor Vardaman had become convinced that the mansion was after all "a suitable house for the Governor" and recommended its preservation. Seventy years later, when the mansion was again in jeopardy, Carroll Waller played a key role in its preservation. It is entirely fitting that a desk carved from the boughs of that historic magnolia should grace the first lady's study.[19]

Other special features of the beautification of the grounds include the parent bush of the "Carroll Waller Camelia" and the Mississippi Flowers of the Month. Developed in honor of the first lady by L. B. Wilson of Gulfport and Helmut Scholl of Columbus, the Carroll Waller Camelia was featured on the cover of the November, 1974, issue of *The Camelia Journal*. A porcelain replica of the blossom designed by famous artist Mrs. Edward Marshall Boehm is also on display in the mansion. The value of the art piece in the mansion is enhanced by the fact that Mrs. Boehm broke the mold after fashioning only two of the designs. On March 29, 1974, Governor Waller by executive proclamation designated an official Flower of the Month for the state of Mississippi. To commemorate this proclamation, Mrs. Waller arranged with Bill Garbo to include a representative of each of these flowers in the formal gardens. The Mississippi Arts Commission, like many other state organizations which responded to the first lady's effort to gain broad public participation in the restoration, commissioned a Mississippi artist to reproduce the Flowers of the Month. These paintings are on display throughout the mansion.[20]

Perhaps for the first time in the mansion's history, officials of the Mississippi Forestry Commission (in consultation with Bill Garbo) made a systematic inventory of the trees and shrubbery on the grounds. These records, which include the age of all the trees, will be of great value to future beautification of the mansion square. The entire restoration and beautification project, at a cost of nearly $100,000, was made possible through the contributions of many individuals, organizations, and businesses.[21]

After waiting, perhaps not always patiently, three and a half years for completion of the restoration which had initially been scheduled for less than two, the first family occupied the Mississippi executive mansion on May 19, 1975. As in the case when Tilghman Tucker first occupied the

A History of the Mississippi Governor's Mansion

mansion in 1842 and again when Edmond F. Noel moved back into the mansion after the renovation in 1908, some interior work remained to be done. Nevertheless, due in part to their excitement about moving in and partly because of the necessity for finalizing the plans for the dedication, the first family decided to occupy the residence. As the Wallers were moving their personal belongings into the private quarters, Jones and Smith were still arranging the antiques in the state rooms and the final touches were being added to the historic portion of the mansion.

Any new building, especially a fifty-room mansion, usually requires a certain period of time to work out all the complications in the various mechanical systems. The moving-in process is no less complicated. There is a great margin for error, both mechanical and human. This has been an enduring problem which all the first families have encountered and to which they all have ultimately adjusted.

As the Wallers settled themselves in their historic new home, the first lady began preparing their first dinner in the mansion. She soon discovered, however, that during the hectic move little thought was given to seeing that food would be available for their first meal. The cupboard was bare, except for a few cans of spaghetti. When the search for a can-opener proved futile, a family member was dispatched to the Eastover residence to retrieve one. After this less than auspicious beginning, the first family retired, weary from the long day, but exhilarated to be in the mansion at last. But, the automatic controls on the cooling system malfunctioned, thus creating a December temperature in the residence. Since no blankets had been brought to the mansion—after all it was the middle of May—the Wallers' first night was reminiscent of that of Governor and Mrs. Brown's when they too endured a wintry night without covers.[22]

The next day brought sunshine and warmth but still more problems. The mansion's telephone system was not yet fully operational, and since the unit at Eastover had been disconnected, communication with the outside world was maintained by an intricate network of runners and couriers. Machines, like men, often fail to perform the simplest tasks in moments of great stress. Such was the case with the washing machines, which overflowed and further complicated the problems of moving into that large and spacious building. When the Wallers' two youngest boys were needed to aid in the cleanup detail, they were nowhere to be found.

Home of Our Heritage

They were later discovered in the dumbwaiter exploring, as young boys would, the secret passages of the mansion's inner recesses.[23]

In the midst of these crises, and during one of the better moments when the communication system was operational, Anita Goodman, the first lady's secretary, received a telephone call from a lady who wished to voice a complaint and offer a suggestion to the new tenants of the mansion. Although it was obvious from the level of activity in and around the mansion that a great deal of work remained to be done and in fact was being done, this lady suggested that someone be assigned to sweep the walk leading from Capitol Street up to the mansion's front portico. This suggestion was prompted by her observation that "You can always tell what kind of housekeeper lives inside by the front walk." After explaining that the beautification of the grounds had not been completed and that the debris would be removed by the workers when the job was finished, Mrs. Goodman thanked the lady for her interest and invited her to come and visit the mansion as soon as it was open to the public.[24]

Perhaps sooner than might have been expected, the most vexatious problems were corrected and the first family soon settled into a less hectic routine. On May 23 Governor Waller held the first official meeting in the governor's study with a distinguished group of officials representing the state and the city of Jackson. The purpose of the meeting was to plan for the reopening of the restored mansion. Dedication ceremonies honoring former first families, their children, and grandchildren were scheduled for June 8, only two weeks away. Later that evening the first formal dinner in the restored mansion was held; the parents of the governor, Mr. and Mrs. Percy A. Waller, were the honored guests. Over the next several days Edward Jones, Berle Smith, Bill Garbo, James Wooldridge, Dewitt Hamilton, James McReynolds, Edwin Lewis, Terrell Wise, Frank Singleton, the first lady, and even the Waller children applied the finishing touches to the mansion. Some of those individuals whose dedication went far beyond what otherwise might have been expected worked far into the night of Saturday, June 7, to get everything as nearly ready as possible for the reopening ceremonies.

During the three years she had served as first lady, Carroll Waller had coordinated and sometimes ramrodded the effort to achieve a special distinction for the Mississippi executive mansion. Her goal, which often appeared just beyond her grasp, was to achieve the designation of the mansion as a National Historic Landmark. There was only one other state residence that had been given this designation. This citation is awarded by the Secretary of the Interior on the advice of a special panel in the U.S. Park Service and is conferred only upon those buildings that are distinguished by architectural design and historical significance. A building's state of preservation and historical authenticity are also carefully considered. Although the designation had been denied once before, largely because William Nichols was not a well-known architect, the first lady intensified her campaign to achieve the recognition she believed the mansion deserved. After compiling additional information about Nichols' other achievements, she invited officials of the Park Service's Office of Archeology and Historic Preservation to come to Jackson and reevaluate the progress of restoration before acting upon the second application. Two representatives of that office came to Jackson and spent two days in late February touring the mansion with Mrs. Waller, Hilliard, Miss Capers, Wooldridge, architects and contractors, and other officials from the Department of Archives and History. After this study and under the contagion of the first lady's enthusiasm, they agreed to present the application to the special panel with their strongest endorsement that the mansion be designated a national landmark. For several anxious months Mrs. Waller and officials at the Archives waited for the final decision. Throughout the long process, the first lady maintained a high level of optimism and was sometimes the only person connected with the effort who believed that the citation could be achieved. Her optimism was vindicated. The special panel which included Mrs. Lady Bird Johnson, whose endorsement of the application was very helpful, recommended that the secretary award the citation to the Mississippi mansion. The announcement and presentation of the bronze plaque emblematic of the designation were made at the reopening. It was a special recognition for the mansion and came on a special day in the life of the executive residence. Carroll Waller accepted the plaque on behalf of the people of Mississippi at the reopening ceremonies.[25]

On Sunday, June 8, 1975, a light, early morning rain bathed the lush, green foliage in the mansion's formal gardens. By mid-morning the rain had stopped, and by noon the sun was shining. The boxwood glistened in

Mississippi school children contributed to the beautification of the Mansion grounds through the "Dimes for the Mansion" project.

Miss Charlotte Capers & James Chastain

Dr. R. A. McLemore & Edward V. Jones

Governor Waller talks to Mansion worker

Early stage of construction

East lawn during final stage of construction

The staircase design of 1908

The original grand staircase design restored in 1975

Southwest Parlor

First Lady's stu[dy]

Northwest bedroom (Bilbo room)

Dining room

Security reception room

Family living room—includes Victorian furniture once owned by Governor T.M.Tucker's family.

Southeast Parlor

Northwest Parlor

Family dining room

Five governors—Paul Johnson, John Bell Williams, Bill Waller, J. P. Coleman, Ross Barnett

Members of the first graduating class of the Governor's Mansion Docent Training Course are shown with Governor and Mrs. William Waller and Miss Charlotte Capers and Elbert R. Hilliard of the Department of Archives and History, who conducted the course.

The gazebo on the east lawn was contributed by the Mississippi Federated Women's Clubs.

Home of Our Heritage

the sunlight and the gazebo's copper dome sparkled. Fresh and rain-swept, the grounds had never been more beautiful. Restored in splendor under a cloudless summer sky, the classical mansion had never appeared more stately.

By noon, two hours before the ceremony, the mansion's parlors were overflowing. Visiting dignitaries, former governors and first ladies, their children, and grandchildren were already arriving. Hosts and hostesses for each of the state rooms were getting last-minute instructions about the historic furnishings and occupants of those rooms. On the front portico, chairs were being arranged for the honored guests and the sound system was being tested.

Shortly after two o'clock Governor Waller asked Dr. R. A. McLemore, former director of the Department of Archives and History and chairman of the Mississippi Executive Mansion Commission, to deliver the invocation. Governor Waller then welcomed the visitors and introduced the former governors and their families. Each of four former governors—James P. Coleman, Ross R. Barnett, Paul B. Johnson, Jr., and John Bell Williams—spoke briefly, recalling their years in that historic home and each lauded its new look. Governor and Mrs. Dolph Briscoe of Texas, Governor and Mrs. Ray Blanton of Tennessee, and Governor Ricardo Bordalto of Guam were also introduced. After other introductions and announcements, and a brief ribbon-cutting ceremony, the governor's mansion was declared officially reopened. Then the governor and the first lady "threw open the doors of the Executive Mansion" and extended its traditional hospitality to the 2,000 visitors attending the ceremonies. It is worthy of note that among those visitors were several black Mississippians who for the first time in a hundred years enjoyed the mansion's hospitality.[26]

Volunteer hosts and hostesses were on hand to provide information and answer questions as the throng of visitors filed through the mansion's spacious state rooms and family quarters. Refreshments were served in the garden to the accompaniment of a string ensemble. Many visitors, awed by its beauty and serenity, lingered on the shaded lawn until late afternoon. Later that evening, Governor and Mrs. Waller left for New Orleans to attend the National Governor's Conference and enjoy a brief respite from the long hours leading up to the reopening of the mansion.

A History of the Mississippi Governor's Mansion

When the first lady returned from New Orleans, she immediately began preparation for the next open house honoring the Governor's Colonels and their wives. This reception, held on June 21, lasted thirteen hours and attracted approximately 8,000 visitors to the mansion. The very next day another open house was held to afford all state employees an opportunity to tour the state's official executive residence. Far exceeding the first lady's anticipation, almost 4,000 state officials turned out for that occasion, making a total of 12,000 visitors to the mansion in a period of about twenty-four hours. At the request of many state employees who were unable to see the mansion on the first date but were anxious to do so, a second open house was scheduled a few weeks later. Many other special days were held for various groups, including a Senior Citizens Day, Girl Scout Day, and 4-H Day. Special tours were arranged for the alumni of state universities when they had football games scheduled for Memorial Stadium in Jackson. Over a period of several weeks following the reopening, each of Mississippi's eighty-two counties was honored on a certain day when county residents were extended a special invitation to tour the mansion. In appreciation for the valued service they rendered during the campaign to preserve the mansion and during its restoration, women from across the state were invited to a series of formal luncheons which the first lady gave in their honor. The traffic through the restored mansion in the six months from June, 1975, through the Christmas holidays was no less than remarkable. The mansion staff estimated that over 60,000 visitors toured the mansion during that period.[27]

The extensive list of dignitaries visiting the mansion during those same six months is indicative of the active pace maintained by Governor Waller and the first lady. It is also an index of the variety of public functions that continue to augment the mansion's social calendar. In addition to those already mentioned, celebrities who visited the mansion included Van Cliburn, Mary Ann Mobley, Senator Lloyd Bentson of Texas, Pat Boone, Sargent Shriver, Jerome Hines, performers from Ringling Brothers Circus, and members of a trade mission from Kuwait. An amusing incident occurred during the Kuwait officials' visit. In the European tradition, they placed their shoes outside their room to be shined prior to the next day's round of conferences. Since the first family no longer enjoys the luxury of

Home of Our Heritage

live-in servants, the Waller sons were recruited to perform this chore. In the mansion's best tradition of hospitality, they did so cheerfully.[28]

Holidays, and especially Christmas, are always happy times at the mansion and usually extend the first lady's creativity in selecting and arranging decorations for the fifty-room dwelling. In their first year in office, although they were not then living in the mansion, Governor and Mrs. Waller established a Christmas tradition which will be continued for years to come. To commemorate Mississippi's admission to the Union on December 10, 1817, the first family held a Christmas tree lighting ceremony on the mansion lawn on December 10, 1972. The mansion's new magnolia was decorated in the 1975 ceremony which was conducted amid the continued excitement occasioned by the restoration.[29]

For the first family's first Christmas in the mansion, Mrs. Waller employed traditional decorations dating from the period of the mansion's construction. Wreaths of pine and cedar were placed throughout the historic portion and a medallion wreath of cedar and fresh fruit was placed on the mansion's main entrance. Other entrances were adorned by wreaths of balsam featuring red apples, pineapples, and lemons. The gazebos were wreathed in boxwood. For the mansion's main Christmas tree, located in the grand-stair hallway, the first lady decorated a double balsam grown in Yazoo County and donated by Mrs. W. M. Link. K. K. Hill, a Mississippi College student and a friend of the first family's daughter, arranged for the donation of the tree and assisted in its decoration. As a boy he had played in and around this particular tree. When K. K. informed Mrs. Link—who had at first declined to sell the tree—why he wanted it, she then graciously donated the beautiful balsam for use as the first Christmas tree in the restored mansion. Decorations on the tree included garlands of popcorn and cranberries strung by 4-H members from across the state, red velvet bows, gingerbread men, fresh fruits, and handmade ornaments.[30] The period decorations which so beautifully complemented the mansion's classical decor were acclaimed by the thousands of visitors who toured the mansion during the holiday season.

In early January, 1976, the first family began preparing to vacate the mansion which they had occupied for a brief but busy seven months. As a courtesy to Governor-elect Cliff Finch and his family, the Wallers moved

A History of the Mississippi Governor's Mansion

out of the executive residence before the expiration of the governor's term to allow the new first family to occupy the mansion prior to the inaugural ceremonies. The last major event of the Wallers' exciting residency was the marriage of their mansion director. On January 10, 1976, Gary Freeman and Barbara Mosley were married in the west parlor which had been the scene of so many mansion weddings. A few days after these nuptials, the first family left the Mississippi executive mansion.[31]

Governor Waller had fulfilled his promise to live in the executive residence, and the first lady had achieved not only the mansion's rescue and restoration but also its recognition as a National Historic Landmark. And perhaps as never before, the "suitable house for the Governor" had become the Mississippi Mansion whose hospitality was extended to all the people.

In 1841, when he was seeking the legislature's continued support for its construction, Governor Alexander G. McNutt reminded the lawmakers that the mansion was not being provided "for the benefit of the Chief Magistrate alone, but to enable him to receive his fellow citizens on suitable occasions." Although McNutt never lived in the mansion, he perceived accurately the central theme of its history. Through those intervening years many traditions have developed, and even a few mansion myths have found their way into Mississippi folklore. The mansion has often been the focus of controversy and its residents the center of angry dispute. But in all those years, even when its condition and appearance were not a source of pride to the people, its tradition of hospitality was. The mansion has outlasted the controversies, survived the dogs of war and time, and escaped even the blind hand of progress. Like Mississippi, it has endured. It is a link to the past, a landmark, a monument, the "home of our heritage." Within its walls the full human drama of birth, life, and death has been played. "It has witnessed," as Governor Bailey said, "all the changing life of Mississippi." And like Mississippi, the mansion's future has never been so bright.

Notes

NOTES TO CHAPTER I

1. *Natchez Free Trader,* January 10, February 8, 24, 1842; *Canton Creole,* January 15, 1842.
2. For a description of early Jackson see "Thomas J. Wharton's First Visit to Jackson in 1837, as told by him," J. L. Power Papers, Series Z100, box 4, folder 65, Mississippi Department of Archives and History, Jackson, Mississippi, hereinafter cited as Power Papers; J. L. Power, "Le Fleurs Bluff," typescript copy of speech of March 13, 1897 in Power Papers, Z100, box 6, folder 88; Jackson *Southron,* November 17, 1837. For activity building up to the completion of the mansion see William Nichols to Morris Emanuel, December 13, 1841, and Nichols to Andrew and Kline, January 7, 1842 in Auditor's Records, Record Group 29, Mississippi Department of Archives and History, Jackson, Mississippi, hereinafter cited as Auditor's Records, and *Natchez Free Trader,* February 8, 1842. For a history of Jackson see William D. McCain, *The Story of Jackson,* 2 vols. (Jackson, 1953). For a brief account of the construction of the mansion and a survey of its history see David N. Young, "A History of the Construction of State Buildings in Jackson, Mississippi, 1822-1860" (unpublished M.A. thesis, Mississippi College, Clinton, Mississippi, 1954), and Gene Holcomb, "The Mississippi Governor's Mansion," *Journal of Mississippi History,* II (January, 1940), 3-21. All manuscript collections, public documents, and other sources cited in subsequent footnotes are located in the Mississippi Department of Archives and History unless otherwise noted.
3. *Natchez Free Trader,* February 24, 1842.
4. For a general discussion of this period see Edwin Miles, *Jacksonian Democracy in Mississippi* (Chapel Hill, N.C., 1960) and John F. H. Claiborne, *Mississippi, A Province, Territory and State* (Jackson, 1880).
5. For a discussion of the Flush Times see R. A. McLemore, *Mississippi, A History,* 2 vols. (Jackson, 1973), I, 284-310; for Walker's speech see John K. Bettersworth, *Mississippi, Yesterday and Today* (Austin, Texas, 1964), 132.
6. Jackson *Clarion,* February 14, 1867.
7. The *Southron* of November 17, 1837, reported that the entire population of 1830 "could have been comfortably seated in one wagon."
8. *Laws of Mississippi 1833,* 468; A. G. McNutt special message to the legislature, January 7, 1840, in *House Journal 1840,* 30-31; *House Journal 1842,* 270-71.
9. *House Journal 1842,* 271.
10. The original manuscript notes taken by the clerk during Tucker's debate have been preserved in the Mississippi Archives in Legislative Records, Record Group 47 (hereinafter

Notes to Chapter I

cited as Legislative Records), vol. 15, folder labeled "Rough Notes." For an excellent guide to official records in the Department of Archives and History see Thomas Henderson and Ronald E. Tomlin, *Guide to Official Records in the Mississippi Department of Archives and History* (Jackson, 1975).

11. Abram Scott to David Morrison, May 20, 1833, Governors Correspondence, Record Group 27, Mississippi Department of Archives and History, Jackson, Mississippi (hereinafter cited as Governors Correspondence), vol. 18; Morrison to Scott (undated) reprinted in *Official and Statistical Register of Mississippi 1917*, 387.

12. Charles Lynch to Morrison, June 22, 1833, Governors Correspondence, vol. 18.

13. Nichols to Lynch, October 12, 1833, Governors Correspondence, vol. 18. For a resumé of the problem of selecting an architect see Lynch's special message to the legislature of November 19, 1833, in *House Journal 1833*, 34, and report of special committee in *Senate Journal 1836*, 214–18.

14. Jackson *Mississippian*, December 2, 1833, and February 7, 1835.

15. *Ibid.*, November 28, 1834; Hiram G. Runnells' special message to the legislature of January, 1835, in *House Journal 1835*, 41–42.

16. *House Journal 1835*, 109.

17. Jackson *Mississippian*, November 11, 1835; *Senate Journal 1836*, 214–18; for Nichols' manuscript bond and commission see Secretary of State Records, Record Group 28, vols. 256–58, in folder labeled "Bonds and Oaths." On February 10, 1836, Nichols wrote to the secretary of state asking for another copy of his commission as someone had stolen the original.

18. Jackson *Mississippian*, January 1, 19, 1836; Lawrence to Lynch, July 10, Governors Correspondence, vol. 18; *Senate Journal 1836*, 218.

19. Lynch to Nichols, March 22, 1836, Governors Correspondence, vol. 22. Nichols designed the penitentiary along the Auburn system. Nichols to Lynch (undated), Governors Correspondence, vol. 18; Jackson *Mississippian*, January 6, April 14, May 19, August 11, 1837.

20. Jackson *Mississippian*, April 27, 1839.

21. Nichols' special report is preserved in Legislative Records, vol. 22.

22. Talbot Hamlin, *Greek Revival in American Architecture* (New York, 1943.) See Introduction by Leopold Arnaud, xvi, and 212. For a more detailed study of Mississippi architecture see Mary Wallace Crocker, *Historic Architecture in Mississippi* (Jackson, 1973).

23. Biographical data on Nichols are derived from U.S. Census of 1830 and 1840; Thornton W. Mitchell to Alice McCardle, March 4, 1975; Milo B. Howard to Alice McCardle, March 4, 1975, in files of Mrs. Carroll Waller; Board of Trustees of the State University, Minutes of January, 1845; *Yazoo Democrat*, October 17, 1850; Author's interview with Edward Tye Neilson and Louie B. Nichols of Lexington, Mississippi, on March 21, 1975; L. L. McNees, *Cemetery Records of Holmes County* (Lexington, Miss., 1955). Henry F. Withey and Elsie R. Withey, *Biographical Dictionary of American Architects* (New York, 1956), 441, seem to confuse William Nichols with a George Nichols but divide William Nichols' achievements between them. Leslie Frank Crocker in "Domestic Architecture of the Middle South" (Ph.D. dissertation, University of Missouri, 1971), 155, does the same.

24. Nichols to McNutt (undated), Governors Correspondence, vol. 27, Miscellaneous.

25. For an itemized audit of the expenditures of the governor's mansion see the report of the state auditor in *House Journal 1842*, 281–314, 665–71. See also the *Journal of Expenditures of the Commissioners of Public Buildings*, 32, 41, 66–71, 73, 75, 78–79, 83, 87.

26. Auditor's Records, vols. 66–67; *House Journal 1842*, 281–314; *Journal of Expenditures*, passim.

27. *Journal of Expenditures*, 83.

28. See William Gibbons' and William Nichols' reports to the legislature in *House Journal 1844*, 162–67.

Notes to Chapter I

29. See manuscript report of committee on public buildings in Legislative Records, vol. 21 and *Southron*, December 31, 1840.

30. Nichols to Emanuel, December 13, 1841, Nichols to Andrew and Kline, January 7, 1842 in Governors Correspondence, vols. 66–67; *House Journal 1842*, 270–71; *Natchez Free Trader*, February 24, June 15, 1842.

31. See Graves' report in *House Journal 1842*, 661–77.

32. *Ibid.*

33. *Ibid.*, 816–19.

34. *Ibid.*, 1065–71.

35. William L. Coker, *Repudiation and Reaction: Tilghman M. Tucker and the Mississippi Bond Question* (New York, 1969), 61–73; *Natchez Free Trader*, March 21, 1843.

36. *Southron*, December 31, 1840.

37. *De Bow's Review*, I (April, 1859), 467; *Harper's New Monthly Magazine*, XC (May, 1895), 831.

NOTES TO CHAPTER II

1. J. A. Orr, "A Trip from Houston to Jackson, Mississippi in 1845," *Publications of the Mississippi Historical Society*, IX (1906), 175–76.

2. For a general discussion of the bond question see Coker, *Repudiation and Reaction*; on party problems see John A. Quitman to Robert J. Walker, February 14, 1842, Robert J. Walker Papers, Series Z659f.

3. For a discussion of the campaign see Miles, *Jacksonian Democracy*, 146–59 and Claiborne, *Mississippi*, 433ff.

4. *Ibid.*

5. Tilghman M. Tucker Subject File in Mississippi Department of Archives and History; Claiborne, *Mississippi*, 433.

6. *Canton Creole*, January 15, 1842.

7. *Natchez Free Trader*, January 7, 10, February 8, 24, 1842; *House Journal 1842*, 240, 270, 365.

8. *Laws of Mississippi 1842*, 138; *Natchez Free Trader*, June 15, 1842.

9. *Natchez Free Trader*, October 6, 1841, June 15, 1842; Claiborne, *Mississippi*, 433; H. Hobbs to Tucker at Columbus, November 29, 1842, Bird Safford to Tucker, February 18, 1843, Governors Correspondence; Kate Markham Power Papers, Series Z118. The latter is the material and correspondence collected by Kate Markham Power for her book on the "Mistresses of the Mansion" which she began in the 1930s but was not able to complete. The material is conveniently arranged in folders for each first lady. It is hereinafter cited as Power, "Mistresses of the Mansion."

10. *Southron*, November 24, 1842.

11. *Ibid.*, February 23, 1843; *Natchez Free Trader*, February 20, 1843.

12. *Southron*, April 26, May 3, 1843.

13. Reuben Davis, *Recollections of Mississippi and Mississippians* (New York, 1889), 100. Davis' book has been reprinted by the Mississippi Historical Society.

14. Tucker to Robert J. Walker, January 8, 1843, Walker Papers.

15. Coker, *Repudiation and Reaction*, 61–73; *Natchez Free Trader*, February 27, March 21, 24, 1842. See also Tucker's special message to the legislature in *House Journal 1843*, 14–15.

16. Auditor's Records, vols. 66–67.

17. *Southron*, May 30, 1843; Coker, *Repudiation and Reaction*, 61–73.

18. *Vicksburg Sentinel* quoted in *Natchez Free Trader*, March 21, 1843. One paper reported Tucker's farewell address as follows: "Nothing was wanting to convince us that

Notes to Chapter II

Governor Tucker was as stupid as any blockhead, but his farewell message certainly caps the climax of his own precious stupidity itself." *The (Panola) Weekly Register*, January 27, 1844.

19. Thomas Williams to General Jessie Spieght, April 2, 1843, in Thomas H. Williams Papers, Series Z695f.
20. *Southron*, January 9, 10, 1844; Jackson *Southern Weekly Reformer*, January 9, 1844.
21. Jackson *Mississippian*, January 10, 1844.
22. *Ibid.*
23. At the close of Brown's second administration a local paper contrasted his residence at the mansion with that of Tucker: "But when [Jacksonians] contrast the marks of civilization and refinement which now surround the Executive Mansion with the African Lily of former times, they are reminded that, for the last four years, a *lady* has been the inmate and controling spirit of that Mansion." *Southron*, December 16, 1847.
24. Jackson *Mississippian*, January 9, 1844.
25. Dunbar Rowland, *Encyclopedia of Mississippi History*, 2 vols. (Atlanta, 1916), I, 310–13; Davis, *Recollections of Mississippi*, 189.
26. Jackson *Mississippian*, June 18, 1847.
27. *The (Panola) Lynx*, January 24, 1846.
28. Jackson *Mississippian*, January 14, 1846.
29. *Ibid*, May 7, November 25, 1847; Power, "Mistresses of the Mansion"; Auditor's Records, vols. 66–67.
30. See text of Brown's speech in Jackson *Clarion*, January 7, 1875; see also James Byrne Ranck, *Albert Gallatin Brown* (New York, 1937), 267–68.
31. See William Gibbons' report to the legislature in *House Journal 1844*, 162–65, and Nichols' report to the same legislature, 165–67; *Laws of Mississippi 1844*, 181, 228–29. Although there were other appropriations for mansion repair and furnishings passed during Brown's administration, they were for work completed and furnishings purchased prior to his term. See *House Journal 1843*, 59, 94–101, and several claims against the state in Auditor's Records, vols. 66–67, and *Southron*, January 10, 1844.
32. Jackson *Mississippian*, July 6, 1847.
33. Joseph W. Matthews Subject File.
34. Davis, *Recollections of Mississippi*, 213; Power, "Mistresses of the Mansion."
35. *Ibid.*
36. Jackson *Mississippian*, January 22, 1848.
37. *Ibid.*
38. See reminiscences of Mrs. Sidney E. Stevens who attended Matthews' inaugural levee in Power, "Mistresses of the Mansion."
39. Goodspeed's *Biographical and Historical Memoirs of Mississippi*, 2 vols. (Chicago, 1891,) I, 19.
40. *The Literary American*, II (January 6, 1849), 20. A copy of this article was obtained from the Joseph Regenstein Library of the University of Chicago through the courtesy of Mrs. Gilbert Longstreet, head reference librarian. See also Jackson *Mississippian*, January 24, 1849.
41. *Jacksonian* quoted in Jackson *Mississippian*, January 12, 1849; *Yazoo Democrat* quoted in Jackson *Mississippian*, April 20, 1849.
42. Jackson *Mississippian*, June 27, 1849.

NOTES TO CHAPTER III

1. Davis, *Recollections of Mississippi*, 137–39.
2. Jackson *Mississippian*, October 29, 1849. All election statistics are from *Official and Statistical Register of Mississippi 1912*, 110–12 and Glenn Abney, *Mississippi Election*

Notes to Chapter III

Statistics 1900-1967 (University, Mississippi, 1968). Population figures are from Mississippi Power and Light Company, *Mississippi: Statistical Summary of Population, 1800-1960* (Jackson, 1962).

3. James Hayes McLendon, ("John A. Quitman" Ph.D. dissertation, University of Texas, 1949), 302-303.
4. *Ibid.*
5. *Ibid.*, "Mistresses of the Mansion."
6. Power, "Mistresses of the Mansion."
7. *House Journal 1850*, 113, 318, 355; *Senate Journal of 1850*, 319; *Laws of Mississippi 1850*, 113.
8. For biographical information on Quitman see John F. H. Claiborne, *The Life and Correspondence of John A. Quitman, Major General, U. S. A. and Governor of the State of Mississippi*, 2 vols. (New York, 1860), and John A. Quitman Subject File.
9. Claiborne, *Life of Quitman*, I, 492-99.
10. *Ibid.*
11. Ray Broussard, "Governor John A. Quitman and the Lopez Expeditions of 1851-1852," *Journal of Mississippi History*, XXVIII (May, 1966), 103-20. See also McLendon, "John A. Quitman," 328, 334.
12. Jackson *Mississippian*, November 29, 1850.
13. For a discussion of this crisis see Cleo Hearon, "Mississippi and the Compromise of 1850," *PMHS* 14 (1914), 7-229.
14. *Ibid.*; Jackson *Mississippian and State Gazette*, February 7, 1851.
15. Jackson *Mississippian and State Gazette*, May 16, 1851; *Flag of the Union*, a Whig paper, quoted in Jackson *Mississippian and State Gazette*, May 16, 1851.
16. For a study of Foote's role in the secession crisis of 1851 see John E. Gonzales, "The Public Career of Henry S. Foote (1804-1880)" (Ph.D. dissertation, University of North Carolina, 1957). See also Jackson *Mississippian*, November 1, 1850, and Jackson *Mississippian and State Gazette*, February 14, September 12, 1851.
17. Jackson *Mississippian and State Gazette*, September 19, 1851. Gonzales, "The Public Career of Henry Foote," 109, 119.
18. Rosalie Quitman Duncan, "Life of General John A. Quitman", *PMHS*, 4 (1901, 415-24.
19. Jackson *Mississippian and State Gazette*, February 10, August 8, 1851; George T. Swann to John I. Guion, February 6, 1851, Governors Correspondence, vol 29.
20. Jackson *Mississippian and State Gazette*, November 28, 1851; *Flag of the Union*, December 19, 1851.
21. *Senate Journal 1852*, 358; *Flag of the Union*, February 6, 1852. Ironically, J. J. Pettus would be living in the mansion during the Civil War when the executive residence sustained its most serious damage and loss of furnishings.
22. *Flag of the Union*, January 8, 1852; *Senate Journal 1852*, 325, 331-32, 349-50, 509, *Laws of Mississippi 1852*, 429; Auditor's Records, vols. 66-67.
23. See Auditor's Report of 1852 in *House Journal 1852*, 34, and vouchers in Auditor's Records, vols. 66-67; for establishment of Executive Mansion Contingency Fund see *Laws of Mississippi 1856*, 434.
24. Power, "Mistresses of the Mansion."
25. Gonzales, "The Public Career of Henry Foote," 148; Jackson *Mississippian and State Gazette*, January 2, 28, March 26, 1852; *Flag of the Union*, March 26, 1852.
26. *Natchez Free Trader*, May 12, 1842; Henry Stuart Foote Subject File.
27. McLemore, *Mississippi*, I, 308-309. Certainly adding to Foote's disappointment was his failure to win re-appointment to the U.S. Senate.
28. *Natchez Free Trader*, April 29, 1842; Power Papers Z100, box 7, folder 117; *The*

Notes to Chapter III

(Jackson) Southern Sun, February 12, December 22, 1839, clipping in John J. McRae Subject File.

29. *House Journal 1854*, 571, 581; *Laws of Mississippi 1854*, 213. For vouchers submitted by Hull (?) to Auditor see Auditor's Records, vol. 68, folder labeled "Work Vouchers, etc., 1855–56." The fence and gates are described by Kate M. Power in typescript pages in Power Papers Z100, box 6, folders 58, 62, 92. These descriptions were prepared as part of the Federal Writers Project during the 1930s. They also appeared in the WPA Source Material for Jackson.

30. *Laws of Mississippi 1854*, 213; see Caleb Parker's vouchers submitted to Auditor in Auditor's Records, vols. 66–67, folder labeled "Work Vouchers, etc., 1850–52." These vouchers seem to be misplaced as the date is January 9, 1856 and should be in the folder for 1855–56. For other vouchers dealing with this work see Auditor's Records, vol. 68, unlabeled folders; Auditor's Report for January 1 to December 31, 1856 in *House Journal 1856–1857*, 105; *Laws of Mississippi 1854*, 367.

31. Jackson *Mississippian*, August 3, 1855, January 10, February 22, 1856.
32. See reminiscences of J. L. Power in Power Papers Z100, box 7, folder 117.
33. Jackson *Mississippian*, August 31, 1855.
34. Power Papers, Z100, box 7, folder 117.
35. Jackson *Mississippian*, January 5, 1858.
36. Lexington *Advertiser*, undated clipping in Power Papers Z100, box 7, folder 117.
37. Biographical information in William McWillie Subject File; Joel M. Acker, "Diary of Judge Joel M. Acker, January 1st 1854 to October 25th 1856," quoted in McLemore, *Mississippi*, I, 435.
38. Lexington *Advertiser*, undated clipping in Power Papers Z100, box 7, folder 117.
39. For information on the McWillie residency see Power, "Mistresses of the Mansion"; for menu of inaugural reception see Governors Correspondence, vol. 33.
40. *Laws of Mississippi 1857*, 120. The vouchers for those purchases are in Governors Correspondence, vol. 33. McWillie to Pettus, March 10, 1860, Governors Correspondence, vol. 35; see Auditor's Records, vol. 71 for McWillie's receipt for the $164.62 he received from Pettus on March 12, 1860.
41. Power, "Mistresses of the Mansion."
42. S. McWillie Harris to Kate Markham Power, August 5, 1937, Power Papers.

NOTES TO CHAPTER IV

1. William Howard Russell, *My Diary North and South* (Boston, 1863), 299. For additional information on Pettus see, Robert W. Dubay, *John Jones Pettus, Mississippi Fire-eater* (Jackson, 1975).
2. *Ibid.*, 298–300.
3. *Ibid.*, 299; *Senate Journal 1859*, 190, 237; reminiscences of Mrs. Sidney E. Stevens in Power, "Mistresses of the Mansion". A *Vicksburg Sun* clipping tells of Pettus joining the militia as a private and going through drills and parades as other enlisted men, although as governor he was the commander-in-chief of the state militia; see clipping in Power, "Mistresses of the Mansion."
4. Percy L. Rainwater, *Mississippi, Storm Center of Secession; 1856–1861* (Baton Rouge, 1938), 170–75.
5. For a full discussion of the reaction to secession see John K. Bettersworth, *Confederate Mississippi* (Baton Rouge, 1943).
6. Rainwater, *Mississippi, Storm Center of Secession*, 216.
7. Davis, *Recollections of Mississippi*, 393.
8. See J. L. Power's resumé of Mississippi troops in the Confederate Army in *Natchez*

Notes to Chapter IV

Democrat, November 28, 1865. For a brief account of the military phase of the war in Mississippi see McLemore, *Mississippi*, I, 447-91.

9. McLemore, *Mississippi*, I, 460.

10. For more detailed accounts see John C. Pemberton, *Pemberton, Defender of Vicksburg* (Chapel Hill, N.C., 1942), and Joseph E. Johnston, *Narrative of Military Operations* (Bloomington, Ind., 1959). For vouchers to Jackson Gas, Light Company see Governors Correspondence, vol. 54.

11. Pettus to Brigadier General John Adams May 5, 1863, executive directive dated May 5, 1863, in Governors Correspondence, vol. 54.

12. Jackson *Mississippian*, April 29, May 5, 1863.

13. Dr. D. W. Yandell to Dr. John M. Johnson, June 17, 1863; copy in Dunbar Rowland (ed.), *Jefferson Davis Constitutionalist, His Letters, Papers and Speeches* (Jackson, 1923), VI, 2-3, 6.

14. Edward Newsome, "Experience in the War of the Great Rebellion," typescript copy in the MDAH, XVI. Sylvanus Cadwallader, *Three Years with Grant* (New York, 1955), 75; Johnston, *Narrative*, 210; Shelby Foote, *The Civil War, A Narrative*, 2 vols. (New York, 1963), I, 365.

15. *Natchez Daily Courier*, May 20, 1863; U. S. Grant, *Personal Memoirs of U. S. Grant* (New York, 1894), 298; Cadwallader, *Three Years with Grant*, 73-75; William T. Sherman, *Memoirs of General William T. Sherman*, 2 vols. (New York, 1875), I, 321.

16. Grant, *Memoirs*, 298.

17. Sherman, *Memoirs*, I, 321-22; Brandon *Republican*, May 21, 1863; "Pioneer Club Scrapbook; A Summary of the Dest uction of Jackson is presented by Anabel Power" in *Jackson Daily News*, September 7, 1947.

18. Sherman, *Memoirs*, I, 322.

19. *Natchez Daily Courier*, May 20, 21, 22, 26, 1863.

20. Dr. R. N. Anderson to Pettus, May 29, 1863, Governors Correspondence, vol. 54.

21. See Executive Journal of Governor Pettus, *ibid.*, vol. 43, pp. 392, 394.

22. *Harper's Weekly*, August 15, 1863, 526; Adam Badeau, *Military History of U. S. Grant*, 3 vols. (New York, 1881), II, 395-97; Sherman, *Memoirs*, I, 344-47; *The War of the Rebellion: A Compilation of the Official Records of the Union and Confederate Armies* (Washington, 1889), Series I, vol. 24, pt. 3, pp. 315, 529, 531-32.

23. Recollections of J. L. Power quoted by Anabel Power in *Jackson Daily News*, September 7, 1947. Much of the furniture Pettus transferred to Macon had been only recently purchased. The legislature voted a $1200 appropriation for that purchase in 1859. See *Laws of Mississippi 1859*, 315.

24. *War of the Rebellion*, 531-32.

25. *Ibid.*

26. Sherman to Mayor C. H. Manship, July 21, 1863, copy of letter in Power Papers Z100, box 6, folder 98; Badeau, *Military History of U. S. Grant*, II, 396; Sherman, *Memoirs*, I, 322.

27. *Everybody Magazine*, October, 1918, copy in Jackson, Mississippi Subject File. This claim is made by John Koolbeck of Harlan, Iowa, who stated that he was one of the men to whom Sherman shouted his famous statement. There are many other claims that the statement was made at different times and at different places.

28. C. H. Manship to Pettus, October 20, 1863, Governors Correspondence, vol. 54.

29. Jackson *Mississippian*, October 10, 15, 1863.

30. Pettus, *Executive Journal*, 391; Governors Correspondence, vol 43.

31. Governor Charles Clark, *Executive Journal*, 409; Governors Correspondence, vol 43.

32. J. S. McNeily, "War and Reconstruction in Mississippi," *PMHS* Centenary Series II (1918), 227.

Notes to Chapter IV

33. See excerpts from the diary of Captain Louis Keller reprinted in *The National Observer*, October 8, 1962; McLemore, *Mississippi*, I, 503-504.

34. Jackson *Clarion*, February 14, 1867; *Vicksburg Daily Times*, January 18, 1868, July 7, 1870. The *Clarion*, formerly printed at Paulding and Meridian, was moved to Jackson by J. J. Shannon on November 4, 1865, when Shannon was appointed state printer.

NOTES TO CHAPTER V

1. For an excellent account of Johnsonian reconstruction see, William C. Harris, *Presidential Reconstruction in Mississippi* (Baton Rouge, 1967).
2. *Ibid.*, 37-61.
3. *Ibid.* Governor Sharkey did not occupy the mansion while he served as provisional governor. See reminiscences of Mrs. Sidney E. Stevens, Power, "Mistresses of the Mansion."
4. *Senate Journal 1865*, 22, 84, Appendix 23-24; *House Journal 1865*, Appendix 11, 46-47; *Laws of Mississippi 1865*, 197.
5. *Laws of Mississippi, 1865*, 197; *Vicksburg Daily Journal*, December 20, 1865.
6. *Senate Journal: Called Session*, October 1866, 12-13, 344, 367-368; see vouchers for this work in Auditor's Records, vol. 82.
7. *Vicksburg Daily Times*, November 1, 1866; *Senate Journal: Called Session, 1866*, 367-368.
8. Power, "Mistresses of the Mansion."
9. Benjamin G. Humphreys Subject File. During Humphreys' brief residency Jefferson Davis and Varina Howell Davis were overnight guests at the mansion on January 30-31, 1868. Jackson *Clarion*, January 30, 1868; *Vicksburg Daily Times*, January 31, February 2, 1868.
10. David G. Sansing, "The Failure of Johnsonian Reconstruction in Mississippi," *Journal of Mississippi History* XXXIV (November, 1972), 307-331.
11. McLemore, *Mississippi*, I, 557-67.
12. Percy L. Rainwater (ed.), "The Autobiography of Benjamin Grubb Humphreys, August 26, 1808-December 20, 1882," *Mississippi Valley Historical Review* XXI (September, 1934), 231-56.
13. The correspondence between General Ames and Governor Humphreys is reprinted in *Appleton's Annual Cyclopedia 1869*, 514-15. Ames explains this confrontation in a letter of January 17, 1900, to James W. Garner who was writing a history of reconstruction in Mississippi. See Garner Papers Z432f and James W. Garner, *Reconstruction in Mississippi* (New York, 1901), 213-16.
14. *Appleton's Annual Cyclopedia 1869*, 515.
15. *Vicksburg Times*, quoted in Garner, *Reconstruction in Mississippi*, 215.
16. *Appleton's Annual Cyclopedia 1869*, 515.
17. Mrs. Humphreys' letter is printed in the *PMHS* III (1900), 99-106.
18. Reminiscences of Lizzie George Henderson printed in PMHS III (1900), 99-106 and Jackson *Clarion-Ledger*, April 16, 1908.
19. PMHS III (1900), 99-106.
20. Rainwater (ed.), "Autobiography of Benjamin Grubb Humphreys," 251-52; Jackson *Clarion-Ledger*, May 3, 1899, April 16, 1908, July 7, 1968; (Jackson) *Clarion Ledger-Jackson Daily News*, October 28, 1955.
21. McLemore, *Mississippi*, I, 571-72.
22. *Grenada Sentinel* quoted in Jackson *Pilot*, December 18, 1869; *Columbus Democrat* quoted in Jackson *Clarion*, February 20, 1873. For more discussion of the "Jackson clique"

Notes to Chapter V

see *Vaiden Times* quoted in Jackson *Pilot*, December 25, 1869; Jackson *Pilot*, January 8, 1870, September 20, 1871, April 10, 1875; *Hinds County Gazette* quoted in Jackson *Clarion*, February 6, 1873.

23. *Senate Journal 1870*, 37; *House Journal 1870*, 75, 161-62, 286-87, 401, 491, 536, 596, 699. The appropriation was increased to $25,000 and subsequently approved. See *Laws of Mississippi 1870*, 472. See vouchers for repair in Auditor's Records, vols. 68 and 71.

24. Jackson *Clarion*, February 11, 1870; Jackson *Pilot*, February 12, 19, 1870.

25. Jackson *Clarion*, February 11, 1870; *Columbus Index* quoted in Jackson *Clarion*, February 11, 1870. The expenditure of $25,000 on the mansion sparked a lively controversy. The *Clarion* referred to the mansion as a "State Palace" and objected to the squandering of state funds on the executive residence. Surprisingly, the *Vicksburg Daily Times and Republican* agreed with the *Clarion*. The *Republican* editor considered "the whole Mansion investment [as] an expensive humbug" and could see no "moral obligation incumbent on the state to furnish its Chief Executive with an elemosinary [sic] residence." The editor felt that hospitals, schools, and other state services were a much more pressing need. However, with the endorsement of Governor Alcorn, the legislature authorized the repairs and the work was eventually completed. See Jackson *Clarion*, June 21, 1871; *Vicksburg Daily Times and Republican*, August 10, 1871.

26. Jackson *Pilot*, March 5, 1870. For a detailed study of Alcorn see Lillian A. Pereryra, *James Lusk Alcorn, Presistent Whig* (Baton Rouge, 1966); Will J. Carpenter, 1905 newspaper clipping in Power Papers.

27. *Biloxi Herald* undated clipping in Governor's Mansion Subject File; and other typescript histories of the mansion in this subject file. For a revisionist study of Mississippi scalawags see David G. Sansing, "The Role of the Scalawag in Mississippi Reconstruction" (Ph.D. dissertation, University of Southern Mississippi, 1969).

28. Jackson *Clarion*, May 25, 1871.

29. Sansing, "The Role of the Scalawag," 86-107.

30. *Ibid.*

31. Power, "Mistresses of the Mansion."

32. Sansing, "The Role of the Scalawag," 86-107.

33. Blanche Butler Ames (comp.), *Chronicles From the Nineteenth Century: Family Letters of Blanche Butler and Adelbert Ames*, 2 vols. (Clinton, Mass., 1957), 640-88. Blanche Butler Ames was the daughter of Governor Ames but was not born until after her father had served as governor of Mississippi.

34. *Ibid.*, 651. Mrs. Ames told her mother that a reception for the legislature which was integrated would be held but "without ladies," presumably to avoid any embarrassment to anyone. *Ibid.*, 656.

35. *Ibid.*, 667.

36. Butler Ames to Kate Markham Power, October 29, 1937, Power Papers.

37. See Ames' inaugural address in *House Journal 1874*.

38. Adelbert Ames to Mississippi Legislature March 28, 1876, Adelbert Ames Subject File.

39. R. H. Thompson to Dunbar Rowland, February 15, 1929, in Dunbar Rowland Papers.

NOTES TO CHAPTER VI

1. L. Q. C. Lamar to John Marshall Stone, March 31, 1876, in John Marshall Stone Papers Z26, folder 2.

2. Jackson *Clarion*, November 14, 18, 1865; Paul Gaston, *The New South Creed* (New York, 1970), 43.

Notes to Chapter VI

3. *Proceedings of the Mississippi Press Association* . . . *1866-1884* (Jackson, 1884), 101-103.
4. Jackson *Mississippian*, May 27, 1891.
5. Jackson *Clarion*, March 3, 1892.
6. Ralph D. Cross and Robert Wales (eds.), Charles Traylor (cartographer), *Atlas of Mississippi* (Jackson, 1974), 43.
7. Jackson *Clarion*, April 7, 1876; Frank A. Critz to Stone, May 18, 1876, Governors Correspondence, vol. 107; Power, "Mistresses of the Mansion"; Jackson *Clarion-Ledger*, November 14, 1889, John Marshall Stone Subject File; Jackson *Clarion*, August 14, 21, November 6, 28, 1878; *Jackson Daily News*, July 24, 1949.
8. *House Journal 1882*, 37; Jackson *Clarion*, January 4, 1882.
9. Jackson *Clarion*, October 6, 1881.
10. See Stone's farewell address in *House Journal 1882*, 36-37.
11. Robert H. Lowry Subject File.
12. *Ibid.*; Albert K. Kirwan, *Revolt of the Rednecks* (New York, 1951, Torchbook edition), 52-55.
13. Power, "Mistresses of the Mansion" (two-page undated newspaper article in Governor's Mansion Subject File).
14. Jackson *Clarion-Ledger*, January 26, June 14, 1888; Lowry-Jayne Papers Z694. 1, box 5.
15. Jackson *Clarion-Ledger*, January 19, 1888.
16. Power, "Mistresses of the Mansion" (in Governor's Mansion Subject File).
17. Jackson *Clarion*, December 28, 1857. Power, "Mistresses of the Mansion" (in Governor's Mansion Subject File).
18. All visitors to the mansion during Lowry's residency were not honored guests. On one occasion a thief crept into the mansion during the night and stole almost a hundred dollars' worth of pistols and other firearms from Dr. C. A. Rice and J. M. Jayne who were overnight guests of Governor Lowry. Jackson *Clarion-Ledger*, March 1, 1888.
19. Power, "Mistresses of the Mansion" (in Governor's Mansion Subject File).
20. Jackson *Clarion-Ledger*, March 15, 22, 28, 29, April 11, May 17, 31, June 14, 1888; Jackson *Clarion*, March 29, June 7, June 19, 1882.
21. *House Journal 1884*, 186, 442, 478.
22. Power, "Mistresses of the Mansion" (in Governor's Mansion Subject File); for additional clippings covering Davis' visit see Lowry-Jayne Papers Z694.1, box 5.
23. *Ibid.*; Power Papers Z100, box 6, folder 95; newspaper clippings in Anabel Power Subject File; Lowry-Jayne Papers Z694.1, box 5; Stone Papers Z26, folder 4; Jackson *Clarion-Ledger*, May 10, 31, 1888.
24. Jackson *Clarion-Ledger*, April 19, 1888.
25. *Brookhaven Leader*, March 14, 1889.
26. Kirwan, *Revolt of the Rednecks*, 40-49, 63-64.
27. *Ibid.*, 58-84; Jackson *Clarion-Ledger*, July 18, 1889.
28. Jackson *Clarion-Ledger*, August 15, November 14, 1889, January 16, 1890; J. W. Martin to Stone, February 28, 1892, Stone Papers Z26, folder 4.
29. *House Journal 1896*, 43-45.
30. *Laws of Mississippi 1892*, 20.
31. Newspaper clipping in Anselm J. McLaurin Subject File.
32. *House Journal 1896*, 43-45.
33. "Pages From An Old Scrap Book," column by Anabel Power in *Jackson Daily News*, January 23, 1849, copy in Anabel Power Subject File.
34. Mary Duval, *History of Mississippi and Civil Government* (Louisville, Ky., 1892), xi.
35. *House Journal 1896*, 43-45.
36. *Ibid.*, 611-12; *Laws of Mississippi 1896*, 20-21.

Notes to Chapter VI

37. Wilbur J. Cash, *Mind of the South* (New York, 1941), 170.
38. Power, "Pages From An Old Scrap Book."
39. Mrs. Anselm McLaurin to Mary, January 25, 1896, McLaurin Papers Series Z509f.
40. "Auntie" to Mary, February 5, 1896, *ibid.*
41. *Ibid.*
42. Newspaper clipping in Anselm J. McLaurin Subject File.
43. *Vicksburg Sunday Journal*, June 4, 1899; Kirwan, *Revolt of the Rednecks*, 118–21.
44. Davis, *Recollections of Mississippi*, 195.

NOTES TO CHAPTER VII

1. Power, "Mistresses of the Mansion"; Interview with Governor Andrew H. Longino, July, 1936 and Mrs. Longino, June, 1936 in WPA Source Material for Hinds County.
2. *Winona Times* newspaper clipping in Andrew H. Longino Subject File.
3. *House Journal 1904*, 29–30.
4. Jackson *Clarion-Ledger*, April 26, 1888, October 3, 1889; *House Journal 1896*, 894; *House Journal of Called Session 1897*, 194–209; 210–29, 240–45.
5. Interview with Governor Longino in WPA Source Material for Hinds County; *House Journal 1900*, 93–94; McLemore, *Mississippi*, II, 31–32; *House Journal 1904*, 26–27.
6. *Winona Times* newspaper clipping in Andrew Longino Subject File; *House Journal 1904*, 26–27.
7. Power, "Mistresses of the Mansion"; Jackson *Clarion-Ledger*, July 25, 1902.
8. Interview with Mrs. Longino in WPA Source Material for Hinds County; Power, "Mistresses of the Mansion."
9. Minute Book, Ladies Aid Society, First Baptist Church, Jackson, Mississippi under date of January 7, 1901, Z484f.
10. Power, "Mistresses of the Mansion."
11. *House Journal 1904*; Jackson *Clarion-Ledger*, February 27, 1908; William F. Holmes, *The White Chief: James Kimble Vardaman* (Baton Rouge, 1970), 116.
12. Holmes, *The White Chief*, 102–15.
13. *Ibid.*, 116–17.
14. *House Journal 1904*, 153–54.
15. Holmes, *The White Chief*, 119.
16. *Ibid.*, 119–20.
17. Percy Bell to Mrs. Mary Dinkins, January 26, 1938 in Power Papers.
18. *Ibid.*; James K. Vardaman, Jr. to Kate Markham Power, January 28, 1938; Aletha Vardaman Fairly to Kate Markham Power, July 1, 1937; Ruth Shearer to Mrs. Dinkins, February 1, 1938, all in Power Papers; Minnie Vardaman Ratliff to Mrs. Waller, February 26, 1975; Mrs. James K. Vardaman Jr. to Mrs. Waller, March 14, 1975.
19. George C. Osborn, *John Sharp Williams, Planter Statesman of the Deep South* (Baton Rouge, 1943), 174.
20. James K. Vardaman, Jr. to Kate Markham Power, January 28, 1938, Power Papers.
21. Ruth Shearer to Mrs. Dinkins, January 26, 1938; James K. Vardaman, Jr. to Kate Markham Power, January 28, 1938, *ibid.*
22. James K. Vardaman Jr. to Kate Markham Power, January 28, 1938, *ibid.*
23. Typescript article by Mrs. Chandler C. Emery (Sallie Winter) in Power, "Mistresses of the Mansion."
24. Minnie Vardaman Ratliff to Mrs. Waller, February 26, 1975.
25. *Ibid.*
26. *House Journal 1908*, 61–62.
27. Jackson *Clarion-Ledger*, January 21, 22, February 22, March 6, 1908, April 17, 1909.

Notes to Chapter VII

28. *House Journal 1908*, 514–15. A bill to sell the mansion was introduced but did not pass. *Ibid.*, 446, 626.
29. *Ibid.*, 656–58, 1072.
30. Jackson *Clarion-Ledger*, February 27, March 6, April 16, 1908.
31. Holcomb, *The Mississippi Governor's Mansion*, 16; W. S. Hull, "Report of W. S. Hull, Architect, Subject: Governor's Mansion" (Jackson, 1908), 3.
32. A great deal of debate resulted from the dispute over the amount of money to be appropriated for the renovation. The sum varied from a low of $20,000 to a high of $40,000. Finally, when the figure of $30,000 was agreed upon, more confusion resulted from the fact that the Senate bill authorizing the renovation did not include an appropriation for that purpose. Another bill containing the appropriation was introduced in the House and hastily passed. See *House Journal 1908*, 858–60, 1066–67, 1071–72, 1081–82; *Senate Journal 1908*, 329, 632, 706; *Laws of Mississippi 1908*, 31, 142; Jackson *Clarion-Ledger*, April 7, 1908.
33. Jackson *Clarion-Ledger*, May 28, 1908.
34. *Ibid.*, June 21, 30, July 1, 1908.
35. *Ibid.*, September 15, 1908.
36. *Ibid.*, June 30, July 1, 1908, April 28, 1909.
37. *House Journal 1910*, 496–97; *House Journal 1912*, 154–55; *Laws of Mississippi 1910*, 31–32.
38. Jackson *Clarion-Ledger*, November 1, 2, 1909.
39. For a lengthy report of Roosevelt's visit see Power, "Pages From An Old Scrap Book," October 17, 1948.
40. For the details on the "Teddy bear" story see Inez and Marshall McClintock, *Toys in America* (Washington, D.C., 1961). 353. Leslie Daiken, *Children's Toys Throughout the Ages* (New York, 1953), 118–19, gives a different origin for the Teddy bear but seems in error. For the Holt Collier story see Jackson *Clarion-Ledger*, November 15, 1902.

NOTES TO CHAPTER VIII

1. Kirwan, *Revolt of the Rednecks*, 212; Wigfall Green, *The Man Bilbo* (Baton Rouge, 1963), 38.
2. For details on Brewer's inaugural see Power, "Pages From An Old Scrap Book," March 27, 1949.
3. *Ibid.*; *Jackson Daily News*, January 16, 1912.
4. Author's interview with Mrs. Gertrude Butler, Governor Brewer's secretary, April 21, 1975.
5. Mrs. Claudia Brewer Strite to Mrs. Carroll Waller, February 25, 1975.
6. Power, "Mistresses of the Mansion"; Claudia Strite to Carroll Waller, February 25, 1975.
7. Claudia Strite to Carroll Waller, February 25, 1975.
8. *Ibid.*
9. *Ibid.*; *Laws of Mississippi 1912*, 460.
10. Claudia Strite to Carroll Waller, February 25, 1975.
11. *Ibid.*
12. *Ibid.*
13. *Ibid.*; *Jackson Daily News*, January 23, 1938.
14. *House Journal 1912*, 1599, 1629.
15. Claudia Strite to Carroll Waller, February 25, 1975.
16. Green, *The Man Bilbo*, 45–54; Kirwan, *Revolt of the Rednecks*, 258. See also but read with caution G. A. Hobbs, *Bilbo, Brewer and Bribery* (Jackson, 1917).
17. Green, *The Man Bilbo*, 54.
18. *House Journal 1916*, 176–77.

Notes to Chapter VIII

19. Author's telephone interview with Mrs. Theodore G. Bilbo and Theodore G. Bilbo, Jr., February, 1975; *Laws of Mississippi* 1916, 89.
20. *House Journal* 1916, 176; Green, *The Man Bilbo*, 56.
21. Green, *The Man Bilbo*, 62.
22. (Jackson) *Clarion Ledger-Jackson Daily News*, December 14, 1975. Mrs. Bilbo said politics was her husband's "hobby and his life."
23. Power, "Mistresses of the Mansion"; Laura D. Harrell Sturdivant, "First Ladies of Mississippi, 1920–1964" (unpublished typescript prepared for Mrs. Paul B. Johnson, Jr., while she was serving as first lady of the state).
24. Telephone interview with Mrs. Bilbo and Theodore G. Bilbo, Jr., February, 1975.
25. *House Journal* 1920, 59–60.
26. Lee M. Russell Subject File; *House Journal* 1920, 219–20.
27. *Laws of Mississippi* 1920, 676–77.
28. *Ibid.*, 89.
29. Kirwan, *Revolt of the Rednecks*, 292–99; Green, *The Man Bilbo*, 65–69; Undated clipping of *Aberdeen Weekly* in Lee M. Russell Subject File.
30. Green, *The Man Bilbo*, 65–69.
31. *Natchez Democrat* quoted in Kirwan, *Revolt of the Rednecks*, 299; Newspaper clipping in Lee M. Russell Subject File.
32. Jackson *Clarion-Ledger*, February 7, 1924; *Senate Journal* 1926, 1032, 1228–79.
33. Mrs. Henry B. Whitfield to Kate Markham Power, November 24, 1937, Power Papers. For a recent biography of Whitfield see Bill R. Baker, *Catch the Vision, The Life of Henry L. Whitfield of Mississippi* (Jackson, 1974).
34. Baker, *Catch the Vision*, 107–10.
35. *Ibid.*
36. *Ibid.*, Chapter 4.
37. Mrs. Henry Whitfield to Kate Markham Power, November 24, 1937, Power Papers.
38. Baker, *Catch the Vision*, 104–106.
39. *Ibid.*, 114–15.
40. Mrs. Henry Whitfield to Kate Markham Power, November 24, 1937, Power Papers.
41. Baker, *Catch the Vision*, 146–48; *Jackson Daily News*, March 20, 1927.
42. *Ibid.*
43. *Ibid.*; Author's interview with Mrs. Mary Frances Murphree Ford, daughter of Governor Murphree, March 3, 1975.
44. *Ibid.*
45. *Ibid.*
46. Green, *The Man Bilbo*, 70–71; *Laws of Mississippi* 1928, 342, 350; Interview with Mrs. Bilbo, February, 1975; *Laws of Mississippi* 1934, 48. There is some controversy about the famous "Bilbo bed." Mrs. Claudia Strite asserts that the suite was given to the mansion by a Brandon man, but Mrs. Bilbo recalls that it was given by one of her husband's supporters from Vicksburg.
47. Interview with Mrs. Bilbo, February, 1975.
48. Green, *The Man Bilbo*, 71.
49. *Ibid.*, 72–88.
50. *Ibid.*, 86–87.
51. *Ibid.*, 88.

NOTES TO CHAPTER IX

1. *House Journal* 1932, 102; Theodore G. Bilbo Papers Z386f.
2. Martin Sennett Conner Subject File; *Jackson Daily News*, August 31, 1931.

Notes to Chapter IX

3. Author's interview with Mrs. Martin S. Conner and Lady Rachel Conner Biggs, February 24, 1975.
4. *Ibid.*
5. Claudia Strite to Carroll Waller, February 25, 1975; *Laws of Mississippi 1932*, 18, 65; *Laws of Mississippi 1934*, 42. Mrs. Strite accompanied Mrs. Somerville on that inspection tour of the mansion.
6. Interview with Mrs. Martin Conner, February 24, 1975.
7. Author's interview with R. H. Singleton, May 6, 1975; Claudia Strite to Carroll Waller, February 25, 1975.
8. McLemore, *Mississippi*, II, 103.
9. *Ibid.*, 104.
10. *Ibid.*, 109.
11. Claudia Strite to Carroll Waller, February 25, 1975; *Jackson Daily News*, September 17, 1950.
12. McLemore, *Mississippi*, II, 110, 117.
13. Power, "Mistresses of the Mansion"; Author's interview with Mrs. Russlin, Governor White's secretary, April 22, 1975.
14. Sam Y. Wilhite to Mrs. Waller, May 29, 1975. The legislature appropriated $6,972.00 for general repairs at the mansion and for the installation of the elevator. *Laws of Mississippi 1936*, 32. During White's administration a very important change occurred in financing repairs at the mansion and other public buildings in Mississippi. House Bill No. 518 (*Laws of Mississippi 1938*, 52–54) created the State Building Commission which was given "large discretionary powers and authority in the expending or allocation of any funds" for construction and repair of public buildings. Allocations for expenditures on the mansion since 1938 are not usually a separate appropriation but a part of the total allocation to the Building Commission, which in turn designates a part of the total allocation to the executive residence and other state-owned buildings. Subsequent references to mansion expenditures will cite the minutes maintained by the Commission. Mr. James Chastain, executive director of the State Building Commission and Mrs. Judy Schute, especially, were very helpful in making those minutes available.
15. Interview with Mrs. Russlin, April 22, 1975.
16. Kate Markham Power to Mrs. Sallie H. Gwin, undated, Power Papers.
17. Jackson *Clarion-Ledger*, December 27, 1943.
18. See interview with Mrs. Paul B. Johnson, Sr. in Jackson *State Times*, December 6, 1959.
19. Author's interview with Mrs. D. C. Lee, Governor Johnson's secretary, February 24, 1975.
20. Jackson *State Times*, December 6, 1959.
21. Author's interview with Mrs. Paul B. Johnson, Jr. and Patricia Johnson Boykin, February 25, 1975; interview with Mrs. Dorothy Power Johnson by Eleana Turner, April 10, 1973, in MDAH.
22. Jackson *Clarion-Ledger*, October 30, 1943; Jackson *State Times*, December 6, 1959; *Jackson Daily News*, July 24, 1942.
23. Jackson *State Times*, December 6, 1959.
24. Interview with Mrs. Paul B. Johnson, Jr. and Patricia Johnson Boykin, February 25, 1975; interview with Mrs. Dorothy Power Johnson, April 10, 1973.
25. Undated clipping of an article by James B. Gibson, "My Mississippi," in Governor's Mansion Subject File. Although the article is not dated it seems certain that it was written in 1940 or 1941.
26. Information in Governor's Mansion Subject File. See also Minutes of State Building Commission (hereinafter SBC), August 29, 1944, for payment of $2,775.10 to Capital Paint and Glass Company of Jackson.

Notes to Chapter IX

27. Interview with Mrs. D. C. Lee, February 24, 1975.
28. *Jackson Daily News*, December 27, 1943.
29. Interview with Mrs. W. R. McKinley, Governor Bailey's secretary, February 25, 1975; Governor Bailey Subject File; Mrs. Thomas L. Bailey Subject File; Mrs. Thomas L. Bailey speech to Etruscan Club of Jackson as reported under the title "Life in Governor's Mansion Described By Mrs. Bailey," *Jackson Daily News*, February 15, 1953.
30. Interview with Mrs. W. R. McKinley, February 25, 1975.
31. Mary Alice Bookhart, "A History of the Governor's Mansion," typescript copy of an article in Governor's Mansion Subject File. The minutes of the Building Commission do not reflect the date or the amount of that purchase.
32. Interview with Mrs. W. R. McKinley; *Jackson Daily News*, February 15, 1953; Jackson *Clarion-Ledger*, November 3, 1943; Telephone interview with Rev. Otis Goodwin, March 17, 1975.
33. Jackson *Clarion-Ledger*, March 17, May 3, July 11, August 7, October 1, 1946; *Jackson Daily News*, October 13, 14, 1946.
34. Author's interview with Harold Bailey, Governor Bailey's son, August 14, 1975. Harold Bailey was a law student at the University of Mississippi and was home visiting his father when Bilbo arrived. As he stood up to leave, both men requested that he remain.
35. Report of an interview with Governor Bailey in *Jackson Daily News*, January 18, 1948. *Jackson Daily News*, January 15, 1946; Jackson *Clarion-Ledger*, November 3, 1946.
36. Telephone interview with Rev. Otis Goodwin, March 17, 1975; Author's interview with Mrs. Fielding L. Wright and Elaine Wright Hunt, February 6, 1975; *Jackson Daily News*, November 3, December 4, 8, 1946; Jackson *Clarion-Ledger*, December 10, 1946.
37. Interview with Mrs. Fielding Wright, February 6, 1975. Fielding, Jr. also served as an administrative assistant to Senator John C. Stennis during part of his father's tenure in office.
38. *Ibid.*
39. *Ibid.*
40. *Ibid.*
41. The interview appears in the *Jackson Daily News*, January 18, 1948.
42. Minutes of the SBC, January 14, April 22, 1949; *Laws of Mississippi 1950*, 968–69; Jackson *Clarion-Ledger*, February 26, 1950.
43. Interview with Mrs. Fielding Wright and Elaine Wright Hunt, February 6, 1975.
44. For a survey of the civil rights movement in Mississippi see McLemore, *Mississippi*, II, 154–76.
45. Wilhite to Mrs. Waller, May 29, 1975. Another modern convenience was also added during White's second residency. At a cost of nearly $80,000 the mansion was rewired and air-conditioned. See Minutes SBC, July 12, 1954, through June 3, 1955.
46. *Clarion-Ledger-Jackson Daily News*, February 27, March 6, 13, 20, 27, 1955.
47. *Ibid.*
48. *Ibid.*, March 20, 1955.
49. Interview with Mrs. Russlin, April 22, 1975.
50. Wilhite to Mrs. Waller, May 29, 1975.
51. *Ibid.*

NOTES TO CHAPTER X

1. For an account of the years of adjustment following the Brown decision see J. Oliver Emmerich, *Two Faces of Janus, The Saga of Deep South Change* (Jackson, 1973). For a briefer survey of those years see McLemore, *Mississippi*, II, 140–76.
2. Author's interview with Judge and Mrs. James P. Coleman, February 5, 1975; *Jackson Daily News*, May 19, 1956. *Clarion-Ledger-Jackson Daily News*, August 4, 1957, printed a

Notes to Chapter X

picture of Governor Coleman's old home place, the governor's mansion, and the national capitol. The captions read: "From here, his old home place in Choctaw County, Governor Coleman moved to here, the Governor's Mansion in Jackson, fulfilling a boyhood dream. Now will he try to move to the nation's capitol? That is the question posed on the political front in Mississippi today." After the expiration of his term as chief magistrate, Coleman did not seek higher office. He was elected by his friends and neighbors to represent Choctaw County in the state legislature. Following an unsuccessful race for governor in 1963, Coleman was appointed to the U.S. Fifth Circuit Court of Appeals.

3. James P. Coleman, *Choctaw County Chronicles* (Jackson, 1975); Interview with Judge Coleman, February 5, 1975.

4. See clippings in Anabel Power Subject File.

5. Interview with Judge and Mrs. Coleman, February 5, 1975. The architectural firm which restored the old capitol was subsequently appointed to restore the mansion also.

6. Like many of his predecessors and all of his successors, Governor Coleman found his office space in the capitol crowded if not inadequate. Interview with Judge Coleman, February 5, 1975. *Jackson Daily News*, February 26, 1957.

7. Interview with Judge and Mrs. Coleman, February 5, 1975.

8. Jackson *State Times*, January 1, 1960.

9. For details of this story see *Jackson Daily News*, January 20, 1958 and Jackson *State Times*, January 21, 1958. This was the second time that General Ames' picture in the capitol had sparked a controversy. In 1902, during a general discussion leading to the selection of suitable pictures to hang in the new capitol, it was suggested that portraits of all governors and senators be included. That would mean that pictures of General Ames and the state's two Negro senators, Hiram Revels and Blanche Bruce, would appear in the new capitol which gave such pride to most Mississippians. This suggestion evoked the following response from the Lexington *Progress-Advertiser*: "God pity the Mississippi Anglo-Saxon who can think with tolerance even for one moment of the hanging of such pictures upon her capitol's beautiful walls," quoted in Jackson *Clarion-Ledger*, November 5, 1902.

10. Jackson *Clarion-Ledger*, August 26, 1959; *Clarion-Ledger-Jackson Daily News*, April 17, 1960; James Howard Meredith, *Three Years in Mississippi* (Bloomington, Ind., 1966).

11. Author's interview with Mrs. Gladys Seeley, mansion hostess under Governors Barnett, Johnson, and Williams, over a period of several weeks from February to May, 1975.

12. Author's interview with Governor Ross Barnett and Ross Barnett, Jr., February 17, 1975, and with Mrs. Ross Barnett, February 24, 1975.

13. Interviews with Barnett Family, February, 1975; *Jackson Daily News*, August 8, 1960.

14. *Ibid.*

15. Mrs. George Yarborough to Mrs. Waller; an undated picture of the Yarborough twins playing in the mansion; *Jackson Daily News*, June 21, 1961.

16. Minutes of SBC, July 10, 1960.

17. *Jackson Daily News*, May 5, 1961, Minutes of SBC, November 9, 1960, March 3, April 12, May 21, June 14, July 12, 1961.

18. Interview with Barnett Family, February, 1975; *Jackson Daily News*, September 14, 1961.

19. There are numerous newspaper references to the renovation. The following are only a few but will enable the reader to follow the controversy: Jackson *State Times*, September 14, 17, 1961; *Jackson Daily News*, September 14, 16, 18, 20, 1961; Memphis *Commercial Appeal*, September 17, 1961; Jackson *Clarion-Ledger*, September 24, 1961. Clippings of most of these article are in Governor's Mansion Subject File.

20. For reports of the tour see *Jackson Daily News*, September 17, 1961, and Jackson *State Times*, September 17, 1961.

21. *Ibid.*

22. *Jackson Daily News*, March 28, 1961.

Notes to Chapter X

23. *Ibid.*; Walter Lord, *The Past That Would Not Die* (New York, 1965), 194–232.
24. Johnson's inaugural received national attention. See *Time*, January 31, 1964, and *Newsweek*, June 29, 1964.
25. Interviews with Johnson family, February 25, 1975, and April 10, 1973.
26. *Ibid.*
27. *Ibid.*; *Clarion-Ledger-Jackson Daily News*, April 4, 1965.
28. Interviews with Johnson family, February 25, 1975, and April 10, 1973.
29. *Ibid.*
30. Interviews with Gladys Seeley, February–May, 1975. See also feature article on Mrs. Seeley in *Clarion-Ledger-Jackson Daily News*, January 14, 1968.
31. Interview with Mrs. Paul B. Johnson and Patricia Johnson Boykin, February 25, 1975.
32. Jackson *Clarion-Ledger*, August 4, 1967.
33. Interview with Johnson family, February 25, 1975.
34. *Ibid.*; Jackson *Clarion-Ledger*, May 28, 1964.
35. Interview with Johnson family, February 25, 1975.
36. *Ibid.*
37. *Jackson Daily News*, February 11, 1967.
38. Author's interview with Governor John Bell Williams, February 10, 1975, and with Mrs. Betty Williams, February 13, 1975.
39. *Ibid.*
40. *Ibid.*; Jackson *Clarion-Ledger*, March 15, 1968. For an article which surveys the use of convict labor in the mansion see Jackson *Clarion-Ledger*, August 4, 1967.
41. *Ibid.*, February 6, 1969.
42. Interview with Betty Williams, February 13, 1975.
43. Jackson *Clarion-Ledger*, April 4, 1968.
44. Minutes of SBC, August 8, 1969; Jackson *Clarion-Ledger*, February 6, 1969.
45. Jackson *Clarion-Ledger*, December 14, 1969.
46. *Ibid.*, July 30, 1970; Minutes of SBC, July 8, 1970.
47. *Jackson Daily News*, November 3, 1970.
48. *Ibid.*; Minutes of SBC, February 11, 1971.
49. Minutes of SBC, July 8, 1971; *Jackson Daily News*, July 14, 15, 1971.

NOTES TO CHAPTER XI

1. Jackson *Clarion-Ledger*, October 13, 1971.
2. Minutes of SBC, December 16, 1971; Jackson *Clarion-Ledger*, December 17, 1971.
3. Jackson *Clarion-Ledger*, December 26, 1971; Minutes of SBC, January 13, 1972.
4. Minutes of SBC, February 7, 17, 1972; Joseph T. Ware, A.I.A., and Edwin R. Lewis, N.S.P.E., "Mississippi Governor's Mansion, Preliminary Report and Evaluation of Existing Conditions" (Jackson, February 7, 1972).
5. Ware and Lewis, "Preliminary Report."
6. *Ibid.*
7. Minutes of SBC, February 17, March 9, 1972; Author's interviews with Edwin Lewis, Dewitt Hamilton, representing SBC, April 14, 1975; *Jackson Daily News*, March 28, 1975.
8. Information in the files of Mrs. Carroll Waller; *Jackson Daily News*, August 20, 1972; Author's interview with James Chastain, director of Building Commission, April 14, 1975; Minutes of SBC, August 10, 1972.
9. Minutes of SBC, July 13, August 10, 1972.
10. *Ibid.*, March 12, 1973; Author's interviews with Edward Jones, Berle Smith, Terrell Wise, April 14, 1975.

Notes to Chapter XI

11. Minutes of SBC, February 1, 27, 1973; Jackson *Clarion-Ledger*, February 2, 1973.
12. *Clarion Ledger-Jackson Daily News*, September 16, 1973; *Jackson Daily News*, December 18, 1973; interview with Terrell Wise, April 14, 1975.
13. Minutes of SBC, July 11, August 8, September 12, December 12, 1974; *Laws of Mississippi 1973*, 299.
14. See article on mansion grounds by Alice McCardle in Jackson *Clarion-Ledger*, December 8, 1974. Jackson *Clarion-Ledger*, January 5, 1975; *Jackson Daily News*, February 21, 1975.
15. Jackson *Clarion-Ledger*, March 26, 1973.
16. Author's interview with Bill Garbo, April 14, 1975.
17. Information in the files of Mrs. Waller.
18. *Ibid.*
19. The desk was designed by Bill Garbo and constructed by Bob Brooks.
20. Information in files of Mrs. Waller.
21. Telephone interview with Bill Garbo, May 8, 1975.
22. Notes taken by Mrs. Anita Goodwin, Mrs. Waller's secretary.
23. *Ibid.*
24. *Ibid.*
25. *Clarion Ledger-Jackson Daily News*, November 11, 1973; *Jackson Daily News*, February 27, 1975; information in files of Mrs. Waller.
26. See Program of Ceremonies for June 8, 1975, and *The Oxford Eagle*, June 9, 1975.
27. Information in files at the Mississippi executive mansion.
28. *Ibid.*
29. *Jackson Daily News*, December 7, 10, 1972; Jackson *Clarion-Ledger*, December 11, 1975.
30. See Mrs. Carroll Waller, "News From Your Mansion," in *The Oxford Eagle*, December 10, 1975.
31. *Clarion Ledger-Jackson Daily News*, January 11, 1976.

Index

Acker, Joel M., 43
Ackerman, Miss., 153
Alabama, 10, 11, 18
Alcorn, Amelia Glover, 64-66
Alcorn, James L., 44, 64-67, 77
Ames, Adelbert, 63, 65, 67-71, 77, 157
Ames, Blanche Butler, 68
Ames, Butler, 69
Anderson, Dr. R. N., 52
Architect. *See* Nichols, William
Architectural design of Mansion, 9-10, 12-13

Bache, Lieutenent, 61-63
Bailey, Harold, 140
Bailey, Nella Massey, 140-141, 144
Bailey, Nellah, 140-141
Bailey, Rosa Powell, 142
Bailey, Thomas L., 122, 140-144, 194
Balance Agriculture With Industry (BAWI), 134, 136
Baptist Church, 116-117
Barkley, Alben, 151-152
Barksdale, Ethelbert, 77, 83
Barksdale, General William, 59
Barksdale, William, 44
Barnett, Pearl Crawford, 158-159, 162
Barnett, Ross, 151,158-165, 171, 191
Batte, Mrs., 78
Belhaven College, 166
Benny, Jack, 173
Bentson, Lloyd, 192
Bilbo bed, 128, 156, 182
Bilbo, Linda Gaddy Bedgood, 116, 118-119, 128-129
Bilbo, Theodore G., 98-105, 108-109, 114-121, 127-130, 137, 142-143, 157, 161
Bilbo, Theodore G., Jr., 11
Birkhead, Frances, 121
Births in Mansion, 45, 95, 141

Black and Tan Convention, 60
Black Codes, 60
Boone, Pat, 192
Bordallo, Ricardo, 191
"Bourbon Democrats," 82
Bowman House, 50
Boy Scouts, 106
Bradford, Major A. B., 27
Brandon, Miss., 48, 77
Brewer, Claudia, 111-115
Brewer, Earl Leroy, 108-116
Brewer, Earlene, 110
Brewer, Minnie Block, 110-111
Briscoe, Dolph & Mrs., 191
Brown, Albert Gallatin, 23-26, 43-44
Brown, Roberta Young, 23-25
Brown vs. Board of Education, 151
Bryan, William Jennings, 99
Building Commission, 146
Buckles, J. C., 21
Buckley, Gay, 95
Burkitt, Frank, 83, 86
Butler, Benjamin "Spoons," 68
Butler, Paul M., 151

Cain, Mary D., 152
Calhoun County, Miss., 126
Calhoun, John C., 33
Campaigns, gubernatorial, 17-18, 27, 31-32, 54, 60, 108, 115, 121, 123, 127, 133, 136, 140, 152-153, 158, 165, 177
Canby, General Edward, 55, 183
Canton, Miss., 158
Canton Creole, 18
Capers, Charlotte, 180, 183, 190
Capitol: construction of old, 7-9; Old Capitol Museum, 168; restoration of old, 155; construction of new, 92-93
Capitol, construction of, 5-9

213

Index

Capitol Commission, 103, 105, 118
Carvel, Elbert, 159
Cash, Wilbur J., 87
Casket of Reminiscences, A, 40
Catholic Church (Jackson, Miss.), 51
Central High School (Jackson, Miss.), 125, 146
Chastain, James, 180
Chennault, Claire, 141
Choctaw County, Miss., 152
Choctaw County Chronicles, 154
Citizens' Council, 164
Civil War: Mansion during, 50-55; Jackson during, 48-56; centennial, 158
Claiborne bed, 182
Claiborne County, Miss., 59
Claiborne, John F. H., 3, 34
Clark, Charles, 54-55, 58
Clark, Reuben, 12, 13
Clarksdale, Miss., 111, 115
Clay, Henry, 20
Clement, Frank, 151
Cliburn, Van, 192
Coahoma County, Miss., 65
Cobb, Ty, 113
Coleman, James P., 152-158, 165, 191
Coleman, Judge S. R., 89
Coleman, Margaret Dennis, 154
Collier, Holt, 107
Columbia, Miss., 133
Columbus Democrat, 64
Columbus Index, 65
Columbus, Miss., 21, 54-55
Committee of One Hundred, 123
Compromise of 1850, 34
Confederate Congress, 40
Confederate House, 51
Conner, Alma Lucille Graham, 131
Conner, Lady Rachel, 131
Conner, Martin Sennett (Mike), 122, 130-134, 136, 140
Constitutions of Mississippi: 1817, 5; 1832, 4, 5; 1890, 83
Construction of Mansion: original building, 12-14; 1908 annex, 103-105; 1975 addition, 178, 180-184
Cook, Mrs. Sam, 112
Cooper, Dr. Tim, 95
Copiah County, Miss., 26
Cost of Mansion: original construction, 6, 12-16; renovations, 103, 105-106, 128, 147, 160-162, 181, 183-185, 187; repairs, 33, 38-39, 58-59, 65, 75-76, 84, 86, 96, 120, 131, 147; furnishings, 18-21, 26, 33, 38, 44, 58-59, 65, 76-77, 84, 96, 106, 112, 120, 128, 131, 160-161, 183

Crawford, Joan, 173
Critz, F. A., 96
Cuban independence, 34

Daughters of the American Revolution, 118
Daughters of 1812, 102
Davis, Jefferson, 36, 43, 44, 81, 93
Davis, Mrs. Jefferson, 95
Davis, Jefferson Hayes, 82
Davis, Jimmie, 170
Davis, Reuben, 27, 44, 54, 89-90
Davis, Varinna Anne, 74
Davis, Varina Howell, 81
Davis, Winnie, 81
DeBow's Review, 16
Debutante Club of Mississippi, 144
Delta, 107, 108, 145
Democratic party: attitude toward Mansion, 16; Panic of 1837, 17-18; Henry Clay's visit, 20; convention of 1843, 22-23; unification, 24; convention of 1847, 26; Jackson cliques, 29; influence of press on, 29; presidential election of 1849, 30; Quitman campaign, 36; know-nothing challenge, 41; sectional rivalry, 42; nomination of McWillie, 43; nomination of Pettus, 46; slavery, 47; election of 1868, 60; defeat of 1868 constitution, 64; reunification, 64; press coverage of Alcorn, 66; participation of whites, 69-70; control since 1876, 71; split within party, 73, 77, 80, 82-83; Populist faction, 86-87; convention of 1899, 89; redneck faction, 108-109; splintering in 1918, 120-211; "Dixiecrats," 148; breech with national party, 148, 151-152, 155-56
Democratic States Rights party, 148
Demonstrations at Mansion, 21, 41-42, 132, 164
Deneen, Charles S., 98
Design of Mansion, 9-10, 12-13
DeSoto County, Miss., 58
Dickson, David, Mrs., 18
Dinner with Dot, 169
"Dimes for the Mansion," 184
Disbrough, Louis, 113
"Dixiecrats," 148, 151
"Dream House," 117-118
Dulles, Allen, 169

East garden, 185-186
Eastland, James O., 156
Economic conditions in Mississippi, 9, 14-15, 17, 75, 82, 92, 120, 123, 129-134, 136, 148
Edwards House, 101, 103, 105-106, 109

214

Index

Ellington, Buford, 156
Entertainment in Mansion. *See* Social life in Mansion, Inaugural Activities, Public use of Mansion, Visiting dignitaries, Weddings
Evers, Charles, 151, 177
Evers, Medgar, 177
Executive Contingency Fund, 66
Executive Mansion Contingency Fund, 39, 44

Farmer's Alliance, 86
Family life in Mansion, 45, 79-80, 87-89, 95, 98, 100, 110-114, 119, 124-129, 136-139, 144-150, 154-155, 159, 166-167, 172, 188-189, 193. *See also* Births in Mansion, Weddings in Mansion
Faubus, Orval, 170
Featherstone, W. S., 83
Fence around Mansion, 12, 38, 41, 69, 104, 174
Finch, Cliff, 193
First Ladies of Mississippi: Tucker, Sara F. McBee, 19; Brown, Roberta Young, 23-25; Matthews, Martha Ann Jones, 28; Quitman, Eliza Turner, 32-33; Foote, Rachel Smiley, 38-39, 41, 94; McRae, Mrs. John J., 42; McWillie, Catherine Anderson, 44-45; Pettus, Mrs. John J., 47; Humphreys, Mildred Maury, 58-59, 62-63; Alcorn, Amelia Glover, 64, 66; Ames, Blanche Butler, 68; Stone, Mary Gillam Coman, 75-76, 78, 83; McLaurin, Mrs. Anselm J., 87-88; Longino, Marion Buckley, 91, 95; Vardaman, Anna Burleson Robinson, 97-100; Noel, Alice Tye Neilson, 102-103, 106-107, 109; Brewer, Minnie Block, 110-111; Bilbo, Linda Gaddy Bedgood, 116, 118-119, 128-129; Russell, Ethelmary Day, 120; Whitfield, Mary Dampeer White, 122-123, 126; Murphree, Clara Martin, 126-127; Conner, Alma Lucille Graham, 131; White, Judith Weir, 134-135, 148-152; Johnson, Corinne Venable, 137, 166; Bailey, Nella Massey, 140-141, 144; Wright, Nan Kelly, 144-147; Coleman, Margaret Dennis, 154; Barnett, Pearl Crawford, 158-159, 162; Johnson, Dorothy Power, 137-138, 166, 168-169; Williams, Elizabeth Ann Wells, 172-175; Waller, Carroll, 177, 180-194
Flournoy, Robert W., 66
Flowers of the Month, 187
Flush Times, 14, 17
Folsom, James E., 155
Foote, Henry Stuart, 36-40

Foote, Mary, 79
Foote, Rachel Smiley, 38-39, 41, 94
Ford, Ernie, 173
Fort Pulaski, Ga., 55
Fraley, Martin, 169
Freeman, Gary, 194
Freeman, John D., 22
Fulkerson, H. S., 48
Furnishings. *See* Interior decoration

Garbo, Bill, 185, 187, 189
Garden Clubs of Mississippi, 173, 186
Gartin, Carroll, 158
Gaston, Mrs. Paul, Sr., 124
Gayle, John, 7
Gibbon, William, 13
Godbold Wells, Miss., 108
Gold bathroom, 162, 182
Goodman, Anita, 189
Goodwin, Otis, 141
Governors of Mississippi: Scott, Abram, 6, 7, 9; Lynch, Charles, 7; Runnels, Hiram G., 7-9; McNutt, Alexander G., 6, 14, 16-18, 194; Tucker, Tilghman G., 3, 4, 6, 14, 17-23, 77, 187; Brown, Albert Gallatin, 23-26, 43-44; Matthews, Joseph W., 27-29; Quitman, John Anthony, 29-37, 43-44, 77, 153; McRae, John J., 40-44; McWillie, William, 42-45, 150; Pettus, John J., 44, 46-50, 52, 54; Clark, Charles, 54-55, 58; Sharkey, William L., 57; Humphreys, Benjamin G., 57-63, 65, 183; Alcorn, James L., 64-67, 77; Powers, Ridgely C., 67; Ames, Adelbert, 63, 65, 67-71, 77, 157; Lowry, Robert, 77-83, 85; Stone, John Marshall, 71-77, 83-86, 144; McLaurin, Anselm J., 77, 86-89; Longino, Andrew H., 89, 91-97; Vardaman, James Kimble, 83, 87, 89, 96-101, 108, 120, 157; Noel, Edmond F., 101-107, 109, 114, 188; Brewer Earl Leroy, 108-116; Bilbo, Theodore G., 98, 105, 108-109, 114-121, 127-130, 137-143, 157, 161; Russell, Lee M., 119-122; Whitfield, Henry, 122-126, 134; Murphree, Dennis, 126-127, 140; Conner, Martin Sennett (Mike), 122, 127-134, 136, 140; White, Hugh Lawson, 133-136, 147-152; Johnson, Paul B., Sr., 136-140; Bailey, Thomas L., 122, 140-144, 194; Wright, Fielding L., 143-148, 152; Coleman, James P., 152-158, 165, 191; Barnett, Ross, 151, 158-165, 171, 191; Johnson, Paul B., Jr., 136-138, 152, 159-160, 165-171, 191; Williams, John Bell, 171-178, 191; Waller, William L., 71,

Index

115, 171, 177-178, 188-189, 191, 194;
  Finch, Cliff, 193
Graham, Billy, 151
Grant, Gen. U. S., 49-50, 76
Graves, 12
Graves, Richard, 14, 15, 21, 22
Greek Revival architecture, 10, 104, 165
Greenville, Miss., 78
Greenwood, Miss., 99
Grenada Sentinel, 64
Grounds, beautification of, 25, 39, 78, 94, 100, 103-105, 112, 147, 160-161, 173, 174, 185-187
Gubernatorial campaigns. *See* Campaigns
Gubernatorial elections. *See* Campaigns, gubernatorial
Guion, John I., 37
Gwin, William, 17

Halifax, Lord and Lady, 141
Hall of Fame, 157-158
Hall of Governors, 157-158
Hamer, Fannie Lou, 151
Hamilton, Dewitt, 189
Harper's Foundry, 186
Harrison, Byron Patton, 120
Harris, James L., 79-80
Harris, Phil, 173
Hattiesburg, Miss., 136, 138
Hayes, Jefferson Davis, 82
Heidelberg Hotel, 142, 152
Henry, Aaron, 151
Henry, R. H., 80
Henry, Mrs. William, 78
Herff, Mrs. Ferdinand, 184
Hermitage, 7
Herod, A. J., 58
Hershey, Lewis, 141
Hill, K.K., 193
Hilliard, Elbert, 183, 190
Hines, Jerome, 192
Hobbs, G. A., 114
Holbrook, Hal, 173
Holm, Celeste, 173
Holmes, County, Miss., 11
Holmes, William F., 97
Hoover, J. Edgar, 170
Howard, Merriman, 65
Howell, S. D., 12
Hoyle, J. M., 97
Hull, James T., 43
Hull, William S., 103, 181
Humphreys, Benjamin G., 57-63, 65, 183
Humphreys, Mildred Maury, 58-59, 62-63

Illinois Central Railroad, 99, 109

Inaugural activities, 3, 24, 27-28, 32, 41-42, 44, 55, 87, 96-97, 109-110, 116, 128, 159, 170
Industrial development, 134-135, 148
Ingalls Corporation, 134, 147
Interior decoration, 18-21, 25-26, 33, 37-38, 41, 44, 52, 54, 58-59, 65, 69, 84, 86, 96, 100, 102, 104-106, 122, 128, 130-131, 139, 141, 144, 149-150, 155, 160-161, 170, 178, 182-184. *See also* Cost of, furnishings, Bilbo bed, Claiborne bed, Gold bathroom, Renovations
Iuka, Miss., 75

Jackson and Great Northern Railroad, 53
Jackson, Andrew, 7
Jackson Board of Trade, 80
Jackson *Clarion-Ledger* (See also *Eastern Clarion*), 40, 61, 65, 80
"Jackson Clique," 29-30, 42, 64, 69
Jackson First Baptist Church, 95
Jackson, Miss., 4-5, 49-55, 57, 74-75, 91, 94, 104, 133, 154-155, 161, 164, 167, 173, 175. *See also* "Jackson Cliques"
Jackson Mississippian, 7, 8, 9, 23, 24, 25, 29, 35, 42, 49, 51, 54
"Jackson ring," 96
Jackson Southron, 21
Jackson State University, 163
Jacksonian Democracy, 4, 6
James, Harry, 173
Johnson, Andrew, 57, 59-60
Johnson, Corinne Venable, 137, 166
Johnson, Dorothy Power, 137-138, 166, 168-169
Johnson, Lady Bird, 190
Johnson, Lyndon B., 151
Johnson, Patricia, 138, 166
Johnson, Patrick, 136, 138
Johnson, Paul B. Jr., 136-138, 152, 159-160, 165-171, 191
Johnson, Paul B. Sr., 120, 133, 136-140
Johnson, Paul B. III, 167
Johnson, Peggy, 136
Johnson, Richard M., 20
Johnson, Shelby, 167
Johnston, Gen. Joseph E., 50, 52-53
Jones, Edward, 182-184, 189
Juliana, Princess, 138
Juniper Grove, 117

Kearney, Belle, 91, 122
Kemper County, Miss., 46
Kennedy, John F., 157
Kennedy, Robert F., 163-164
Kings Daughters organization, 99

216

Index

Know-Nothing political party, 41, 43
Kossuth, Louis, 39
Ku Klux Klan, 120
Kuwait trade misssion visit, 192-193

Ladies Aid Society, 95
Lafayette County, Miss., 119
Lamar, L. Q. C., 44, 72-73, 82
Land boom, 4-5
Land sale, 4-5
Landscaping of Mansion, 25, 39, 78, 94, 100, 103-105, 112, 147, 160-161, 173, 174, 185-187
Lawrence, John, 7-9
Lee County, Miss., 97
Lee, Robert E., 157
Lee, Stephen D., 83
Lennon Sisters, 173
Lewis, Edwin, 189
Lexington, Miss., 11, 102
Lincoln, Abraham, 51
Link, Mrs. W. M., 193
"Little White House repair job," 147, 155
Long, Huey P., 133
Longino, Andrew H., 89, 91-97
Longino, Marion Buckley, 91, 95
Louisiana Academy, 53
Louisville, Ken., 21
Lowndes, County, Miss., 6, 18
Lowry, "Birdie," 79-80
Lowry, Patrick, 79
Lowry, Robert, 77-83, 85
Lowry, Robert (son), 79
Lyceum, 165
Lynch, Charles, 7

Macon, Miss., 52, 54-55, 58
Manship, C. H., 53-54
Manship House, 186
Mansion, as political issue. *See* Politics, "Sale of Mansion" issue
Mansion security, 156, 170, 171, 173
Marion County, Miss., 134
Marshall County, Miss., 27, 29
Marshall County Jacksonian, 29
Matthews, Elizabeth, 28
Matthews, Joseph W., 27-29
Matthews, Martha Ann Jones, 28
Matthews, Sallie, 28
Meredith, James, 150-151, 163-165
Meridian, Miss., 52, 54, 78, 81, 158
Metcalf brothers, 107
Mexican War, 26, 27, 34
Mississippi Arts Commission, 187
Mississippi Arts Festival, 173
Mississippi Department of Archives and History, 178, 180, 183, 190-191
Mississippi Educational Television, 181
Mississippi Executive Mansion Commission, 191
Mississippi Federal Writers Project, 135
Mississippi Federated Women's Club, 186
Mississippi Forestry Association, 186
Mississippi Forestry Commission, 187
Mississippi Gubernatorial Campaigns. *See* Campaigns, gubernatorial
Mississippi Library Commission, 185
Mississippi Press Association, 73
Mississippi Research and Development Center, 185
Mississippi State College for Women, 122, 125
Mississippi: The Storm Center of Secession, 47
"Mistresses of the Mansion," 135
Mitchell, Henrietta, 150
Mitchell, Stephen, 151
Mobley, Mary Ann, 192
Modernization of Mansion, 26, 80, 104-105, 112, 120, 127, 135, 161, 170, 173-174
Money, H. D., 93
Montgomery, J. S., 81
Moody, Anne, 150-151
Morrison, David, 7
Mosley, Barbara, 194
Murphree, Clara Martin, 126-127
Murphree, Dennis, 126-127, 140

MacArthur, Douglas, 151
McCardle, William, 85
McCargo, W. H., 58-59
McClung, Alexander, 44
McComb, Miss., 137
McIntyre, Carl, 175-176
McKee, James C., 67
McKeithen, John, 170
McKenna, 65
McLacklan, 12
McLaurin, Anselm J., 77, 86-89
McLaurin, Mrs. Anselm J., 87-88
McLaurin, Daisy, 88
McLaurin, Mary, 88
McLemore, R. A., 180, 191
McNutt, Alexander G., 6, 14, 16-18, 194
McRae, John J., 40-44
McRae, Mrs. John J., 42
McReynolds, James, 189
McWillie, Catherine Anderson, 44-45
McWillie, William, 42-45, 150

Nashville, Tenn., 7
Natchez Daily Courier, 52

217

Index

Natchez Free Trader, 3, 19
Natchez, Miss., 4, 20, 78, 150
National Historic Landmark: Mansion designated, 190
Negro suffrage, 90
New Capitol, *See* Capitol
Newton *Ledger*, 80
Nichols, William, 3, 7, 9, 10, 11, 13, 14, 15, 18, 26, 165, 181
Noel, Alice Tye Neilson, 102-103, 106-107, 109
Noel, Edmond F., 96, 101-107, 109, 114, 188
North Carolina, 10, 11
Noxubee County, Miss., 67

Old Capitol. *See* Capitol
Old Ladies Home Association, 102
Otey, Bishop (Episcopal, of Tennessee), 44
Oxford, Miss., 158

Panic of 1837, 9, 15, 17
Panola County, Miss., 24
Parchman (state penitentiary), 114-115, 117, 134, 141-142, 144-145, 156-157, 168-169, 172
Parker, Alton B., 99
Pascagoula, Miss., 134
Paulding *Clarion*, 80
Pearl River, 50
Pearl River County, Miss., 117
Pemberton, Gen. John G., 49, 52
Pendergast, Lucy, 79
Pennypacker, S. W., 99
Percy, Leroy, 108
Peterson, Charles, 181
Pettus, John J., 44, 46-50, 52, 54
Pettus, Mrs. John J., 47
Pettus, Sulky, 47, 49
Pettus, Willie, 47, 49
Philadelphia, Penn., 11
Phillips, Rubel, 165
Planters Bank, 8
Poindexter, George, 33
Politics, Mansion as issue, 16, 23, 94-95, 100-102, 116, 119, 122, 161-162, 174, 176-177
Poole, Eula, 144
Poplarville, Miss., 116-117
Population growth: in Mississippi, 4-5; in Jackson, 94
Populism, 83, 86-87
Porter, Admiral David, 53
Power, Anabel, 155
Power, Kate Markham, 69, 135-136

Powers, Louise, 67
Powers, Ridgely C., 67
Prentiss, Miss., 177
Prentiss, Seargent S., 44
Public use of Mansion, 41, 111, 124, 134-135, 137, 141, 144, 154, 158, 163

Quitman, Eliza Turner, 32-33
Quitman, John Anthony, 29-37, 43-44, 77, 153
Quitman, Rosalie (Duncan), 36, 37

Racial tension, 150-153, 155-157, 163, 171
Radical Republicans, 59-60
Rainwater, Percy L., 47
Ratliff, Minnie Vardaman, 100
Rayburn, Sam, 156
Reconstruction, 57-71
Red Banks, 166
"Redneck," 108, 116
Renovations: 1908 (Noel), 103-106; 1928 (Bilbo), 127-128; 1951 (Wright), 147; 1961 (Barnett), 160-162; 1975 (Waller), 180-187
Repair of Mansion: Needs detailed, 76, 85, 120, 131, 139, 155, 160, 170, 174-176, 178-180; Problems corrected, 37-38, 40-41, 58-59, 64-65, 75-77, 84-86, 96, 103-105, 120, 131-132, 139, 147, 155, 160-161, 170-171, 174-176. *See also* Cost of Mansion, Modernization, Renovations
Republican party, 63-67, 70, 165
Restoration of 1975, dedication, 189
Ringling Brothers Circus, 192
Rogers, Francis M., 40
Rogers, Will, 125
Rolling Fork, Miss., 144
Roosevelt, Franklin D., 138
Roosevelt, Theodore, 106-107
Rowland, Dunbar, 70
Runnels, Hiram G., 7-9
Russell, Ethelmary Day, 120
Russell, Lee M., 119-122
Russell, Richard, 156

Sacred harp association, 159
"Sale of Mansion" issue, 95, 97, 100-102, 116, 119, 127, 138
Scholl, Helmut, 187
School History of Mississippi, 85
Scott, Abram, 6, 7, 9
Secession, 36, 39, 40, 46-48, 57
Security at Mansion, 156, 170, 171, 173
Seeley, Gladys, 168
Servants, Parchman inmates used as, 114-115, 117, 134, 141-142, 144-145, 156-

218

Index

157, 168-169, 172
Sharkey, William L., 57
Shattuck, David, 18
Sherman, Gen., 50-54
Shriver, Sargent, 192
Simrall, Horatio F., 73
Singleton, Frank, 189
Singleton, Otho, 44
Singleton, R. H., 132
Smith, Berle, 183, 189
Sneed, Duncan, 80
Social life in Mansion: Gov. Tucker, 19, 23; Gov. Brown, 24-25; Gov. Matthews, 27-28; Gov. Quitman, 35; Gov. Foote, 39, 41; Gov. McRae, 42; Gov. McWillie, 44-45; Gov. Alcorn, 66; Gov. Ames, 68; Gov. Stone, 75, 84-85; Gov. Lowry, 77-78, 81-82; Gov. McLaurin, 87; Gov. Longino, 91, 94-95; Gov. Vardaman, 97-100; Gov. Noel, 103, 106; Gov. Brewer, 110-113; Gov. Bilbo, 119; Gov. Whitfield, 124-125; Gov. Murphree, 126-127; Gov. White, 135, 147, 151; Gov. Johnson, Sr., 137-138; Gov. Bailey, 141; Gov. Wright, 144; Gov. Barnett, 159; Gov. Johnson, Jr., 167, 169-170; Gov. Waller, 189, 191-192. *See also* Inaugural activities, Public use of Mansion, Visiting dignitaries, Weddings
Somerville, Nellie Nugent, 131
Sons of Confederate Veterans, 185
State Building Commission, 173-174, 176-178, 181-182
Staunton and McKenna (contractors), 65
Stennis, John C., 156
Stevens, Forrest, 88
Stewart family, 150
Stone, Alfred H., 132
Stone, John Marshall, 71-77, 83-86, 144
Stone, Mary Gillam Coman, 75-76, 78, 83
Sullens, Fred, 108, 115, 129-130

Taft, William Howard, 106
Taylor, Gen. Richard, 55, 183
Tecumseh, 20
"Teddy Bear," 107
Teller, Edward, 159
Texas Revolution, 34
Thompson, Jacob, 54
Thompson, R. H., 70
Tombigbee River, 155
Tougaloo College, 163
Tourists, 158, 168, 192
Trott, Henry, 114-115
Tucker, Tilghman G., 3, 4, 6, 14, 17-23, 77, 187

Tucker, Sarah F. McBee, 19

United Confederate Veterans, 102
United Daughters of the Confederacy, 93, 102, 118, 157
University of Mississippi, 11, 133, 158, 163-165

Vardaman, Aletha, 99
Vardaman, Anna Burleson Robinson, 97-100
Vardaman, James K. Jr., 100
Vardaman, James Kimble, 83, 87, 89, 96-101, 108, 120, 157
Vardaman, Mary Ann Fox, 101
Vicksburg, Miss., 49-50, 52-54, 78
Vicksburg National Park, 99
Vicksburg Sentinel, 18, 22
Vicksburg Times, 61
Visiting dignitaries, 20, 39, 44, 81, 99-100, 106, 113, 125, 138, 141, 151-152, 155-156, 159, 169-170, 173, 191-192

Walker, Robert J., 4, 20
Walker and McLacklan, 12
Wallace, George C., 159, 170
Waller, Carroll, 177, 180-194
Waller children, 189
Waller, William L., 71, 115, 171, 177-178, 188-189, 191, 194
Wamble, Helen, 157
Ward, Dr. B. E., 96
Ware and Lewis architectural firm, 180
Water Valley, Miss., 110
Watkins, Tom, 164
Webb, Hunter C., 141
Weddings in Mansion, 45, 79-80, 88-89, 95, 126, 137-138, 141, 147, 167, 195
Williams, John Bell, 171-178, 191
West, A. M., 54
Western Union, 113
Wharton, T. J., 54
Whig party, 16, 17, 18, 20, 21, 26, 36, 43, 54, 64
White, Hugh Lawson, 133-136, 147-152
White, Judith Weir, 134-135, 148-152
Whitfield, Henry, 122-126, 134
Whitfield, James, 37
Whitfield, Mary Dampeer White, 122-123, 126
Williams, Elizabeth Ann Wells, 172-175
Williams, Ezra, 13
Williams, John Bell, 171-178, 191
Williams, J. Benjamin, 185
Williams, John D., 164
Williams, John Sharp, 98
Williams, Thomas, 22

219

Index

Wilson, L. B., 187
Wise Construction Company, 183
Wise, Terrell, 183, 189
Woodville, Miss., 32, 33
Women's Christian Temperance Union, 91, 95, 102
Women's suffrage, 91, 123
Wooldridge, James, 183, 189-190
World War II, 137, 140-143
Wright, Elaine, 144, 146-147

Wright, Fielding L., 143-148, 152
Wright, Fielding, Jr., 144
Wright, Nan Kelly, 144-147
Wright, Sophie, 99

Yandell, Dr. D. W., 50
Yarbrough, George, 160
Yazoo County, Miss., 11
Yazoo Democrat, 11, 29
Yellow fever, 75

www.ingramcontent.com/pod-product-compliance
Lightning Source LLC
Chambersburg PA
CBHW030340240426
43661CB00052B/1697